Programming Algorithms in Lisp

Writing Efficient Programs with Examples in ANSI Common Lisp

Vsevolod Domkin

Apress®

Programming Algorithms in Lisp: Writing Efficient Programs with Examples in ANSI Common Lisp

Vsevolod Domkin
Kyiv, Ukraine

ISBN-13 (pbk): 978-1-4842-6427-0   ISBN-13 (electronic): 978-1-4842-6428-7
https://doi.org/10.1007/978-1-4842-6428-7

Managing Director, Apress Media LLC: Welmoed Spahr
Acquisitions Editor: Steve Anglin
Development Editor: Matthew Moodie
Coordinating Editor: Mark Powers

Cover designed by eStudioCalamar

Distributed to the book trade worldwide by Apress Media, LLC, 1 New York Plaza, New York, NY 10004, U.S.A. Phone 1-800-SPRINGER, fax (201) 348-4505, e-mail orders-ny@springer-sbm.com, or visit www. springeronline.com. Apress Media, LLC is a California LLC and the sole member (owner) is Springer Science + Business Media Finance Inc (SSBM Finance Inc). SSBM Finance Inc is a **Delaware** corporation.

For information on translations, please e-mail booktranslations@springernature.com; for reprint, paperback, or audio rights, please e-mail bookpermissions@springernature.com.

Apress titles may be purchased in bulk for academic, corporate, or promotional use. eBook versions and licenses are also available for most titles. For more information, reference our Print and eBook Bulk Sales web page at http://www.apress.com/bulk-sales.

Any source code or other supplementary material referenced by the author in this book is available to readers on GitHub via the book's product page, located at www.apress.com/9781484264270. For more detailed information, please visit http://www.apress.com/source-code.

Printed on acid-free paper

Table of Contents

About the Author

Vsevolod Domkin from Kyiv, Ukraine, is a Lisp programmer and enthusiast, a natural language processing researcher, an occasional writer/blogger, and a teacher.

About the Technical Reviewer

Michał "phoe" Herda is a programmer with contributions to multiple parts of the Common Lisp (CL) ecosystem: CL implementations, existing and widely used CL utilities, documentation, and some of the new library ideas that he slowly pushes forward and works on.

Acknowledgments

I'm very thankful to those who helped me in the work on *Programming Algorithms in Lisp* by providing support, advice, corrections, and suggestions. First of all, many thanks to my wife, Ksenya, who encouraged me to work on it despite the time that was, in part, taken from my family duties. Michał "phoe" Herda contributed a very thorough and detail-oriented review that helped correct a couple of significant misunderstandings on my part and pushed me to add more code and explanations where they were lacking. He has also championed the idea of a separate repository with all the book's code accompanied by a test suite and helped me in this undertaking.

I am very grateful to Dr. Robert Strandh who humbly volunteered his help as an editor of the initial chapters of the book to make it sound more native (as my English is far from perfect since I'm not a native speaker) and point out the mistakes that I made. He and his wife, Kathleen, have contributed lots of improvements to more than half of the chapters, and I tried to follow their advice in the subsequent ones. Thanks to Rainer Joswig for commenting on the Lisp choices. I'm also grateful to my father, Dr. Volodymyr Demkine, for reviewing and proofing the book. Thanks to @dzenicv on reddit who posted links to almost all of the chapters there, which triggered some helpful discussions. Thanks to @tom_mellior on Hacker News for pointing a serious deficiency in the explanation of Union-Find. Thanks to all those people who shared the links to the chapters and contributed their comments and attention.

CHAPTER 1

Introduction

This book started after teaching an intensive course on algorithms to working programmers in Kyiv, in spring 2016. It took more than 3 years to complete, and, meanwhile, I also did three iterations of the course. Its aim is to systematically explain how to write efficient programs and, also, the approaches and tools for determining why the program isn't efficient enough. In the process, it will teach you some Lisp and show in action the technics of algorithmic development. And, even if you won't program in Lisp afterward, you'll still be able to utilize the same approaches and tools or be inclined to ask why they aren't available in your language of choice from its authors. :)

Why Algorithms Matter

In our industry, currently, there seems to prevail a certain misunderstanding of the importance of algorithms for the working programmer. There's often a disconnect between the algorithmic questions posed at the job interviews and the everyday essence of the same job. That's why opinions are voiced that you, actually, don't have to know CS to be successful in the software developer's job. That's true. You don't, but you'd better do if you want to be in the notorious top 10% programmers. For several reasons. One is that, actually, you can find room for algorithms almost at every corner of your work—provided you are aware of their existence. To put it simply, the fact that you don't know a more efficient or elegant solution to a particular programming problem doesn't make your code less crappy. The current trend in software development is that, although the hardware becomes more performant, the software becomes slower faster. There are two reasons for that, in my humble opinion:

1. Most of the application programmers don't know the inner workings of the underlying platforms. And the number of platform layers keeps increasing.

© Vsevolod Domkin 2021
V. Domkin, *Programming Algorithms in Lisp*, https://doi.org/10.1007/978-1-4842-6428-7_1

2. Most of the programmers also don't know enough algorithms
    and algorithmic development technics to squeeze the most from
    their code. And often this means a loss of one or more orders of
    magnitude of performance.

In the book, I'll address, primarily, the second issue but will also try to touch on the first whenever possible.

Besides, learning the art of solving difficult algorithmic problems trains the brain and makes it more apt to solving various other problems, in the course of your day-to-day work.

Finally, you will be speaking the same lingua franca as other advanced programmers—the tongue that transcends the mundane differences of particular programming languages. And you'll gain a more detached view of those differences, freeing your mind from the dictate of a particular set of choices exhibiting in any one of them.

One of the reasons for this gap of understanding of the value of algorithms, probably, originates from how they are usually presented in the computer science curriculum. First, it is often done in a rather theoretical or "mathematical" way with rigorous proofs and lack of connection to the real world. Second, the audience is usually freshmen or sophomores who don't have a lot of practical programming experience and thus can't appreciate and relate how this knowledge may be applied to their own programming challenges (because they didn't have those yet)—rather, most of them are still at the level of struggling to learn well their first programming language and, in their understanding of computing, are very much tied to its choices and idiosyncrasies.

In this book, the emphasis is made on the demonstration of the use of the described data structures and algorithms in various areas of computer programming. Moreover, I anticipate that the self-selected audience will comprise programmers with some experience in the field. This makes a significant difference in the set of topics that are relevant and how they can be conveyed. Another thing that helps a lot is when the programmer has a good command of more than one programming language, especially if the languages are from different paradigms: static and dynamic, object-oriented and functional. These factors allow bridging the gap between "theoretical" algorithms and practical coding, making the topic accessible, interesting, and inspiring.

This is one answer to a possible question: Why write another book on algorithms? Indeed, there are several good textbooks and online courses on the topic, of which I'd recommend the most Steven Skiena's *The Algorithm Design Manual*. Yet, as I said, this book is not at all academic in presentation of the material, which is a norm for other textbooks. Except for simple arithmetic, it contains almost no "math" or proofs. And, although proper attention is devoted to algorithmic complexity, it doesn't deal with theories of complexity or computation and similar scientific topics. Besides, all the algorithms and data structures come with some example practical use cases. Last, but not least, there's no book on algorithms in Lisp, and, in my opinion, it's a great topic to introduce the language. The next chapter will provide a crash course to grasp the basic ideas, and then we'll discuss various Lisp programming approaches alongside the algorithms they will be used to implement.

This is an introductory book, not a bible of algorithms. It will draw a comprehensive picture and cover all topics necessary for further advancement of your algorithm knowledge. However, it won't go too deep into the advanced topics, such as persistent or probabilistic data structures and advanced tree, graph, and optimization algorithms, as well as algorithms for particular fields, such as machine learning, cryptography, or computational geometry. All of those fields require (and usually have) separate books of their own.

A Few Words About Lisp

For a long time, I'd been contemplating writing an introductory book on Lisp, but something didn't add up. I couldn't see the coherent picture, in my mind. And then I got a chance to teach algorithms with Lisp. From my point of view, it's a perfect fit for demonstrating data structures and algorithms (with a caveat that students should be willing to learn it), while discussing the practical aspects of those algorithms allows to explain the language naturally. At the same time, this topic requires almost no endeavor into the adjacent areas of programming, such as architecture and program design, integration with other systems, user interface, and use of advanced language features, such as types or macros. And that is great because those topics are overkill for an introductory text and they are also addressed nicely and in great detail elsewhere (see *Practical Common Lisp* and *ANSI Common Lisp*).

Why Lisp is great for algorithmic programs? One reason is that the language was created with such use case in mind. It has support for all the proper basic data structures, such as arrays, hash-tables, linked lists, strings, and tuples. It also has a numeric tower, which means no overflow errors and, so, a much saner math. Next, it's created for the interactive development style, so the experimentation cycle is very short, there's no compile-wait-run-revise red tape, and there are no unnecessary constraints, like the need for additional annotations (a.k.a. types), prohibition of variable mutation, or other stuff like that. You just write a function in the REPL (Read-Eval-Print Loop), run it, and see the results. In my experience, Lisp programs look almost like pseudocode. Compared to other languages, they may be slightly more verbose at times but are much more clear, simple, and directly compatible with the algorithm's logical representation.

But why not choose a popular programming language? The short answer is that it wouldn't have been optimal. There are four potential mainstream languages that could be considered for this book: C++, Java, Python, and JavaScript (JS). (Surely, there's already enough material on algorithms that use them.) The first two are statically typed, which is, in itself, a big obstacle to using them as teaching languages. Java is also too verbose, while C++ too low level. These qualities don't prevent them from being used in the majority of production algorithm code, in the wild, and you'll, probably, end up dealing with such code sooner than later if not already. Besides, their standard libraries provide great examples of practical algorithm implementation. But I believe that gaining good conceptual understanding will allow to easily adapt to one of these languages if necessary, while learning them in parallel with diving into algorithms creates unnecessary complexity. Python and JS are, in many ways, the opposite choices: they are dynamic and provide some level of an interactive experience (albeit inferior compared to Lisp), but those languages are in many ways anti-algorithmic. Trying to be simple and accessible, they hide too much from the programmer and don't give enough control of the concrete data. Teaching algorithms, using their standard libraries, seems like cheating to me as their basic data structures often are not what they claim to be. Lisp is in the middle: it is both highly interactive and gives enough control of the environment while not being too verbose and demanding. And the price to pay—the unfamiliar syntax—is really small, in my humble opinion.

Mostly, this book will be dedicated to showing Lisp code and explaining it. Yet, all such code snippets will fall into two quite different categories:

- One kind will represent complete code blocks (with occasional small omissions left as exercises for you) that could be run in the Lisp environment, accompanied with the examples of its invocation. These code blocks are accessible in a dedicated GitHub repository.

- The other kind is represented by sketches used to explain how the presented algorithms will be built into larger systems (usually, you'll see these sketches in the "in action" section of each chapter). Such sketches will not be runnable as they may require a lot of supporting code and/or infrastructure and should be treated only as an outline.

CHAPTER 2

Algorithmic Complexity

Complexity is a point that will be mentioned literally on every page of this book; the discussion of any algorithm or data structure can't avoid this topic. After correctness, it is the second most important quality of every algorithm. Moreover, often correctness alone doesn't matter if complexity is neglected, while the opposite is possible: to compromise correctness somewhat in order to get significantly better complexity. By and large, algorithm theory differs from other subjects of CS in that it concerns not about presenting a working (correct) way to solve some problem but about finding an efficient way to do it, where efficiency is understood as the minimal (or admissible) number of operations performed and occupied memory space.

In principle, the complexity of an algorithm is the dependence of the number of operations that will be performed on the size of the input. It is crucial to the computer system's scalability: it may be easy to solve the programming problem for a particular set of inputs, but how will the solution behave if the input is doubled or increased tenfold or millionfold? This is not a theoretical question, and an analysis of any general-purpose algorithm should have a clear answer to it.

Complexity is a substantial research topic: a whole separate branch of CS— complexity theory—exists to study it. Yet, throughout the book, we'll try to utilize the end results of such research without delving deep into rigorous proofs or complex math, especially since, in most of the cases, measuring complexity is a matter of simple counting. Let's look at the following illustrative example:

```lisp
(defun mat-max (mat)
  (let (max)
    (dotimes (i (array-dimension mat 0))
      (dotimes (j (array-dimension mat 1))
        (when (or (null max)
                  (> (aref mat i j) max))
          (setf max (aref mat i j)))))
    max))
```

© Vsevolod Domkin 2021

V. Domkin, *Programming Algorithms in Lisp*, https://doi.org/10.1007/978-1-4842-6428-7_2

This function finds the maximum element of a two-dimensional array (matrix):

```
CL-USER> (mat-max #2A((1 2 3) (4 5 6)))
6
```

What's its complexity? To answer, we can just count the number of operations performed: at each iteration of the inner loop, there are two comparisons involving one array access, and, sometimes, if the planets align, we perform another access for assignment. The inner loop is executed `(array-dimension mat 1)` times (let's call it m where m=3) and the outer one `(array-dimension mat 0)` (n=2, in the example). If we sum this all up, we'll get n `*` m `*` 4 as an upper limit, for the worst case when each sequent array element is larger than the previous. As a rule of thumb, each loop adds multiplication to the formula, and each sequential block adds a plus sign.

In this calculation, there are two variables (array dimensions n and m) and one constant (the number of operations performed for each array element). There exists a special notation—**Big-O**—used to simplify the representation of end results of such complexity arithmetic. In it, all constants are reduced to 1, and thus m `*` 1 becomes just m, and also since we don't care about individual array dimension differences, we can just put n `*` n instead of n `*` m. With such simplification, we can write down the final complexity result for this function: `O(n^2)`. In other words, our algorithm has quadratic complexity (which happens to be a variant of a broader class called "polynomial complexity") in array dimensions. It means that by increasing the dimensions of our matrix ten times, we'll increase the number of operations of the algorithm 100 times. In this case, however, it may be more natural to be concerned with the dependence of the number of operations on the number of **elements** of the matrix, not its dimensions. We can observe that n^2 is the actual number of elements, so it can also be written as just n—if by n we mean the number of elements and then the complexity is linear in the number of elements (`O(n)`). As you see, it is crucial to understand what n we are talking about!

There are just a few more things to know about Big-O complexity before we can start using it to analyze our algorithms:

1. There are six major complexity classes of algorithms:

    -   Constant-time (`O(1)`)

    -   Sublinear (usually, logarithmic—`O(log n)`)

    -   Linear (`O(n)`) and superlinear (`O(n * log n)`)

- Higher-order polynomial ($O(n^c)$, where c is some constant greater than 1)

- Exponential ($O(c^n)$, where c is usually 2 but, at least, greater than 1)

- Just plain lunatic complex ($O(n!)$ and so forth)—I call them $O(mg)$, jokingly

Each class is a step-function change in performance, especially, at scale. We'll talk about each one of them as we'll be discussing the particular examples of algorithms falling into it.

2. Worst-case vs. average-case behavior. In this example, we saw that there may be two counts of operations: for the average case, we can assume that approximately half of the iterations will require assignment (which results in 3,5 operations in each inner loop), and, for the worst case, the number will be exactly 4. As Big-O reduces all numbers to 1, for this example, the difference is irrelevant, but there may be others, for which it is much more drastic and can't be discarded. Usually, for such algorithms, both complexities should be mentioned (alongside ways to avoid worst-case scenarios): a good example is quicksort algorithm described in Chapter 5.

3. We have also seen the so-called "constant factors hidden by the Big-O notation." That is, from the point of view of algorithmic complexity, it doesn't matter if we need to perform 3 operations in the inner loop or 30. Yet, it is quite important in practice, and we'll also discuss it when examining binary search. Even more, some algorithms with better theoretical complexity may be worse in many practical applications due to these hidden factors (e.g., until the dataset reaches a certain size).

4. Finally, besides execution time complexity, there's also space complexity, which instead of the number of operations measures the amount of storage space used proportional to the size of the input. In general, similar approaches are applied to its estimation.

CHAPTER 3

A Crash Course in Lisp

The introductory post for this book, unexpectedly, received quite a lot of attention, which is nice since it prompted some questions, and one of them I planned to address in this chapter.

I expect that there will be two main audiences for this book:

- People who'd like to advance in algorithms and writing efficient programs—the major group

- Lispers, either accomplished or aspiring, who also happen to be interested in algorithms

This chapter is intended primarily for the first group. After reading it, the rest of the Lisp code from the book should become understandable to you. Besides, you'll know the basics to run Lisp and experiment with it if you will so desire.

As for the lispers, you might be interested to glance over this part just to understand my approach to utilizing the language throughout the book.

The Core of Lisp

To effortlessly understand Lisp, you'll have to forget, for a moment, any concepts of how programming languages should work that you might have acquired from your prior experience in coding. Lisp is simpler; and when people bring their Java, C, or Python approaches to programming with it, first of all, the results are suboptimal in terms of code quality (simplicity, clarity, and beauty), and, what's more important, there's much less satisfaction from the process, not to mention very few insights and little new knowledge gained.

© Vsevolod Domkin 2021
V. Domkin, *Programming Algorithms in Lisp*, https://doi.org/10.1007/978-1-4842-6428-7_3

It is much easier to explain Lisp if we begin from a blank slate. In essence, all there is to it is just an evaluation rule: Lisp programs consist of **forms** that are **evaluated** by the compiler. There are 3 + 2 ways how that can happen:

- Self-evaluation: All literal constants (like 1, "hello", etc.) are evaluated to themselves. These literal objects can be either built-in primitive types (1) or data structures ("hello").

- Symbol evaluation: Separate symbols are evaluated as names of variables, functions, types, or classes depending on the context. The default is variable evaluation, that is, if we encounter a symbol foo, the compiler will substitute in its place the current value associated with this variable (more on this a little bit later).

- Expression evaluation: Compound expressions are formed by grouping symbols and literal objects with parentheses. The form (oper 1 foo) is considered a "functional" expression: the operator name is situated in the first position (head) and its arguments, if any, in the subsequent positions (rest).

There are three ways to evaluate a Lisp compound expression:

- There are 25 special operators that are defined in lower-level code and may be considered something like axioms of the language: they are predefined, always present, and immutable. Those are the building blocks, on top of which all else is constructed, and they include the sequential block operator, the conditional expression if, and the unconditional jump go, to name a few. If oper is the name of a special operator, the low-level code for this operator that deals with the arguments in its own unique way is executed.

- There's also ordinary function evaluation: if oper is a function name, first, all the arguments are evaluated with the same evaluation rule, and then the function is called with the obtained values.

- Finally, there's macro evaluation. Macros provide a way to change the evaluation rule for a particular form. If oper names a macro, its code is substituted instead of our expression and then evaluated. Macros are a major topic in Lisp, and they are used to build a large part of the language as well as provide an accessible way, for the users, to extend it. However, they are orthogonal to the subject of this book and won't be discussed in further detail here. You can delve deeper into macros in such books as *On Lisp* or *Let Over Lambda*.

It's important to note that, in Lisp, there's no distinction between statements and expressions, no special keywords, no operator precedence rules, and other similar arbitrary stuff you can stumble upon in other languages. Everything is uniform; everything is an expression in a sense that it will be evaluated and return some value.

A Code Example

To sum up, let's consider an example of the evaluation of a Lisp form. The following one implements the famous binary search algorithm (that we'll discuss in more detail in one of the following chapters):

```
(when (> (length vec) 0)
  (let ((beg 0)
        (end (length vec)))
    (do ()
        ((= beg end))
      (let ((mid (floor (+ beg end) 2)))
        (if (> (aref vec mid) val)
            (setf end mid)
            (setf beg (1+ mid)))))
    (values beg
            (aref vec beg)
            (= (aref vec beg) val))))
```

It is a compound form. In it, the so-called top-level form is when, which is a macro for a one-clause conditional expression: an if with only the true branch. First, it evaluates the expression (> (length vec) 0), which is an ordinary function for a logical operator > applied to two args: the result of obtaining the length of the contents of the variable vec and a constant 0. If the evaluation returns true, that is, the length of vec is greater than 0, the rest of the form is evaluated in the same manner. The result of the evaluation, if nothing exceptional happens, is either false (which is called nil, in Lisp) or three values returned from the last form (values ...). In the following, we'll talk about other operators shown here.

But first I need to say a few words about RUTILS. It is a third-party library developed by me that provides a number of extensions to the standard Lisp syntax and its basic operators. The reason for its existence is that the Lisp standard is not going to change ever, and, as everything in this world, it has its flaws. Besides, our understanding of what constitutes elegant and efficient code evolves over time. The great advantage of the Lisp standard, however, which counteracts the issue of its immutability, is that its authors had put into it multiple ways to modify and evolve the language at almost all levels starting from even the basic syntax. And this addresses our ultimate need, after all: we're not so interested in changing the standard as in changing the language. So RUTILS is one of the ways of evolving Lisp; and its purpose is to make programming in it more accessible without compromising the core principles of the language. So I will utilize a number of RUTILS features throughout this book, explaining them as needed. Surely, using a particular third-party extension is a question of preference and taste, and it might not be approved by some of the Lisp old-times, but no worries: in your code, you'll be able to easily swap them for your favorite alternatives. Yet, completely rejecting this option is puristic and impractical.

The REPL

Lisp programs are supposed to be run not only in a one-off fashion of simple scripts but also as live systems that operate over long periods of time experiencing change not only of their data but also code. This general way of interaction with a program is called Read-Eval-Print Loop (REPL), which literally means that the Lisp compiler reads a form, evaluates it with the aforementioned rule, prints the results back to the user, and loops over.

REPL is the default way to interact with a Lisp program, and it is very similar to the Unix shell. When you run your Lisp (e.g., by entering `sbcl` at the shell), you'll drop into the REPL. We'll precede all REPL-based code interactions in the book with a REPL prompt (`CL-USER>` or similar). Here's an example one:

```
CL-USER> (print "Hello world")
"Hello world"
"Hello world"
```

A curious reader may be asking why `"Hello world"` is printed twice. It's a proof that everything is an expression in Lisp. :) The `print` "statement," unlike in most other languages, not only prints its argument to the console (or other output streams) but also returns it as is. This comes very handy when debugging, as you can wrap almost any form in a `print` not changing the flow of the program.

Obviously, if the interaction is not necessary, just the read-eval part may remain. But, what's more important, Lisp provides a way to customize every stage of the process:

- At the `read` stage, special syntax ("syntax sugar") may be introduced via a mechanism called reader macros.

- Ordinary macros are a way to customize the `eval` stage.

- The `print` stage is conceptually the simplest one, and there's also a standard way to customize object printing via the Common Lisp Object System's (CLOS) `print-object` function.

- The `loop` stage can be replaced by any desired program logic.

Basic Expressions

The structural programming paradigm states that all programs can be expressed in terms of three basic constructs: sequential execution, branching, and looping. Let's see how these operators are expressed in Lisp.

Sequential Execution

The simplest program flow is sequential execution. In all imperative languages, it is what is assumed to happen if you put several forms in a row and evaluate the resulting code block, like this:

```
CL-USER> (print "hello") (+ 2 2)
"hello"
4
```

The value returned by the last expression is returned as the value of the whole sequence.

Here, the REPL interaction forms an implicit unit of sequential code. However, there are many cases when we need to explicitly delimit such units. This can be done with the `block` operator:

```
CL-USER> (block test
           (print "hello")
           (+ 2 2))
"hello"
4
```

Such block has a name (in this example, `test`). This allows to prematurely end its execution by using an operator `return-from`:

```
CL-USER> (block test
           (return-from test 0)
           (print "hello")
           (+ 2 2))
0
```

A shorthand `return` is used to exit from blocks with a `nil` name (which are implicit in most of the looping constructs we'll see further):

```
CL-USER> (block nil
           (return 0)
           (print "hello")
           (+ 2 2))
0
```

Finally, if we don't even plan to ever prematurely return from a block, we can use the progn operator that doesn't require a name:

```
CL-USER> (progn
          (print "hello")
          (+ 2 2))
"hello"
4
```

Branching

Conditional expressions calculate the value of their first form and, depending on it, execute one of several alternative code paths. The basic conditional expression is if:

```
CL-USER> (if nil
            (print "hello")
            (print "world"))
"world"
"world"
```

As we've seen, nil is used to represent logical falsity, in Lisp. All other values are considered logically true, including the symbol t which directly has the meaning of truth.

And when we need to do several things at once, in one of the conditional branches, it's one of the cases when we need to use progn or block:

```
CL-USER> (if (+ 2 2)
            (progn (print "hello")
                   4)
            (print "world"))
"hello"
4
```

However, often we don't need both branches of the expressions, that is, we don't care what will happen if our condition doesn't hold (or holds). This is such a common case that there are special expressions for it in Lisp—when and unless:

```
CL-USER> (when (+ 2 2)
```

```
            (print "hello")
            4)
"world"
4
CL-USER> (unless (+ 2 2)
            (print "hello")
            4)
NIL
```

As you see, it's also handy because you don't have to explicitly wrap the sequential forms in a progn.

One other standard conditional expression is cond, which is used when we want to evaluate several conditions in a row:

```
CL-USER> (cond
            ((typep 4 'string)
             (print "hello"))
            ((> 4 2)
             (print "world")
             nil)
            (t
             (print "can't get here")))
"world"
NIL
```

The t case is a catch-all that will trigger if none of the previous conditions worked (as its condition is always true). The preceding code is equivalent to the following:

```
(if (typep 4 'string)
    (print "hello")
    (if (> 4 2)
        (progn
          (print "world")
          nil)
        (print "can't get here")))
```

There are many more conditional expressions in Lisp, and it's very easy to define your own with macros (it's actually how when, unless, and cond are defined), and when there arises a need to use a special one, we'll discuss its implementation.

Looping

Like with branching, Lisp has a rich set of looping constructs, and it's also easy to define new ones when necessary. This approach is different from the mainstream languages that usually have a small number of such statements and, sometimes, provide an extension mechanism via polymorphism. And it's even considered to be a virtue justified by the idea that it's less confusing for the beginners. It makes sense to a degree. Still, in Lisp, both generic and custom approaches manage to coexist and complement each other. Yet, the tradition of defining custom control constructs is very strong. Why? One justification for this is the parallel to human languages: indeed, when and unless, as well as dotimes and loop, are either directly words from the human language or derived from natural language expressions. Our mother tongues are not so primitive and dry. The other reason is because you can. That is, it's so much easier to define custom syntactic extensions in Lisp than in other languages that sometimes it's just impossible to resist. :) And in many use cases, they make the code much simpler and clearer.

Anyway, for a complete beginner, actually, you have to know the same number of iteration constructs as in any other language. The simplest one is dotimes that iterates the counter variable a given number of times (from 0 to (- times 1)) and executes the body on each iteration. It is analogous to for (int i = 0; i < times; i++) loops found in C-like languages:

```
CL-USER> (dotimes (i 3)
           (print i))
0
1
2
NIL
```

The return value is nil by default, although it may be specified in the loop header.

The most versatile (and low-level) looping construct, on the other hand, is do:

```
CL-USER> (do ((i 0 (1+ i))
              (prompt (read-line) (read-line)))
             ((> i 1) i)
          (print (pair i prompt))
          (terpri))
foo

(0 "foo")
bar

(1 "bar")


2
```

do iterates a number of variables (zero or more) that are defined in the first part (here, i and prompt) until the termination condition in the second part is satisfied (here, (> i 1)) and, as with dotimes (and other do-style macros), executes its body—the rest of the forms (here, print and terpri, which is a shorthand for printing a newline). read-line reads from standard input until newline is encountered, and 1+ returns the current value of i increased by 1.

All do-style macros (and there's quite a number of them, both built-in and provided from external libraries: dolist, dotree, do-register-groups, dolines, etc.) have an optional return value. In do, it follows the termination condition—here, just return the final value of i.

Besides do-style iteration, there's also a substantially different beast in CL ecosystem—the infamous loop macro. It is very versatile, although somewhat unlispy in terms of syntax and with a few surprising behaviors. But elaborating on it is beyond the scope of this book, especially since there's an excellent introduction to loop in Peter Seibel's *LOOP for Black Belts*.

Many languages provide a generic looping construct that is able to iterate an arbitrary sequence, a generator, and other similar-behaving things—usually, some variant of foreach. We'll return to such constructs after speaking about sequences in more detail.

And there's also an alternative iteration philosophy: the functional one, which is based on higher-order functions (map, reduce, and similar)—we'll cover it in more detail in the following chapters also.

Procedures and Variables

We have covered the three pillars of structural programming, but one essential, in fact, the most essential, construct still remains—variables and procedures.

What if I told you that you can perform the same computation many times, but changing some parameters... OK, OK, pathetic joke. So procedures are the simplest way to reuse computations, and procedures accept arguments, which allows to pass values into their bodies. A procedure, in Lisp, is called lambda. You can define one like this: (lambda (x y) (+ x y)). When used, such procedure—also often called a function, although it's quite different from what we consider a mathematical function, and, in this case, called an anonymous function as it doesn't have any name—will produce the sum of its inputs:

```
CL-USER> ((lambda (x y) (+ x y)) 2 2)
4
```

It is quite cumbersome to refer to procedures by their full code signature, and an obvious solution is to assign names to them. A common way to do that in Lisp is via the defun macro:

```
CL-USER> (defun add2 (x y) (+ x y))
ADD2
CL-USER> (add2 2 2)
4
```

The arguments of a procedure are examples of variables. Variables are used to name memory cells whose contents are used more than once and may be changed in the process. They serve different purposes:

- To pass data into procedures

- As temporary placeholders for some varying data in code blocks (like loop counters)

- As a way to store computation results for further reuse

- To define program configuration parameters (like the OS environment variables, which can also be thought of as arguments to the main function of our program)

- To refer to global objects that should be accessible from anywhere in the program (like the *standard-output* stream)

- And more

Can we live without variables? Theoretically, well, maybe. At least, there's the so-called point-free style of programming that strongly discourages the use of variables. But, as they say, don't try this at home (at least, until you know perfectly well what you're doing :) Can we replace variables with constants or single-assignment variables, that is, variables that can't change over time? Such approach is promoted by the so-called *purely* functional languages. To a certain degree, yes. But, from the point of view of algorithm development, it makes life a lot harder by complicating many optimizations if not totally outruling them.

So how to define variables in Lisp? You've already seen some of the variants: procedural arguments and let bindings. Such variables are called local or lexical, in Lisp parlance. That's because they are only accessible locally throughout the execution of the code block, in which they are defined. let is a general way to introduce such local variables, which is lambda in disguise (a thin layer of syntax sugar over it):

```
CL-USER> (let ((x 2))
           (+ x x))
4
CL-USER> ((lambda (x) (+ x x))
          2)
4
```

While with lambda you can create a procedure in one place, possibly assign it to a variable (that's what, in essence, defun does), and then apply many times in various places, with let you define a procedure and immediately call it, leaving no way to store it and reapply again afterward. That's even more anonymous than an anonymous function! Also, it requires no overhead, from the compiler. But the mechanism is the same.

Creating variables via let is called binding, because they are immediately assigned (bound with) values. It is possible to bind several variables at once:

```
CL-USER> (let ((x 2)
               (y 2))
           (+ x y))
4
```

However, we often want to define a row of variables with next ones using the previous ones' values. It is cumbersome to do with let, because you need nesting (as procedural arguments are assigned independently):

```
(let ((len (length list)))
  (let ((mid (floor len 2)))
    (let ((left-part (subseq list 0 mid))
          (right-part (subseq list mid)))
      ...)))
```

To simplify this use case, there's let*:

```
(let* ((len (length list))
       (mid (floor len 2))
       (left-part (subseq list 0 mid))
       (right-part (subseq list mid)))
  ...)
```

However, there are many other ways to define variables: bind multiple values at once; perform the so-called "destructuring" binding when the contents of a data structure (usually, a list) are assigned to several variables, first element to the first variable, second to the second, and so on; access the slots of a certain structure, and so on. For such use cases, there's with binding from RUTILS, which works like let* with extra powers. Here's a very simple example:

```
(with ((len (length list))
       (mid rem (floor len 2))
       ;; this group produces a list of 2 sublists that are bound
       ;; to left-part and right-part
       ;; NB. The ';' character starts a comment here
       ((left-part right-part) (group mid list)))
  ...
```

In the code throughout this book, you'll only see these two binding constructs: `let` for trivial and parallel bindings and `with` for all the rest.

As we said, variables may not only be defined, or they'd be called "constants" instead, but also modified. To alter the variable's value, we'll use the `setf` operator:

```
CL-USER> (let ((x 2))
           (print (+ x x))
           (setf x 4)
           (+ x x))
4
8
```

Modification, generally, is a dangerous construct as it can create unexpected action-at-a-distance effects, when changing the value of a variable in one place of the code affects the execution of a different part that uses the same variable. This, however, can't happen with lexical variables: each `let` creates its own scope that shields the previous values from modification (just as passing arguments to a procedure call and modifying them within the call doesn't alter those values, in the calling code):

```
CL-USER> (let ((x 2))
           (print (+ x x))
           (let ((x 4))
             (print (+ x x)))
           (print (+ x x)))
4
8
4
```

Obviously, when you have two `let`s in different places using the same variable name, they don't affect each other, and these two variables are, actually, totally distinct.

Yet, sometimes it is useful to modify a variable in one place and see the effect in another. The variables, which have such behavior, are called global or dynamic (and also special, in Lisp jargon). They have several important purposes. One of them is defining important configuration parameters that need to be accessible anywhere. The other is referencing general-purpose singleton objects like the standard streams or the state of the random number generator. Yet another is pointing to some context that can be altered in certain places subject to the needs of a particular procedure (for instance, the *package* global variable determines in what package we operate—CL-USER in all previous examples). More advanced uses for global variables also exist. The common way to define a global variable is with defparameter, which specifies its initial value:

```
(defparameter *connection* nil
  "A default connection object.") ; this is a docstring describing the
  variable
```

Global variables, in Lisp, usually have so-called "earmuffs" around their names to remind the user of what they are dealing with. Due to their action-at-a-distance feature, it is not the safest programming language feature, and even a "global variables considered harmful" mantra exists. Lisp is, however, not one of those squeamish languages, and it finds many uses for special variables. By the way, they are called "special" due to a special feature, which greatly broadens the possibilities for their sane usage: if bound in let, they act as lexical variables, that is, the previous value is preserved and restored upon leaving the body of a let:

```
CL-USER> (defparameter *temp* 1)
*TEMP*
CL-USER> (print *temp*)
1
CL-USER> (progn
           (let ((*temp* 2))
             (print *temp*)
             (setf *temp* 4)
             (print *temp*))
           *temp*)
2
4
1
```

Procedures in Lisp are first-class objects. This means the one you can assign to a variable as well as inspect and redefine at runtime and, consequently, do many other useful things with. The funcall operator[1] will call a procedure passed to it as an argument:

---

[1] RUTILS provides an abbreviation of the standard funcall to simply call. It was surely fun to be able to call a function from a variable back in the 1960s, but now it has become so much more common that there's no need for the prefix. ;)

```
CL-USER> (funcall 'add2 2 2)
4
CL-USER> (let ((add2 (lambda (x y) (+ x y))))
           (funcall add2 2 2))
4
```

In fact, defining a function with defun also creates a global variable, although in the function namespace. Functions, types, classes—all of these objects are usually defined as global. However, for functions, there's a way to define them locally with flet:

```
CL-USER> (foo 1)
;; ERROR: The function CL-USER::FOO is undefined.
CL-USER> (flet ((foo (x) (1+ x)))
           (foo 1))
2
CL-USER> (foo 1)
;; ERROR: The function CL-USER::FOO is undefined.
```

Comments

Finally, there's one more syntax we need to know: how to put comments in the code. Only losers don't comment their code, and comments will be used extensively, throughout this book, to explain some parts of the code examples inside of them. Comments, in Lisp, start with a ; character and end at the end of a line. So the following snippet is a comment: ; this is a comment. There's also a common style of commenting, when short comments that follow the current line of code start with a single ;, longer comments for a certain code block precede it, occupy the whole line or a number of lines, and start with ;;, and comments for a code section that include several Lisp top-level forms (global definitions) start with ;;; and also occupy whole lines. Besides, each global definition can have a special comment-like string, called the "docstring," that is intended to describe its purpose and usage and that can be queried programmatically. To put it all together, this is how different comments may look like:

```
;;; Some code section

(defun this ()
  "This has a curious docstring."
```

```
...)
(defun that ()
  ...
  ;; this is an interesting block don't you find?
  (block interesting
    (print "hello"))) ; it prints hello
```

Getting Started

I strongly encourage you to play around with the code presented in the following chapters of the book. Try to improve it, find issues with it, and come up with fixes and measure and trace everything. This will not only help you master some Lisp but also understand much deeper the descriptions of the discussed algorithms and data structures, their pitfalls, and corner cases. Doing that is, in fact, quite easy. All you need is install some Lisp (preferably, SBCL or CCL) and a couple of add-ons.

As I said in the preceding text, the usual way to work with Lisp is interacting with its REPL. Running the REPL is fairly straightforward. On my Linux Mint, I'd run the following commands:

```
$ apt-get install sbcl rlwrap
...
$ rlwrap sbcl
...
*  (print "hello world")

"hello world"
"hello world"
*
```

* is the raw Lisp prompt. It's, basically, the same as the CL-USER> prompt you'll see in SLIME, but less powerful in terms of code completion, debugging, and so on. You can also run a Lisp script file: sbcl --script hello.lisp. If it contains just a single (print "hello world") line, we'll see the "hello world" phrase printed to the console.

This is a working but not the most convenient setup. A much more advanced environment is SLIME that works inside Emacs (a similar project for vim is called

SLIMV). There exist a number of other solutions: some Lisp implementations provide an IDE, and some IDEs and editors provide integration.

In our experiments, we'll often rely on third-party additions to the language. All of them will be prefixed with a package qualifier to clearly distinguish those extensions from the standard Lisp constructs. Most often you'll see RUTILS operators bearing a prefix rtl. This will make the code look a bit heavier than it should (as usually such utility functions are imported and used on par with the standard ones). In the first edition of the book, all the REPL interactions were shown in the context of the RTL-USER package that is, basically, CL-USER + RUTILS, removing the necessity for using the rtl prefix. However, to make the code examples more in line with vanilla Common Lisp, we decided to fall back to the default way of basing the code in the package CL-USER and not importing any libraries, instead referring to their symbols by the fully qualified name.

To access RUTILS and other third-party libraries that will be mentioned throughout the book, you'll first need to load them using Quicklisp—a Lisp extensions manager similar to Debian apt or Python pip. Here is what you'll have to do after starting the REPL to be able to run most of the code examples from the following chapters:

```
* (ql:quickload :rutils)
* (named-readtables:in-readtable  rtl:rutils-readtable)
```

Well, that's enough Lisp you'll need to know to start. We'll get acquainted with other Lisp concepts as they will become needed for the next chapters of this book. Yet, you're all set to read and write Lisp programs. They may seem unfamiliar at first, but as you overcome the initial bump and get used to their parenthesized prefix surface syntax, I promise that you'll be able to recognize and appreciate their clarity and conciseness.

So, as they say in Lisp land, happy hacking!

CHAPTER 4

Data Structures

The next several chapters will be describing the basic data structures that every programming language provides, their usage, and the most important algorithms relevant to them. And we'll start with the notion of a data structure and tuples or structs that are the most primitive and essential ones.

Data Structures vs. Algorithms

Let's start with a somewhat abstract question: What's more important, algorithms or data structures?

From one point of view, algorithms are the essence of many programs, while data structures may seem secondary. Besides, although a majority of algorithms rely on certain features of particular data structures, not all do. Good examples of the data structure–relying algorithms are heapsort, search using BSTs, and Union-Find. And of the other type are the sieve of Eratosthenes and consistent hashing.

At the same time, some seasoned developers state that when the right data structure is found, the algorithm will almost write itself. Linus Torvalds, the creator of Linux, is quoted saying

> Bad programmers worry about the code. Good programmers worry about data structures and their relationships.

© Vsevolod Domkin 2021
V. Domkin, *Programming Algorithms in Lisp*, https://doi.org/10.1007/978-1-4842-6428-7_4

A somewhat less poignant version of the same idea is formulated in *The Art of Unix Programming* by Eric S. Raymond as the "Rule of Representation":

> *Fold knowledge into data so program logic can be stupid and robust.*

> *Even the simplest procedural logic is hard for humans to verify, but quite complex data structures are fairly easy to model and reason about. To see this, compare the expressiveness and explanatory power of a diagram of (say) a fifty-node pointer tree with a flowchart of a fifty-line program. Or, compare an array initializer expressing a conversion table with an equivalent switch statement. The difference in transparency and clarity is dramatic.*

> *Data is more tractable than program logic. It follows that where you see a choice between complexity in data structures and complexity in code, choose the former. More: in evolving a design, you should actively seek ways to shift complexity from code to data.*

Data structures are more static than algorithms. Surely, most of them allow change of their contents over time, but there are certain invariants that always hold. This allows reasoning by simple induction: consider only two (or at least a small number of) cases, the base one(s) and the general. In other words, data structures remove, in the main, the notion of time from consideration, and change over time is one of the major causes of program complexity. In other words, data structures are declarative, while most of the algorithms are imperative. The advantage of the declarative approach is that you don't have to imagine (trace) the flow of time through it.

So this book, like most other books on the subject, is organized around data structures. The majority of the chapters present a particular structure and its properties and interface and explain the algorithms associated with it, showing its real-world use cases. Yet, some important algorithms don't require a particular data structure, so there are also several chapters dedicated exclusively to them.

The Data Structure Concept

Among data structures, there are, actually, two distinct kinds: abstract and concrete. The significant difference between them is that an abstract structure is just an interface (a set of operations) and a number of conditions or invariants that have to be met. Their particular implementations, which may differ significantly in efficiency characteristics and inner mechanisms, are provided by the concrete data structures. For instance, an abstract data structure queue may be described by just two operations: enqueue that adds an item to the end of the queue and dequeue that gets an item at the beginning and removes it. There's also a constraint that the items should be dequeued in the same order they are enqueued. Now, a queue may be implemented using a number of different underlying data structures: a linked or a double-linked list, an array, or a tree. Each one having different efficiency characteristics and additional properties beyond the queue interface. We'll discuss both kinds in the book, focusing on the concrete structures and explaining their usage to implement a particular abstract interface.

The term data structures has somewhat fallen from grace in the recent years, being often replaced by conceptually more loaded notions of types, in the context of the functional programming paradigm, or classes, in the object-oriented one. Yet, both of those notions imply something more than just algorithmic machinery we're exclusively interested in, for this book. First of all, they also distinguish among primitive values (numbers, characters, etc.) that are all non-distinct, in the context of algorithms. Besides, classes form a hierarchy of inheritance, while types are associated with algebraic rules of category theory. So we'll stick to a neutral data structures term, throughout the book, with occasional mentions of the other variants where appropriate.

Contiguous and Linked Data Structures

The current computer architectures consist of a central processor (CPU), memory, and peripheral input-output (IO) devices. The data is someway exchanged with the outside world via the IO devices, stored in memory, and processed by the CPU. And there's a crucial constraint, called the von Neumann's bottleneck: the CPU can only process data that is stored inside of it in a limited number of special basic memory blocks called registers. So it has to constantly move data elements back and forth between the registers and main memory (using intermediate cache to speed up the process). Now, there are things that can fit in a register and those that can't. The first ones are called primitive and mostly unite those items that can be directly represented with integer numbers: integers proper, floats, and characters. Everything that requires a custom data structure to be represented can't be put in a register as a whole.

Another item that fits into the processor register is a memory address. In fact, there's an important constant—the number of bits in a general-purpose register, which defines the maximum memory address that a particular CPU may handle and, thus, the maximum amount of memory it can work with. For a 32-bit architecture it's 2^32 (4 GB) and for 64-bit—you've guessed it—2^64. A memory address is usually called a **pointer**, and if you put a pointer in a register, there are commands that allow the CPU to retrieve the data in-memory from where it points.

So there are two ways to place a data structure inside the memory:

- A contiguous structure occupies a single chunk of memory, and its contents are stored in adjacent memory blocks. To access a particular piece, we should know the offset of its beginning from the start of the memory range allocated to the structure. (This is usually handled by the compiler.) When the processor needs to read or write to this piece, it will use the pointer calculated as the sum of the base address of the structure and the offset. The examples of contiguous structures are arrays and structs.

- A linked structure, on the contrary, doesn't occupy a contiguous block of memory, that is, its contents reside in different places. This means that pointers to a particular piece can't be pre-calculated and should be stored in the structure itself. Such structures are much more flexible at the cost of this additional overhead both in terms of used space and time to access an element (which may require several hops when there's nesting, while in the contiguous structure, it is always constant). There exist a multitude of linked data structures like lists, trees, and graphs.

Tuples

In most languages, some common data structures, like arrays or lists, are "built-in," but, under the hood, they will mostly work in the same way as any user-defined ones. To implement an arbitrary data structure, these languages provide a special mechanism called records, structs, objects, and so on. The proper name for it would be "tuple." It is the data structure that consists of a number of fields, each one holding either a primitive value, another tuple, or a pointer to another tuple of any type. This way a tuple can represent any structure, including nested and recursive ones. In the context of type theory, such structures are called product types.

A tuple is an abstract data structure, and its sole interface is the field accessor function: by name (a named tuple) or index (an anonymous tuple). It can be implemented in various ways, although a contiguous variant with constant-time access is preferred. However, in many languages, especially dynamic, programmers often use lists or dynamic arrays to create throw-away ad hoc tuples. Python has a dedicated tuple data type that is often used for this purpose, which is a linked data structure under the hood. The following Python function will return a tuple (written in parens) of a decimal and remainder parts of the number x:

```python
def truncate(x):
    dec = int(x)
    rem = x - dec
    return (dec, rem)
```

This is a simple and not very efficient way that may have its place when the number of fields is small and the lifetime of the structure is short. However, a better approach both from the point of view of efficiency and code clarity is to use a predefined structure. In Lisp, a tuple is called "struct" and is defined with defstruct, which uses a contiguous representation by default (although there's an option to use a linked list under the hood). The following is the definition of a simple pair data structure that has two fields (called "slots" in Lisp parlance)—left and right:

```lisp
(defstruct pair
  left right)
```

The defstruct macro, in fact, generates several definitions: of the struct type, its constructor that will be called make-pair and have two keyword arguments :left and :right and field accessors pair-left and pair-right. Also, a common print-object method for structs will work for our new structure, as well as a reader macro to restore it from the printed form. Here's how it all fits together:

```lisp
CL-USER> (make-pair :left "foo" :right "bar")
#S(PAIR :LEFT "foo" :RIGHT "bar")
CL-USER> (pair-right (read-from-string (prin1-to-string *)))
"bar"
```

prin1-to-string and read-from-string are complimentary Lisp functions that allow to print the value in a computer-readable form (if an appropriate print-function is provided) and read it back. Good print representations readable to both humans and, ideally, computers are very important to code transparency and should never be neglected.

There's a way to customize every part of the definition. For instance, if we plan to use pairs frequently, we can leave out the pair- prefix by specifying the (:conc-name nil) property. Here is an improved pair definition and shorthand constructor for it from RUTILS, which we'll use throughout the book. It uses :type list allocation to integrate with destructuring macros:

```
(defstruct (pair (:type list) (:conc-name nil))
  "A generic pair with left (LT) and right (RT) elements."
  lt rt)

(defun pair (x y)
  "A shortcut to make a pair of X and Y."
  (make-pair :lt x :rt y))
```

Passing Data Structures in Function Calls

One final remark. There are two ways to use data structures with functions: either pass them directly via copying appropriate memory areas (**call-by-value**)—an approach usually applied to primitive types—or pass a pointer (**call-by-reference**). In the first case, there's no way to modify the contents of the original structure in the called function, while in the second variant it is possible, so the risk of unwarranted change should be taken into account. The usual way to handle it is by making a copy before invoking any changes, although, sometimes, mutation of the original data structure may be intended so a copy is not needed. Obviously, the call-by-reference approach is more general, because it allows both modification and copying, and more efficient because copying is on demand. That's why it is the default way to handle structures (and objects) in most programming languages. In a low-level language like C, however, both variants are supported. Moreover, in C++, the pass-by-reference has two kinds: pass the pointer and pass what's actually called a reference, which is syntax sugar over pointers that allows accessing the argument with non-pointer syntax (dot instead of arrow) and adds a couple of restrictions. But the general idea, regardless of the idiosyncrasies of particular languages, remains the same.

Structs in Action: Union-Find

Data structures come in various shapes and flavors. Here, I'd like to mention one peculiar and interesting example that is both a data structure and an algorithm, to some extent. Even the name speaks about certain operations rather than a static form. Well, most of the more advanced data structures all have this feature that they are defined not only by the shape and arrangement but also via the set of operations that are applicable. Union-Find is a family of data structure–algorithms that can be used for efficient determination of set membership in sets that change over time. They may be used for finding the disjoint parts in networks, detection of cycles in graphs, finding the minimum spanning tree, and so forth. One practical example of such problems is automatic image segmentation: separating different parts of an image, a car from the background or a cancer cell from a normal one.

Let's consider the following problem: How to determine if two points of the graph have a path between them, given a graph that is a set of points (vertices) and edges between some of the pairs of these points? A path in the graph is a sequence of points leading from source to destination with each pair having an edge that connects them. If some path between two points exists, they belong to the same component, and if it doesn't, to two disjoint ones.

Here is a graph with three disjoint components:

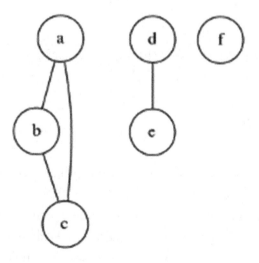

For two arbitrary points, how to determine if they have a connecting path? The naive implementation may take one of them and start building all the possible paths (this may be done in a breadth-first or depth-first manner or even randomly). Anyway, such procedure will, generally, require a number of steps proportional to the number of vertices of the graph. Can we do better? This is a usual question that leads to the creation of more efficient algorithms.

The Union-Find approach is based on a simple idea: when adding, the items record the id of the component they belong to. But how to determine this id? Use the id associated with some point already in this subset or the current point's id if the point is in a subset of its own. And what if we have the subsets already formed? No problem. We can simulate the addition process by iterating over each vertex and taking the id of an arbitrary point it's connected to as the subset's id. The following is the implementation of this approach (to simplify the code, we'll use the pointers to point structs instead of ids, but, conceptually, it's the same idea):

```
(defstruct point
  parent)  ; if the parent is null the point is the root

(defun uf-union (point1 point2)
  "Join the subsets of POINT1 and POINT2."
  (setf (point-parent point1) (or (point-parent point2)
                                  point2)))

(defun uf-find (point)
  "Determine the id of the subset that a POINT belongs to."
  (let ((parent (point-parent point)))
    (if parent
        (uf-find parent)
        point)))
```

Just calling (make-point) will add a new subset with a single item in it to our set.

Note that uf-find uses recursion to find the root of the subset, that is, the point that was added first. So, for each vertex, we store some intermediary data, and, to get the subset id, each time, we'll have to perform additional calculations. This way, we managed to reduce the average-case find time, but, still, haven't completely excluded the possibility of it requiring traversal of every element of the set. Such so-called degraded case may manifest when each item is added referencing the previously added one. That is, there will be a single subset with a chain of its members connected to the next one like this: a -> b -> c -> d. If we call uf-find on a, it will have to enumerate all of the set's elements.

Yet, there is a way to improve uf-find behavior: by compressing the tree depth to make all points along the path to the root point to it, that is, squashing each chain into a wide shallow tree of depth 1:

```
    d
^  ^  ^
|  |  |
a  b  c
```

Unfortunately, we can't do that, at once, for the whole subset, but, during each run of uf-find, we can compress one path, which will also shorten all the paths in the subtree that is rooted in the points on it! Still, this cannot guarantee that there will not be a sequence of enough unions to grow the trees faster than finds can flatten them. But there's another tweak that, combined with path compression, allows to ensure sublinear (actually, almost constant) time of both operations: keep track of the size of all trees and link the smaller tree below the larger one. This will ensure that all trees' heights will stay below (log n). The rigorous proof of that is quite complex, although, intuitively, we can see the tendency by looking at the base case: if we add a two-element tree and a one-element one, we'll still get the tree of the height 2.

Here is the implementation of the optimized version:

```
(defstruct point
  parent
  (size 1))

(defun uf-find (point)
  (let ((parent (point-parent point)))
    (if parent
        ;; here, we use the fact that the assignment will also return
        ;; the value to perform both path compression and find
        (setf (point-parent point) (uf-find parent))
        point)))
```

```
(defun uf-union (point1 point2)
  (rtl:with ((root1 (uf-find point1))
             (root2 (uf-find point2))
             (major minor (if (> (point-size root1)
                                 (point-size root2))
                              (values root1 root2)
                              (values root2 root1))))
    (incf (point-size major) (point-size minor))
    (setf (point-parent minor) major)))
```

Here, Lisp multiple `values` come handy, to simplify the code.[1]

The suggested approach is quite simple in implementation but complex in complexity analysis. So I'll have to give just the final result: m Union-Find operations, with tree weighting and path compression, on a set of n objects will work in $O((m + n)$ $\log^* n)$ (where $\log^*$ is an iterated logarithm—a very slowly increasing function that can be considered a constant, for practical purposes).

Finally, this is how to check if none of the points belong to the same subset in almost $O(n)$ where n is the number of points to check,[2] so in $O(1)$ for two points:

```
(defun uf-disjoint (points)
  "Return true if all of the POINTS belong to different subsets."
  (let ((roots (list)))
    (dolist (point points)
```

---

[1]Moreover, Python has special syntax for destructuring such tuples: `dec, rem = truncate(3.14)`. However, this is not the optimal way to handle returning the primary and one or more secondary values from a function. Lisp provides a more elegant solution called multiple values: all the necessary values are returned via the values form `(values dec rem)` and can be retrieved with `(multiple-value-bind (dec rem) (truncate 3.14) ...)` or `(rtl:with ((dec rem (truncate 3.14))) ...)`. It is more elegant because secondary values may be discarded at will by calling the function in a usual way: `(+ 1 (truncate 3.14))` => 4. This is not possible in Python, because you can't sum a tuple with something.

[2]Actually, the complexity here is $O(n^2)$ due to the use of the function member that performs set membership test in $O(n)$, but it's not essential to the general idea. If `uf-disjoint` is expected to be called with tens or hundreds of points, the roots structure has to be changed to a hash-set that has a $O(1)$ membership operation.

```
    (let ((root (uf-find point)))
      (when (member root roots)
        (return-from uf-disjoint nil))
      (push root roots))))
  t)
```

Takeaways

A couple more observations may be drawn from this simple example:

1. Not always the clever idea that we initially have works flawlessly at once. It is important to check the edge cases for potential problems.

2. We've seen an example of a data structure that directly doesn't exist: pieces of information are distributed over individual data points. Sometimes, there's a choice between storing the information, in a centralized way, in a dedicated structure like a hash-table and distributing it over individual nodes. The latter approach is often more elegant and efficient, although it's not so obvious.

CHAPTER 5

Arrays

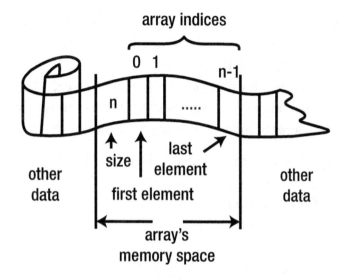

Arrays are, alongside structs, the most basic data structure and, at the same time, the default choice for implementing algorithms. A one-dimensional array that is also called a "vector" is a contiguous structure consisting of the elements of the same type. One of the ways to create such arrays, in Lisp, is this:

```
CL-USER> (make-array 3)
#(0 0 0)
```

The printed result is the literal array representation. It happens that the array is shown to hold 0s, but that's implementation-dependent. Additional specifics can be set during array initialization—for instance, the :element-type, :initial-element, and even full contents:

```
CL-USER> (make-array 3 :element-type 'list :initial-element nil)
#(NIL NIL NIL)
CL-USER> (make-array 3 :initial-contents '(1.0 2.0 3.0))
#(1.0 2.0 3.0)
```

© Vsevolod Domkin 2021
V. Domkin, *Programming Algorithms in Lisp*, https://doi.org/10.1007/978-1-4842-6428-7_5

If you read back such an array, you'll get a new copy with the same contents:

```
CL-USER> #(1.0 2.0 3.0)
#(1.0 2.0 3.0)
```

It is worth noting that the element type restriction is, in fact, not a limitation; the default type is T.[1] In this case, the array will just hold pointers to its elements that can be of arbitrary type. If we specify a more precise type, however, the compiler might be able to optimize storage and access by putting the elements in memory directly in the array space. This is, mainly, useful for numeric arrays, but it makes multiple orders of magnitude difference for them for several reasons, including the existence of vector CPU instructions that operate on such arrays.

The arrays we have created are mutable, that is, we can change their contents, although we cannot resize them. The main operator to access array elements is aref. You will see it in those pieces of code, in this chapter, where we care about performance:

```
CL-USER> (let ((vec (make-array 3 :initial-contents '(1.0 2.0 3.0))))
           (print (aref vec 0))
           (print (rtl:? vec 1))
           (setf (aref vec 2) 4.0))
           (print (rtl:? vec 2))
           (aref vec 3))
1.0
2.0
4.0
; Evaluation aborted on #<SIMPLE-TYPE-ERROR expected-type: (MOD 3) datum: 3>
```

In Lisp, array access beyond its boundary, as expected, causes an error.

It is also possible to create constant arrays using the literal notation #( ). These constants can, actually, be changed in some environments, but don't expect anything nice to come out of such abuse—and the compiler will warn you of that:

```
CL-USER> (let ((vec #(1.0 2.0 3.0)))
           (setf (aref vec 2) nil)
           (print vec))
; caught WARNING:
```

---

[1]...or void* in C, or some other type that allows any element in your language of choice.

```
;   Destructive function (SETF AREF) called on constant data.
;   See also:
;     The ANSI Standard, Special Operator QUOTE
;     The ANSI Standard, Section 3.2.2.3
;
; compilation unit finished
;   caught 1 WARNING condition

#(1.0 2.0 NIL)
```

RUTILS provides more options to easily create arrays with a shorthand notation:

```
RTL-USER> #v(1 2 3)
#(1 2 3)
RTL-USER> (vec 1 2 3)
#(1 2 3)
```

Although the results seem identical, they aren't. The first version creates a mutable analog of #(1 2 3), and the second also makes it adjustable (we'll discuss adjustable or dynamic arrays next).

Arrays as Sequences

Vectors are one of the representatives of the abstract sequence container type that has the following basic interface:

- Inquire the length of a sequence: Performed in Lisp using the function length.

- Access the element by index: The RUTILS ? operator is the most generic variant, while the native one for arrays is aref and a more general elt for all built-in sequences (this also includes lists and, in some implementations, user-defined, so-called, extensible sequences).

- Get the subsequence: The standard provides the function subseq for this purpose.

These methods have some issues that you should mind:

- The length function, for arrays, works in $O(1)$ time as length is tracked in the array structure. There is an alternative (more primitive) way to handle arrays, employed, primarily, in C when the length is not stored and, instead, there's a special termination "symbol" that indicates the end of an array. For instance, C strings have a '\0' termination character, and arrays representing command-line arguments, in the Unix syscalls API for such functions as exec, are terminated with null pointers. Such an approach is, first of all, not efficient from the algorithmic point of view as it requires $O(n)$ time to query the array's length. And, what's even more important, it has proven to be a source of a number of catastrophic security vulnerabilities—the venerable "buffer overflow" family of errors.

- The subseq function creates a copy of the part of its argument, which is an expensive operation. This is the functional approach that is a proper default, but many of the algorithms don't involve subarray mutation, and, for them, a more efficient variant would be to use a shared-structure variant that doesn't make a copy but merely returns a pointer into the original array. Such option is provided, in the Lisp standard, via the so-called displaced arrays, but it is somewhat cumbersome to use. That's why a more straightforward version is present in RUTILS which is named slice:

```
CL-USER> (rtl:with ((vec (rtl:vec 1 2 3))
                    (part (rtl:slice vec 2)))
            (print part)
            (setf (aref part 0) 4)
            (print part)
            vec)
#(3)
#(4)
#(1 2 4)
```

Beyond the basic operations, sequences in Lisp are the target of a number of higher-order functions, such as `find`, `position`, `remove-if`, and so on. We'll get back to discussing their use later in the book.

Dynamic Vectors

Let's examine arrays from the point of view of algorithmic complexity. General-purpose data structures are usually compared by their performance on several common operations and, also, space requirements. These common operations are access, insertion, deletion, and, sometimes, search.

In the case of ordinary arrays, the space used is the minimum possible: almost no overhead is incurred except, perhaps, for some meta-information about array size. Array element access is performed by index in constant time because it's just an offset from the beginning that is the product of index by the size of a single element. Search for an element requires a linear scan of the whole array, or, in the special case of a sorted array, it can be done in $O(\log n)$ using binary search.

Insertion (at the end of an array) and deletion with arrays is problematic, though. Basic arrays are static, that is, they can't be expanded or shrunk at will. The case of expansion requires free space after the end of the array that isn't generally available (because it's already occupied by other data used by the program), so it means that the whole array needs to be relocated to another place in memory with sufficient space. Shrinking is possible, but it still requires relocation of the elements following the deleted one. Hence, both of these operations require $O(n)$ time and may also cause memory fragmentation. This is a major drawback of arrays.

However, arrays definitely should be the default choice for most algorithms. Why? First of all, because of the other excellent properties arrays provide and also because, in many cases, lack of flexibility can be circumvented in a certain manner. One common example is iteration with accumulation of results in a sequence. This is often performed with the help of a stack (as a rule, implemented with a linked list), but, in many cases (especially when the length of the result is known beforehand), arrays may be used to the same effect. Another approach is using dynamic arrays, which add array resizing capabilities. And only in the case when an algorithm requires contiguous manipulation (insertion and deletion) of a collection of items or another advanced flexibility, linked data structures are preferred.

So the first approach to working around the static nature of arrays is possible when we know the target number of elements. For instance, the most common pattern of sequence processing is to map a function over it, which produces the new sequence of the same size filled with results of applying the function to each element of the original sequence. With arrays, it can be performed even more efficiently than with a list. We just need to pre-allocate the resulting vector and set its elements one by one as we process the input:

```
(defun map-vec (fn vec)
  "Map function FN over each element of VEC
   and return the new vector with the results."
  (let ((rez (make-array (length vec))))
    (dotimes (i (length vec))
      (setf (aref rez i) (funcall fn (aref vec i))))
    rez))
```

```
CL-USER> (map-vec '1+ #(1 2 3))
#(2 3 4)
```

It should be noted that the standard map and map-into functions implement the same functionality.

We use a specific accessor aref here instead of generic ? to ensure efficient operation in the so-called "inner loop"—although there's just one loop here, it will be the inner loop of many complex algorithms.

However, in some cases, we don't know the size of the result beforehand. For instance, another popular sequence processing function is called filter or remove- if (-not) in Lisp. It iterates over the sequence and keeps only elements that satisfy/don't satisfy a certain predicate. It is, generally, unknown how many elements will remain, so we can't predict the size of the resulting array. One solution will be to allocate the full-sized array and fill only so many cells as needed. It is a viable approach although suboptimal. Filling the result array can be performed by tracking the current index in it or, in Lisp, by using an array with a **fill-pointer**:

```
(defun clumsy-filter-vec (pred vec)
  "Return the vector with only those elements of VEC
   for which calling pred returns true."
  (let ((rez (make-array (length vec) :fill-pointer 0)))
```

```
   (dotimes (i (length vec))
     (when (funcall pred (aref vec i))
       (vector-push (aref vec i) rez)))
   rez))
CL-USER> (describe (clumsy-filter-vec 'oddp #(1 2 3)))
#(1 3)
  [vector]
Element-type: T
Fill-pointer: 2
Size: 3
Adjustable: yes
Displaced-to: NIL
Displaced-offset: 0
Storage vector: #<(SIMPLE-VECTOR 3) {100E9AF30F}>
```

Another more general way would be to use a "dynamic vector." This is a kind of an array that supports insertion by automatically expanding its size (usually, not one element at a time but proportionally to the current size of the array). Here is how it works:

```
CL-USER> (let ((vec (make-array 0 :fill-pointer t :adjustable t)))
          (dotimes (i 10)
            (vector-push-extend i vec)
            (describe vec)))
#(0)
  [vector]
Element-type: T
Fill-pointer: 1
Size: 1
Adjustable: yes
Displaced-to: NIL
Displaced-offset: 0
Storage vector: #<(SIMPLE-VECTOR 1) {100ED9238F}>#(0 1)
Fill-pointer: 2
Size: 3
```

```
#(0 1 2)
Fill-pointer: 3
Size: 3

#(0 1 2 3)
Element-type: T
Fill-pointer: 4
Size: 7

...

#(0 1 2 3 4 5 6 7)
Fill-pointer: 8
Size: 15

#(0 1 2 3 4 5 6 7 8)
Element-type: T
Fill-pointer: 9
Size: 15

#(0 1 2 3 4 5 6 7 8 9)
Element-type: T
Fill-pointer: 10
Size: 15
```

For such "smart" arrays, the complexity of insertion of an element becomes **asymptotically** constant: resizing and moving elements happens less and less often the more elements are added. With a large number of elements, this comes at a cost of a lot of wasted space, though. At the same time, when the number of elements is small (below 20), it happens often enough, so that the performance is worse than for a linked list that requires a constant number of two operations for each insertion (or one if we don't care to preserve the order). So dynamic vectors are the solution that can be used efficiently only when the number of elements is neither too big nor too small.

Why Are Arrays Indexed from 0

Although most programmers are used to it, not everyone understands clearly why the choice was made, in most programming languages, for 0-based array indexing. Indeed, there are several languages that prefer a 1-based variant (for instance, MATLAB and Lua). This is quite a deep and yet very practical issue that several notable computer scientists, including Dijkstra, have contributed to.

At first glance, it is "natural" to expect the first element of a sequence to be indexed with 1, second with 2, and so on. This means that if we have a subsequence from the first element to the tenth, it will have the beginning index 1 and the ending 10, that is, be a closed interval also called a segment: [1, 10]. The cons of this approach are the following:

1. It is more straightforward to work with half-open intervals (i.e., the ones that don't include the ending index): especially, it is much more convenient to split and merge such intervals and, also, test for membership. With 0-based indexing, our example interval would be half-open: [0, 10).

2. If we consider multidimensional arrays that are most often represented using one-dimensional ones, getting an element of a matrix with indices i and j translates to accessing the element of an underlying vector with an index i*w + j or i + j*h for 0-based arrays, while for 1-based ones, it's more cumbersome: (i-1)*w + j. And if we consider three-dimensional arrays (tensors), we'll still get the obvious i*w*h + j*h + k formula for 0-based arrays and, maybe, (i-1)*w*h + (j-1)*h + k for 1-based ones, although I'm not, actually, sure if it's correct (which shows how such calculations quickly become untractable). Besides, multidimensional array operations that are much more complex than mere indexing also often occur in many practical tasks, and they are also more complex and thus error-prone with base 1.

There are other arguments, but I consider them to be much more minor and a matter of taste and convenience. However, the intervals and multidimensional array issues are quite serious. And here is a good place to quote one of my favorite anecdotes that there are two hard problems in CS: cache invalidation and naming things, and off-by-one errors. Arithmetic errors with indexing are a very nasty kind of bug, and although it can't be avoided altogether, 0-based indexing turns out to be a much more balanced solution.

Now, using 0-based indexing, let's write down the formula for finding the middle element of an array. Usually, it is chosen to be (`floor (length array) 2`). This element will divide the array into two parts, left and right, each one having length at least (`1- (floor (length array) 2)`: The left part will always have such size and will not include the middle element. The right side will start from the middle element and will have the same size if the total number of array elements is even or be one element larger if it is odd.

Multidimensional Arrays

So far, we have only discussed one-dimensional arrays. However, more complex data structures can be represented using simple arrays. The most obvious example of such structures is multidimensional arrays. There are a staggering variety of other structures that can be built on top of arrays, such as binary (or, in fact, any n-ary) trees, hash-tables, and graphs, to name a few. If we have a chance to implement the data structure on an array, usually, we should not hesitate to take it as it will result in constant access time, good cache locality contributing to faster processing, and, in most cases, efficient space usage.

Multidimensional arrays are a contiguous data structure that stores its elements so that, given the coordinates of an element in all dimensions, it can be retrieved according to a known formula. Such arrays are also called **tensors** and, in the case of two-dimensional arrays, matrices. We have already seen one **matrix** example in the discussion of complexity:

```
#2A((1 2 3)
    (4 5 6))
```

A matrix has rows (first dimension) and columns (second dimension). Accordingly, the elements of a matrix may be stored in the row-major or column-major order. In row-major order, the elements are placed row after row—just like the following, that is, the memory will contain the sequence: 1 2 3 4 5 6. In column-major order, they are stored by column (this approach is used in many "mathematical" languages, such as Fortran or MATLAB), so raw memory will look like this: 1 4 2 5 3 6. If row-major order is used, the formula to access the element with coordinates i (row) and j (column) is (`+ (* i n) j`) where n is the length of the matrix's row, that is, its width. In the case of column-major order, it is (+ i (* j m)) where m is the matrix's height. It is necessary to know which storage style is used in a particular language as in numeric computing it is common to intermix libraries written in many languages—C, Fortran, and others—and, in the process, incompatible representations may clash.[2]

Such matrix representation is the most obvious one, but it's not exclusive. Many languages, including Java, use iliffe vectors to represent multidimensional arrays. These are vectors of vectors, that is, each matrix row is stored in a separate one-dimensional array and the matrix is the vector of such vectors. Besides, more specific multidimensional arrays, such as sparse or diagonal matrices, may be represented using more efficient storage techniques at the expense of a possible loss in access speed. Higher-order tensors may also be implemented with the described approaches.

One classic example of operations on multidimensional arrays is matrix multiplication. The following simple straightforward algorithm has the complexity of $O(n^3)$ where n is the matrix dimension. The condition for successful multiplication is equality of height of the first matrix and width of the second one. The cubic complexity is due to three loops— by the outer dimensions of each matrix and by the inner identical dimension:

```
(defun m* (m1 m2)
  (let ((n (array-dimension m1 1))
        (n1 (array-dimension m1 0))
        (n2 (array-dimension m2 1))
        (rez (make-array (list n1 n2))))
    (assert (= n (array-dimension m2 0)))
```

---

[2]Such incompatibility errors are not a cheap thing: for instance, it is reported that the crash of the first Ariane V rocket happened due to interoperation of two programs that used the metric and the imperial measurement systems without explicit conversion of the data. There's an elegant solution to such problem: "dimensional numbers," which are a custom reader macro to encode the measure alongside the number. Here is a formula expressed with such numbers:

```
(defun running-distance-for-1kg-weight-loss (mass)
(* 1/4 (/ #M37600kJ (* #M0.98m/s2 mass))))

CL-USER> (running-distance-for-1kg-weight-loss #M80kg)
119897.96
CL-USER> (running-distance-for-1kg-weight-loss #I200lb)
105732.45
```

The output is, of course, in metric units. Unfortunately, this approach will not be useful for arrays encoded by different languages as they are obtained not by reading the input but by referencing external memory. Instead, a wrapper struct/class is, usually, used to specify the element order.

```
(dotimes (i n1)
  (dotimes (j n2)
    (let ((cur 0))
      (dotimes (k n)
        (incf cur (* (aref m1 i k)
                     (aref m2 k j))))
      (setf (aref rez i j) cur))))
rez))
```

There are more efficient albeit much more complex versions using the divide-and-conquer approach that can work in only $O(n^{2.37})$, but they have significant hidden constants and, that's why, are rarely used in practice, although if you're relying on an established library for matrix operations, such as the Fortran-based BLAS/ATLAS, you will find one of them under the hood.

Binary Search

Now, let's talk about some of the important and instructive array algorithms. The most prominent ones are searching and sorting.

A common sequence operation is searching for the element either to determine if it is present, to get its position, or to retrieve the object that has a certain property (key-based search). The simple way to search for an element in Lisp is using the function find:

```
CL-USER> (let ((vec (make-array 2 :initial-contents
                                  (list (rtl:pair :foo :bar)
                                        (rtl:pair :baz :quux)))))
          (print (find (rtl:pair :foo :bar) vec))
          (print (find (rtl:pair :foo :bar) vec :test 'equal))
          (print (find (rtl:pair :bar :baz) vec :test 'equal))
          (print (find :foo vec :key 'lt)))
NIL
(:FOO :BAR)
NIL
(:FOO :BAR)
```

In the first case, the element was not found due to the wrong comparison predicate: the default eql will only consider two structures to be the same if they're the same object, and, in this case, there will be two separate pairs with the same content. So the second search is successful as equal performs deep comparison. Then the element is not found as it is just not present. And, in the last case, we did the key-based search looking just at the lt element of all pairs in vec.

Such search is called sequential scan because it is performed in a sequential manner over all elements of the vector starting from the beginning (or end if we specify :from-end t) until either the element is found or we have examined all the elements. The complexity of such search is, obviously, O(n), that is, we need to access each element of the collection (if the element is present, we'll look, on average, at n/2 elements and, if not present, always at all n elements).

However, if we know that our sequence is sorted, we can perform the search much faster. The algorithm used for that is one of the most famous algorithms that every programmer has to know and use, from time to time—binary search. The more general idea behind it is called "divide and conquer": if there's some way, looking at one element, to determine the outcome of our global operation for more than just this element, we can discard the part for which we already know that the outcome is negative. In binary search, when we're looking at an arbitrary element of the sorted vector and compare it with the item we search for

- If the element is the same, we have found it.

- If it's smaller, all the previous elements are also smaller and thus uninteresting to us—we need to look only on the subsequent ones.

- If it's greater, all the following elements are not interesting.

Here is an example of search for the value 5 in the array #(1 3 4 5 7 9):

```
1  3  4  5  7  9
--x--x--^

5  7  9
   ^--x--

5  7
^--x--

5 (found)
```

Thus, each time, we can examine the middle element and, after that, can discard half of the elements of the array without checking them. We can repeat such comparisons and halving until the resulting array contains just a single element.

Here's the straightforward binary search implementation using recursion:

```
(defun bin-search (val vec &optional (pos 0))
  (if (> (length vec) 1)
      (rtl:with ((mid (floor (length vec) 2))
                 (cur (aref vec mid)))
        (cond ((< cur val) (bin-search val
                                       (rtl:slice vec mid)
                                       (+ pos mid)))
              ((> cur val) (bin-search val
                                       (rtl:slice vec 0 mid)
                                       pos))
              (t (+ pos mid))))
      (when (= (aref vec 0) val)
        pos)))
```

If the middle element differs from the one we're looking for, it halves the vector until just one element remains. If the element is found, its position (which is passed as an optional third argument to the recursive function) is returned. Note that we assume that the array is sorted. Generally, there's no way to quickly check this property unless we examine all array elements (and thus lose all the benefits of binary search). That's why we don't assert the property in any way and just trust the programmer. :)

An important observation is that such recursion is very similar to a loop that at each stage changes the boundaries we're looking in between. Not every recursive function can be matched with a similar loop so easily (for instance, when there are multiple recursive calls in its body, an additional memory data structure is needed), but when it is possible, it usually makes sense to choose the loop variant. The pros of looping are the avoidance of both the function calls' overhead and the danger of hitting the recursion limit or the stack overflow associated with it, while the pros of recursion are simpler code and better debuggability that comes with the possibility to examine each iteration by tracing using the built-in tools.

Another thing to note is interesting counterintuitive arithmetic of additional comparisons. In our naive approach, we had three cond clauses, that is, up to two comparisons to make at each iteration. In total, we'll look at (log n 2) elements of our array, so we have no more than (/ (1- (log n 2)) n) chance to match the element with the = comparison before we get to inspect the final one-element array. That is, with the probability of (- 1 (/ (1- (log n 2)) n)), we'll have to make all the comparisons up to the final one. Even for such small n as 10, this probability is 0.77 and for 100 0.94. And this is an optimistic estimate for the case when the element searched for is actually present in the array, which may not always be so. Otherwise, we'll have to make all the comparisons. Effectively, these numbers prove the equality comparison meaningless and just a waste of computation, although from "normal" programmer intuition it might seem like a good idea to implement early exit in this situation...

Finally, there's also one famous nonobvious bug associated with the binary search that was still present in many production implementations for many years past the algorithm's inception. It's also a good example of the dangers of forfeiting boundary condition check that is the root of many severe problems plaguing our computer systems by opening them to various exploits. The problem, in our code, may manifest in systems that have limited integer arithmetic with potential overflow. In Lisp, if the result of summing two fixnums is greater than most-positive-fixnum (the maximum number that can be represented directly by the machine word), it will be automatically converted to bignums, which are a slower representation but with unlimited precision:

```
CL-USER> most-positive-fixnum
4611686018427387903
CL-USER> (type-of most-positive-fixnum)
(INTEGER 0 4611686018427387903)
CL-USER> (+ most-positive-fixnum most-positive-fixnum)
9223372036854775806
CL-USER> (type-of (+ most-positive-fixnum most-positive-fixnum))
(INTEGER 4611686018427387904)
```

In many other languages, such as C or Java, what will happen is either silent overflow (the worst), in which case we'll get just the remainder of division of the result by the maximum integer, or an overflow error. Both of these situations are not accounted for in the (floor (+ beg end) 2) line. The simple fix to this problem, which makes sense to keep in mind for future similar situations, is to change the computation to the following equivalent form: (+ beg (floor (- end beg) 2)). It will never overflow. Why? Try to figure out on your own. ;)

Taking all that into account and allowing for a custom comparator function, here's an "optimized" version of binary search that returns three values:

- The final element of the array.

- Its position.

- Has it, actually, matched the element we were searching for?

```
(defun bin-search (val vec &key (less '<) (test '=) (key 'identity))
  (when (plusp (length vec))
    (let ((beg 0)
          (end (1- (length vec))))
      (do ()
          ((= beg end))
        (let ((mid (+ beg (floor (- end beg) 2))))
          (if (funcall less (funcall key (aref vec mid)) val)
              (setf beg (1+ mid))
              (setf end mid))))
      (values (aref vec beg)
              beg
              (funcall test (funcall key (aref vec beg)) val)))))
```

How many loop iterations do we need to complete the search? If we were to take the final one-element array and expand the array from it by adding the discarded half, it would double in size at each step, that is, we'll be raising 2 to the power of the number of expansion iterations (initially, before expansion—after zero iterations—we have one element, which is 2^0; after one iteration, we have two elements; after two iterations, we have four elements, and so on). The number of iterations needed to expand the full array may be calculated by the inverse of exponentiation—the logarithmic function. That is, we'll need (log n 2) iterations (where n is the initial array size). Shrinking the array takes the same as expanding, just in the opposite order, so the complexity of binary search is O(log n).

How big is the speedup from linear to logarithmic complexity? Let's do a quick-and-dirty speed comparison between the built-in (and optimized) sequential scan function find and our bin-search:

```
CL-USER> (rtl:with ((size 100000000)
                    (mid (1+ (/ size 2)))
                    (vec (make-array size)))
           (dotimes (i size)
             (setf (aref vec i) i))
           (time (find mid vec))
           (time (bin-search mid vec)))
Evaluation took:
  0.591 seconds of real time
  0.595787 seconds of total run time (0.595787 user, 0.000000 system)
  100.85% CPU
  ...
Evaluation took:
  0.000 seconds of real time
  0.000000 seconds of total run time (0.000000 user, 0.000000 system)
  100.00% CPU
  ...
```

Unfortunately, I don't have enough RAM on my notebook to make bin-search take at least a millisecond of CPU time. We can count nanoseconds to get the exact difference, but a good number to remember is that (log 1000000 2) is approximately 20, so, for the million-element array, the speedup will be 50000×!

The crucial limitation of binary search is that it requires our sequence to be presorted because sorting before each search already requires at least linear time to complete, which kills any performance benefit we might have expected. There are multiple situations when the presort condition may hold without our intervention:

- All the data is known beforehand, and we can sort it just once prior to running the search, which may be repeated multiple times for different values.

- We maintain the sorted order as we add data. Such an approach is feasible only if addition is performed less frequently than search. This is often the case with databases, which store their indices in sorted order.

57

A final note on binary search: Obviously, it will only work fast for vectors and not linked sequences.

Binary Search in Action: A Fast Specialized In-Memory DB

In one consumer Internet company I was working for, a lot of text processing (which was the company's bread and butter) relied on access to a huge statistical dataset called "ngrams." Ngrams is a simple natural language processing concept: basically, they are phrases of a certain length. A unigram (onegram) is a single word, a bigram a pair of words, and a fivegram a list of five words. Each ngram has some weight associated with it, which is calculated (estimated) from the huge corpus of texts (we used the crawl of the whole Internet). There are numerous ways to estimate this weight, but the basic one is to just count the frequency of the occurrence of a specific ngram phrase in the corpus.

The total number of ngrams may be huge: for our case, the whole dataset, on disk, measured in tens of gigabytes. And the application requires constant random access to it. Using an off-the-shelf database would have incurred us too much overhead as such systems are general-purpose and don't optimize for the particular use cases, like the one we had. So a special-purpose solution was needed. In fact, now there is readily available ngrams handling software, such as KenLM. We have built our own, and, initially, it relied on binary search of the in-memory dataset to answer the queries. Considering the size of the data, what do you think was the number of operations required? I don't remember it exactly, but somewhere between 25 and 30. For handling tens of gigabytes or hundreds of millions/billions of ngrams, quite a decent result. And, most important, it didn't exceed our application's latency limits! The key property that enabled such solution was the fact that all the ngrams were known beforehand and hence the dataset could be presorted. Yet, eventually, we moved to an even faster solution based on perfect hash-tables (that we'll discuss later in this book).

We can outline the operation of such a datastore with the following key structures and functions.

A dictionary *dict* will be used to map words to numeric codes. (We'll discuss hash-tables that are employed for such dictionaries several chapters later. For now, it will be sufficient to say that we can get the index of a word in our dictionary with (rtl:? *dict* word)). The number of entries in the dictionary will be around one million.

All the ngrams will be stored alphabetically sorted in 2-gigabyte files with the following naming scheme: ngram-rank-i.bin. rank is the ngram word count (we were specifically using ngrams of ranks from 1 to 5), and i is the sequence number of the file. The contents of the files will constitute the alternating ngram indices and their frequencies. The index for each ngram will be a vector of 32-bit integers with the length equal to the rank of an ngram. Each element of this vector will represent the index of the word in *dict*. The frequency will also be a 32-bit integer.

All these files will be read into memory. As the structure of the file is regular—each ngram corresponds to a block of (1+ rank) 32-bit integers—it can be treated as a large vector.

For each file, we know the codes of the first and last ngrams. Based on this, the top-level index will be created to facilitate efficiently locating the file that contains a particular ngram.

Next, binary search will be performed directly on the contents of the selected file. The only difference with regular binary search is that the comparisons need to be performed rank times: for each 32-bit code.

A simplified version of the main function get-freq intended to retrieve the ngram frequency for ranks 2–5 will look something like this:

```
(defun get-freq (ngram)
  (rt:with ((rank (length ngram))
            (codes (ngram-codes ngram))
            (vec index found?
                (bin-search codes
                            (ngrams-vec rank codes)
                            :less 'codes<
                            :test 'ngram=)))
    (if found?
        (aref vec rank)
        0)))
```

where

```
(defun ngram-codes (ngram)
  (map-vec (lambda (word) (rtl:? *dict* word))
           ngram))
```

```
(defun ngrams-vec (rank codes)
  (loop :for ((codes1 codes2) ngrams-vec) :across *ngrams-index*
        :when (and (<= (aref codes1 0) (aref codes 0))
                   (codes< codes codes2 :when= t))
        :do (return ngrams-vec)))

(defun codes< (codes1 codes2 &key when=)
  (dotimes (i (length codes1)
              ;; this will be returned when all
              ;; corresponding elements of codes are equal
              when=)
    (cond ((< (aref codes1 i)
              (aref codes2 i))
           (return t))
          ((> (aref codes1 i)
              (aref codes2 i))
           (return nil)))))

(defun ngram= (block1 block2)
  (let ((rank (1- (length block1))))
    (every '= (rtl:slice block1 0 rank)
              (rtl:slice block2 0 rank))))
```

We assume that the *ngrams-index* array containing pairs of codes for the first and last ngrams in the file and the ngram data from the file itself were already initialized. This array should be sorted by the codes of the first ngrams in the pairs. A significant drawback of the original version of this program was that it took quite some time to read all the files (tens of gigabytes) from disk. During this operation, which measured in several dozens of minutes, the application was not responsive. This created a serious bottleneck in the system as a whole and complicated updates as well as put normal operation at additional risk. The solution we utilized to counteract this issue was a common one for such cases: switching to lazy loading using the Unix mmap facility. With this approach, the bounding ngram codes for each file should be precalculated and stored as metadata, to initialize the *ngrams-index* before loading the data itself.

Sorting

Sorting is another fundamental sequence operation that has many applications. Unlike searching, there is no single optimal algorithm for sorting, and different data structures allow different approaches to it. In general, the problem of sorting a sequence is to place all of its elements in a certain order determined by the comparison predicate. There are several aspects that differentiate sorting functions:

- In-place: This kind of sorting is a destructive operation, but it is often desired because it may be faster and also it preserves space (especially relevant when sorting big amounts of data at once). The alternative is copying sort.

- Stable: Whether two elements, which are considered the same by the predicate, retain their original order or may be shuffled.

- Online: Does the function require to see the whole sequence before starting the sorting process, or can it work with each element one by one, always preserving the result of processing the already seen part of the sequence in the sorted order?

One more aspect of a particular sorting algorithm is its behavior on several special kinds of input data: already sorted (in direct and reversed order), almost sorted, and completely random. An ideal algorithm should show better than average performance (up to $O(1)$) on the sorted and almost sorted special cases.

Over the history of CS, sorting was and still remains a popular research topic. Not surprisingly, several dozens of different sorting algorithms were developed. But before discussing the prominent ones, let's talk about "stupid sort" (or "bogosort"). It is one of the sorting algorithms that has a very simple idea behind, but an outstandingly nasty performance. The idea is that among all permutations of the input sequence, there definitely is the completely sorted one. If we were to take it, we wouldn't need to do anything else. It's an example of the so-called "generate and test" paradigm that may be employed when we know next to nothing about the nature of our task: then, put some input into the black box and see the outcome. In the case of bogosort, the number of possible inputs is the number of all permutations that's equal to $n!$, so considering that we need to also examine each permutation's order, the algorithm's complexity is $O(n * n!)$ (in both time and space)—quite a nasty number, especially, since some specialized sorting algorithms can work as fast as $O(n)$ (for instance, bucket sort for integer numbers). On the other hand, if generating all permutations is a library function and we don't care about complexity, such an algorithm will have a rather simple implementation that looks quite innocent. So the performance characteristics of third-party functions should always be considered as well and not taken for granted. And, by the way, your standard library sort function is also a good example of this rule:

```
(defun bogosort (vec comp)
  (dolist (variant (all-permutations vec))
    (dotimes (i (1- (length variant)))
                  ;; this is the 3rd optional argument of dotimes header
                  ;; that is evaluated only after the loop finishes normally
                  ;; if it does we have found a completely sorted
                      permutation!
                  (return-from bogosort variant))
      (when (funcall comp (aref variant (1+ i)) (aref variant i))
        (return)))))  ; current variant is not sorted, skip it
```

O(n^2) Sorting

Although we can imagine an algorithm with even worse complexity factors than this, bogosort gives us a good lower bound on the sorting algorithm's performance and an idea of the potential complexity of this task. However, there are much faster approaches that don't have a particularly complex implementation. There are a number of such simple algorithms that work in quadratic time. A very well-known one, which is considered by many a kind of "Hello world" algorithm, is bubble sort. Yet, in my opinion, it's quite a bad example to teach (sadly, often it is taught) because it's both not very straightforward and has poor performance characteristics. That's why it's *never* used in practice. There are two simple quadratic sorting algorithms that you actually have a chance to encounter in the wild: selection adn Insertion sort. Amond then, insertion sort is used quite frequently. Their comparison is quite insightful, so we'll take a look at both, instead of focusing just on the former.

   Selection sort is an in-place sorting algorithm that moves left to right from the beginning of the vector one element at a time and builds the sorted prefix to the left of the current element. This is done by finding the "largest" (according to the comparator predicate) element in the right part and swapping it with the current element:

```
(defun selection-sort (vec comp)
  (dotimes (i (1- (length vec)))
    (let ((best (aref vec i))
          (idx i))
      (dotimes (j (- (length vec) i 1))
        (when (call comp (aref vec (+ i j 1)) best)
          (setf best (aref vec (+ i j 1))
                idx (+ i j 1))))
      (rotatef (aref vec i) (aref vec idx))))  ; this is the Lisp swap
    operator
  vec)
```

Selection sort requires a constant number of operations regardless of the level of sortedness of the original sequence: (/ (* n (- n 1)) 2)—the sum of the arithmetic progression from 1 to n, because, at each step, it needs to fully examine the remainder of the elements to find the maximum and the remainder's size varies from n to 1. It handles equally well both contiguous and linked sequences.

Insertion sort is another quadratic-time in-place sorting algorithm that builds the sorted prefix of the sequence. However, it has a few key differences from selection sort: instead of looking for the global maximum on the right-hand side, it looks for a proper place of the current element on the left-hand side. As this part is always sorted, it takes linear time to find the place for the new element and insert it there leaving the side in sorted order. Such change has great implications:

- It is stable.

- It is online. The left part is already sorted, and, in contrast with selection sort, it doesn't have to find the maximum element of the whole sequence in the first step. It can handle encountering it at any step.

- For sorted sequences, it works in the fastest possible way—in linear time—as all elements are already inserted into proper places and don't need moving. The same applies to almost sorted sequences, for which it works in almost linear time. However, for reverse sorted sequences, its performance will be the worse. In fact, there is a clear proportion of the algorithm's complexity to the average offset of the elements from their proper positions in the sorted sequence: $O(k * n)$, where k is the average offset of the element. For sorted sequences k=0 and for reverse sorted sequences, it's (/ (- n 1) 2).

```
(defun insertion-sort (vec comp)
  (dotimes (i (1- (length vec)))
    (do ((j i (1- j)))
        ((minusp j))
      (if (funcall comp (aref vec (1+ j)) (aref vec j))
          (rotatef (aref vec (1+ j)) (aref vec j))
          (return)))))
  vec)
```

As you see, the implementation is very simple: we look at each element starting from the second and compare it to the previous element, and if it's better, we swap them and continue the comparison with the previous element until we reach the array's beginning.

So where's the catch? Is there anything that makes selection sort better than insertion? Well, if we closely examine the number of operations required by each algorithm, we'll see that selection sort needs exactly (/ (* n (- n 1)) 2) comparisons and on average n/2 swaps. For insertion sort, the number of comparisons varies from n-1 to (/ (* n (- n 1)) 2), so, in the average case, it will be (/ (* n (- n 1)) 4), that is, half as many as for the other algorithm. In the sorted case, each element is already in its position, and it will take just one comparison to discover that, in the reverse sorted case, the average distance of an element from its position is (/ (- n 1) 2) and, for the middle variant, it's in the middle, that is, (/ (- n 1) 4), times the number of elements (n). But, as we can see from the implementation, insertion sort requires almost the same number of swaps as comparisons, that is, (/ (* (- n 1) (- n 2)) 4) in the average case, and it matches the number of swaps of selection sort only in the close to best case, when each element is on average one-half step away from its proper position. If we sum up all comparisons and swaps for the average case, we'll get the following numbers:

- Selection sort: `(+ (/ (* n (- n 1)) 2) (/ n 2)) = (/ (+ (* n n) n) 2)`

- Insertion sort: `(+ (/ (* n (- n 1)) 2) (+ (/ (* (- n 1) (- n 2)) 4) = (/ (+ (* 1.5 n n) (* -2.5 n) 1) 2)`

The second number is slightly higher than the first. For small ns, it is almost negligible: for instance, when n=10, we get 55 operations for selection sort and 63 for insertion. But, asymptotically (for huge ns like millions and billions), insertion sort will need 1.5 times more operations. Also, it is often the case that swaps are more expensive operations than comparisons (although the opposite is also possible).

In practice, insertion sort ends up being used more often. In general, quadratic sorts are only used when the input array is small (and so the difference in the number of operations doesn't matter), and Insertion sort has the most useful properties. However, one situation where selection sort's predictable performance is an important factor is in the systems with deadlines.

Quicksort

There are a number of other $O(n^2)$ sorting algorithms similar to selection and insertion sorts, but studying them quickly turns boring, so we won't, as there are also a number of significantly faster algorithms that work in `O(n * log n)` time (almost linear). They usually rely on the **divide-and-conquer** approach when the whole sequence is recursively divided into smaller subsequences that have some property, thanks to which it's easier to sort them, and then these subsequences are combined back into the final sorted sequence. The feasibility of such performance characteristics is justified by the observation that ordering relations are recursive, that is, if we have compared two elements of an array and then compare one of them to the third element, with a probability of half a step away, we'll also know how it relates to the other element.

Probably, the most famous of such algorithms is quicksort. Its idea is, at each iteration, to select some element of the array as the "pivot" point and divide the array into two parts—all the elements that are smaller and all those that are larger than the pivot—and then recursively sort each subarray. As all left elements are below the pivot and all right above, when we manage to sort the left and right sides, the whole array will be sorted. This invariant holds for all iterations and for all subarrays. The word "invariant," literally, means some property that doesn't change over the course of the algorithm's execution when other factors, for example, bounds of the array we're processing, are changing.

There're several tricks in quicksort implementation. The first one has to do with pivot selection. The simplest approach is to always use the last element as the pivot. Now, how do we put all the elements greater than the pivot after it if it's already the last element? Let's say that all elements are greater—then the pivot will be at index 0. Now, if moving left to right over the array we encounter an element that is not greater than the pivot, we should put it before, that is, the pivot's index should increment by 1. When we reach the end of the array, we know the correct position of the pivot, and in the process, we can swap all the elements that should precede it in front of this position. Now, we have to put the element that is currently occupying the pivot's place somewhere. Where? Anywhere after the pivot, but the most obvious thing is to swap it with the pivot:

```
(defun quicksort (vec comp)
  (when (> (length vec) 1)
    (with ((pivot-i 0)
           (pivot (aref vec (1- (length vec)))))
      (dotimes (i (1- (length vec)))
        (when (funcall comp (aref vec i) pivot)
          (rotatef (aref vec i)
                   (aref vec pivot-i))
          (incf pivot-i)))
      ;; swap the pivot (last element) in its proper place
      (rotatef (aref vec (1- (length vec)))
               (aref vec pivot-i))
      (quicksort (rtl:slice vec 0 pivot-i) comp)
      (quicksort (rtl:slice vec (1+ pivot-i)) comp)))
  vec)
```

Although recursion is employed here, such implementation is space-efficient as it uses array displacement ("slicing") that doesn't create new copies of the subarrays, so sorting happens in-place. Speaking of recursion, this is one of the cases when it's not so straightforward to turn it into looping (this is left as an exercise to the reader :)).

What is the complexity of such implementation? Well, if, on every iteration, we divide the array in two equal halves, we'll need to perform n comparisons and n/2 swaps and increments, which totals to 2n operations. And we'll need to do that (log n 2) times, which is the height of a complete binary tree with n elements. At every level in the recursion tree, we'll need to perform twice as many sorts with twice as little data, so each level will take the same number of 2n operations. Total complexity is 2n * (log n 2), that is, O(n * log n), in the ideal case.

However, we can't guarantee that the selected pivot will divide the array into two ideally equal parts. In the worst case, if we were to split it into two totally unbalanced subarrays, with n-1 and 0 elements, respectively, we'd need to perform sorting n times and perform a number of operations that will diminish in the arithmetic progression from 2n to 2. This sums to (* n (- n 1))—a dreaded O(n^2) complexity. So the worst-case performance for quicksort is not just worse, but in a different complexity league than the average-case one. Moreover, the conditions for such performance (given our pivot selection scheme) are not so uncommon: sorted and reverse sorted arrays. And the almost sorted ones will result in the almost worst-case scenario.

It is also interesting to note that if, at each stage, we were to split the array into parts that have a 10:1 ratio of lengths, this would have resulted in n * log n complexity! How come? The 10:1 ratio, basically, means that the bigger part each time is shortened at a factor of around 1.1, which still is a power-law recurrence. The base of the algorithm will be different, though: 1.1 instead of 2. Yet, from the complexity theory point of view, the logarithm base is not important because it's still a constant: (log n x) is the same as (/ (log n 2) (log x 2)), and (/ 1 (log x 2)) is a constant for any fixed logarithm base x. In our case, if x is 1.1, the constant factor is 7.27. This means that quicksort, in the quite bad case of recurring 10:1 splits, will be just a little more than seven times slower than in the best case of recurring equal splits. Significant, yes. But, if we were to compare n * log n (with base 2) vs. n^2 performance for n=1000, we'd already get a 100 times slowdown, which will only continue increasing as the input size grows. Compare this to a constant factor of 7...

So how do we achieve at least 10:1 split or, at least, 100:1 or similar? One of the simple solutions is called the 3-medians approach. The idea is to consider not just a single point as a potential pivot but three candidates—first, middle, and last points—and select the one which has the median value among them. Unless accidentally two or all three points are equal, this guarantees that we won't be taking the extreme value. Thus, the all-to-nothing split can be avoided. Also, for a sorted array, this should produce a nice near to equal split. How probable is stumbling at the special case when we'll always get at the extreme value due to equality of the selected points? The calculations here are not so simple, so I'll give just the answer: it's extremely improbable that such condition will hold for all iterations of the algorithm due to the fact that we'll always remove the last element and all the swapping that is going on. More precisely, the only practical variant when it may happen is when the array consists almost or just entirely of the same elements. And this case will be addressed next. One more refinement to the three-median approach that will work even better for large arrays is nine-median that, as is apparent from its name, performs the median selection not among three but nine equidistant points in the array.

Dealing with equal elements is another corner case for quicksort that should be addressed properly. The fix is simple: to divide the array not in two but three parts, smaller, larger, and equal to the pivot. This will allow for the removal of the equal elements from further consideration and will even speed up sorting instead of slowing it down. The implementation adds another index (this time, from the end of the array) that will tell us where the equal-to-pivot elements will start, and we'll be gradually swapping them into this tail as they are encountered during array traversal.

Production Sort

I was always wondering how it's possible, for quicksort, to be the default sorting algorithm when it has such bad worst-case performance and there are other algorithms like merge sort or heap sort that have guaranteed $O(n * \log n)$ ones. With all the mentioned refinements, it's apparent that the worst-case scenario, for quicksort, can be completely avoided (in the probabilistic sense), while it has a very nice property of sorting in-place with good cache locality, which significantly contributes to better real-world performance. Moreover, production sort implementation will be even smarter by utilizing quicksort while the array is large and switching to something like insertion sort when the size of the subarray reaches a certain threshold (10–20 elements). All this, however, is applicable only to arrays. When we consider lists, other factors come into play that make quicksort much less plausible.

Here's an attempt at such—let's call it "production sort"—implementation (the function 3-medians is left as an exercise to the reader). Essentially, it is a more hardened version of quicksort that has to do additional bookkeeping due to the adaptive selection of the pivot (with 3-medians) and falls back to insertion sort when the vector size falls below ten elements:

```
(defun prod-sort (vec comp &optional (eq 'eql))
  (cond ((< (length vec) 2)
         vec)
        ((< (length vec) 10)
         (insertion-sort vec comp))
        (t
         (rotatef (aref vec (1- (length vec)))
                  (aref vec (3-medians vec comp)))
         (rtl:with ((pivot-i 0)
                    (pivot-count 1)
                    (last-i (1- (length vec)))
                    (pivot (aref vec last-i)))
           (do ((i 0 (1+ i)))
               ((> i (- last-i pivot-count)))
             (cond ((funcall comp (aref vec i) pivot)
                    (rotatef (aref vec i)
                             (aref vec pivot-i))
                    (incf pivot-i))
                   ((funcall eq (aref vec i) pivot)
                    (rotatef (aref vec i)
                             (aref vec (- last-i pivot-count)))
                    (incf pivot-count)
                    (decf i))))  ; decrement i to reprocess newly swapped
                                 point
           (dotimes (i pivot-count)
             (rotatef (aref vec (+ pivot-i i))
                      (aref vec (- last-i i))))
           (prod-sort (rtl:slice vec 0 pivot-i) comp eq)
           (prod-sort (rtl:slice vec (+ pivot-i pivot-count)) comp eq))))
  vec)
```

All in all, the example of quicksort is very interesting, from the point of view of complexity analysis. It shows the importance of analyzing the worst-case and other corner-case scenarios and, at the same time, teaches that we shouldn't give up immediately if the worst case is not good enough, for there may be ways to handle such corner cases that reduce or remove their impact.

Performance Benchmark

Finally, let's look at our problem from another angle: simple and stupid. We have developed three sorting functions' implementations: insertion, quick, and prod. Let's create a tool to compare their performance on randomly generated datasets of decent sizes. This may be done with the following code and repeated many times to exclude the effects of randomness (obviously, that could be automated as well):

```
(defun random-vec (size)
  (let ((vec (make-array size)))
    (dotimes (i size)
      (setf (aref vec i) (random size)))
    vec))

(defun print-sort-timings (sort-name sort-fn vec)
  ;; we'll use in-place modification of the input vector VEC
  ;; so we need to copy it to preserve the original for future use
  (let ((vec (copy-seq vec))
        (len (length vec)))
    (format t "= ~Asort of random vector (length=~A) =~%"
            sort-name len)
    (time (funcall sort-fn vec '<))
    (format t "= ~Asort of sorted vector (length=~A) =~%"
            sort-name len)
    (time (funcall sort-fn vec '<))
    (format t "= ~Asort of reverse sorted vector (length=~A) =~%"
            sort-name len)
    (time (funcall sort-fn vec '>))))

CL-USER> (let ((vec (random-vec 10000)))
          (print-sort-timings "Insertion " 'insertion-sort vec)
          (print-sort-timings "Quick" 'quicksort vec)
          (print-sort-timings "Prod" 'prod-sort vec))
= Insertion sort of random vector (length=10000) =
Evaluation took:
```

```
  0.632 seconds of real time
...
= Insertion sort of sorted vector (length=10000) =
Evaluation took:
  0.000 seconds of real time
...
= Insertion sort of reverse sorted vector (length=10000) =
Evaluation took:
  1.300 seconds of real time
...
= Quicksort of random vector (length=10000) =
Evaluation took:
  0.039 seconds of real time
...
= Quicksort of sorted vector (length=10000) =
Evaluation took:
  1.328 seconds of real time
...
= Quicksort of reverse sorted vector (length=10000) =
Evaluation took:
  1.128 seconds of real time
...
= Prodsort of random vector (length=10000) =
Evaluation took:
  0.011 seconds of real time
...
= Prodsort of sorted vector (length=10000) =
Evaluation took:
  0.011 seconds of real time
...
= Prodsort of reverse sorted vector (length=10000) =
Evaluation took:
  0.021 seconds of real time
...
```

Overall, this is a really primitive approach that can't serve as conclusive evidence on its own, but it has value as it aligns well with our previous calculations. Moreover, it once again reveals some things that may be omitted in those calculations: for instance, the effects of the hidden constants of the Big-O notation or of the particular programming vehicles used. We can see that, for their worst-case scenarios, where quicksort and insertion sort both have $O(n^2)$ complexity and work approximately on par with each other. Yet, the difference between logarithmic and quadratic runtimes is clearly seen in the random vector scenario. Also, our prodsort algorithm demonstrates its expected performance that is ~100× better than the basic algorithms for their worst cases. It is also four times faster than quicksort for the random case—probably due to the use of three-median pivot selection. As you see, such simple testbeds quickly become essential in testing, debugging, and fine-tuning our algorithms' implementations. So it's a worthy investment.

Finally, it is worth noting that array sort is often implemented as in-place sorting, which means that it will modify (spoil) the input vector. We use that in our test function: first, we sort the array and then sort the sorted array in direct and reverse orders. This way, we can omit creating new arrays. Such destructive sort behavior may be both the intended and surprising behavior. The standard Lisp's `sort` and `stable-sort` functions also exhibit it, which is, unfortunately, a source of numerous bugs due to the application programmer forgetfulness of the function's side effects (at least, this is an acute case, for myself). That's why RUTILS provides an additional function `safe-sort` that is just a thin wrapper over standard `sort` to free the programmer's mind from worrying or forgetting about this treacherous `sort` 's property.

Takeaways

1. Array is a goto structure for implementing your algorithms.
    First, try to fit it before moving to other things like lists, trees,
    and so on.

2. Complexity estimates should be considered in context: of the particular task's requirements and limitations, of the hardware platform, and so on. Performing some real-world benchmarking alongside back-of-the-napkin abstract calculations may be quite insightful.

3. It's always worth thinking of how to reduce the code to the simplest form: checking of additional conditions, recursion, and many other forms of code complexity, although rarely are a game changer, often may lead to significant unnecessary slowdowns.

CHAPTER 6

Linked Lists

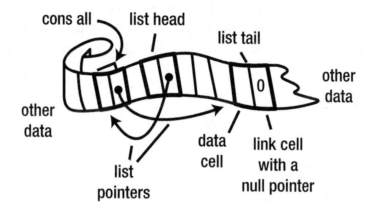

Linked data structures are in many ways the opposite of the contiguous ones that we have explored to some extent in the previous chapter using the example of arrays. In terms of complexity, they fail where those ones shine (first of all, at random access), but prevail at scenarios when a repeated modification is necessary. In general, they are much more flexible and so allow the programmer to represent almost any kind of a data structure, although the ones that require such level of flexibility may not be too frequent. Usually, they are specialized trees or graphs.

The basic linked data structure is a singly linked list.

Just like arrays, lists in Lisp may be created both with a literal syntax for constants and by calling a function—make-list—that creates a list of a certain size filled with nil elements. Besides, there's a handy list utility that is used to create lists with the specified content (the analog of rtl:vec):

```
CL-USER> '("hello" world 111)
("hello" WORLD 111)
CL-USER> (make-list 3)
```

© Vsevolod Domkin 2021
V. Domkin, *Programming Algorithms in Lisp*, https://doi.org/10.1007/978-1-4842-6428-7_6

```
(NIL NIL NIL)
CL-USER> (list "hello" 'world 111)
("hello" WORLD 111)
```

An empty list is represented as (), and, interestingly, in Lisp, it is also a synonym of logical falsehood (nil). This property is used very often, and we'll have a chance to see that.

If we were to introduce our own lists, which may be quite a common scenario in case the built-in ones' capabilities do not suit us, we'd need to define the structure "node," and our list would be built as a chain of such nodes. We might have wanted to store the list head and, possibly, tail, as well as other properties like size. All in all, it would look like the following:

```
(defstruct list-cell
  data
  next)

(defstruct our-own-list
  (head nil :type (or list-cell null))
  (tail nil :type (or list-cell null)))

CL-USER> (let ((tail (make-list-cell :data "world")))
           (make-our-own-list
             :head (make-list-cell
                     :data "hello"
                     :next tail)
             :tail tail))
#S(OUR-OWN-LIST
   :HEAD #S(LIST-CELL
             :DATA "hello"
             :NEXT #S(LIST-CELL :DATA "world" :NEXT NIL))
   :TAIL #S(LIST-CELL :DATA "world" :NEXT NIL))
```

Lists as Sequences

Alongside arrays, list is the other basic data structure that implements the sequence abstract data type. Let's consider the complexity of basic sequence operations for linked lists:

- So-called random access, that is, access by index of a random element, requires $O(n)$ time as we have to traverse all the preceding elements before we can reach the desired one ($n/2$ operations on average).

- Yet, once we have reached some element, removing it or inserting something after it takes $O(1)$.

- Subsequencing is also $O(n)$.

Getting the list length, in the basic case, is also $O(n)$, that is, it requires full list traversal. It is possible, though, to store list length as a separate slot, tracking each change on the fly, which means $O(1)$ complexity. Lisp, however, implements the simplest variant of lists without size tracking. This is an example of a small but important decision that real-world programming is full of. Why is such a solution the right thing in this case? Adding the size counter to each list would have certainly made this common length operation more effective, but the cost of doing that would've included increase in occupied storage space for all lists, a need to update size in all list modification operations, and, possibly, a need for a more complex cons cell implementation.[1] These considerations make the situation with lists almost opposite to arrays, for which size tracking is quite reasonable because they change much less often and not tracking the length historically proved to be a terrible security decision. So what side to choose? A default approach is to prefer the solution which doesn't completely rule out the alternative strategy. If we were to choose a simple cons cell sans size (what the authors of Lisp did), we'd always be able to add the "smart" list data structure with the size field on top of it. Yet, stripping the size field from built-in lists won't be possible. Similar reasoning is also applicable to other questions, such as "Why aren't lists, in Lisp, doubly linked?" Also, it helps that there's no security implication as lists aren't used as data exchange buffers, for which the problem manifests itself.

---

[1]However, in the Lisp machines, cons cells even had special hardware support, and such change would have made it useless.

For demonstration, let's add the size field to `our-own-list` (and, meanwhile, consider all the functions that will need to update it...):

```
(defstruct our-own-list
  (head nil :type (or list-cell null))
  (tail nil :type (or list-cell null))
  (size 0 :type (integer 0)))
```

Given that obtaining the length of a list, in Lisp, is an expensive operation, a common pattern in programs that require multiple requests of the length field is to store its value in some variable at the beginning of the algorithm and then use this cached value, updating it if necessary.

As we see, lists are quite inefficient in random access scenarios. However, many sequences don't require random access and can satisfy all the requirements of a particular use case using just the sequential one. That's one of the reasons why they are called sequences, after all. And if we consider the special case of list operations at index 0, they are, obviously, efficient: both access and addition/removal are $O(1)$. Also, if the algorithm requires a sequential scan, list traversal is rather efficient too. Yet, it is not as good as array traversal for it still requires jumping over the memory pointers. There are numerous sequence operations that are based on sequential scans. The most common is `map`, which we analyzed in the previous chapter. It is the functional programming alternative to looping, a more high-level operation, and thus simpler to understand for the common cases, although less versatile.

`map` is a function that works with different types of built-in sequences. It takes as the first argument the target sequence type (if `nil` is supplied, it won't create the resulting sequence and so will be used just for side effects). Here is a polymorphic example involving lists and vectors:

```
CL-USER> (map 'vector '+
              '(1 2 3 4 5)
              #(1 2 3))
#(2 4 6)
```

`map` applies the function provided as its second argument (here, addition) sequentially to every element of the sequences that are supplied as other arguments, until one of them ends, and records the result in the output sequence. `map` would have been even more intuitive, if it just had used the type of the first argument for the result sequence, that is, be a "do what I mean" dwim-map, while a separate advanced variant with result-type selection might have been used in the background. Unfortunately, the current standard scheme is not for change, but we can define our own wrapper function:

```
(defun dwim-map (fn seq &rest seqs)
  "A thin wrapper over MAP that uses the type of the first SEQ for the
  result."
  (apply 'map (type-of seq) fn seqs))
```

Historically, map in Lisp was originally used for lists in its list-specific variants that predated the generic map. Most of those functions like mapcar, mapc, and mapcan (replaced in RUTILS by a safer flat-map) are still widely used today.

Now, let's see a couple of examples of using mapping. Suppose that we'd like to extract odd numbers from a list of numbers. Using mapcar as a list-specific map, we might try to call it with an anonymous function that tests its argument for oddity and keeps it in such a case:

```
CL-USER> (mapcar (lambda (x) (when (oddp x) x))
                 (rtl:range 1 10))
(1 NIL 3 NIL 5 NIL 7 NIL 9)
```

However, the problem is that non-odd numbers still have their place reserved in the result list, although it is not filled by them. Keeping only the results that satisfy (or don't) certain criteria and discarding the others is a very common pattern that is known as "filtering." There's a set of Lisp functions for such scenarios: remove, remove-if, and remove-if-not, as well as RUTILS' complements to them keep-if and keep-if-not. We can achieve the desired result adding remove to the picture:

```
CL-USER> (remove nil (mapcar (lambda (x) (when (oddp x) x))
                             (rtl:range 1 10)))
(1 3 5 7 9)
```

A more elegant solution will use the remove-if(-not) or rtl:keep-if(-not) variant. remove-if-not is the most popular among these functions. It takes a predicate and a sequence and returns the sequence of the same type holding only the elements that satisfy the predicate:

```
CL-USER> (remove-if-not 'oddp (range 1 10))
(1 3 5 7 9)
```

Using such high-level mapping functions is very convenient, which is why there are a number of other -if(-not) operations, like find(-if(-not)), member(-if(-not)), position(-if(-not)), and so on.

The implementation of mapcar or any other list mapping function, including your own task-specific variants, follows the same pattern of traversing the list accumulating the result into another list and reversing it in the end:

```
(defun simple-mapcar (fn list)
  (let ((rez (list)))
    (dolist (item list)
      (setf rez (cons (funcall fn item) rez)))
    (reverse rez)))
```

The function cons is used to add an item to the beginning of the list. It creates a new list head that points to the previous list as its tail.

From the complexity point of view, if we compare such iteration with looping over an array, we'll see that it is also a linear traversal that requires twice as many operations as with arrays because we need to traverse the result fully once again, in the end, to reverse it. Its advantage, though, is higher versatility: if we don't know the size of the resulting sequence (e.g., in the case of remove-if-not), we don't have to change anything in this scheme and just add a filter line ((when (oddp item) ...), while for arrays we'd either need to use a dynamic array (that will need constant resizing and so have at least the same double number of operations) or pre-allocate the full-sized result sequence and then downsize it to fit the actual accumulated number of elements, which may be problematic when we deal with large arrays.

Lists as Functional Data Structures

The distinction between arrays and linked lists in many ways reflects the distinction between the imperative and functional programming paradigms. Within the imperative or, in this context, procedural approach, the program is built out of low-level blocks (conditionals, loops, and sequentials) that allow for the most fine-tuned and efficient implementation, at the expense of abstraction level and modularization capabilities. It also heavily utilizes in-place modification and manual resource management to keep overhead at a minimum. An array is the most suitable data structure for such a way of programming. Functional programming, on the contrary, strives to bring the abstraction level higher, which may come at a cost of sacrificing efficiency (only when necessary and, ideally, only for noncritical parts). Functional programs are built by combining referentially transparent computational procedures (a.k.a. "pure functions") that operate on more advanced data structures (either persistent ones or having special access semantics, e.g., transactional) that are also more expensive to manage but provide additional benefits.

Singly linked lists are a simple example of functional data structures. A **functional** or **persistent** data structure is the one that doesn't allow in-place modification. In other words, to alter the contents of the structure, a fresh copy with the desired changes should be created. The flexibility of linked data structures makes them suitable for serving as functional ones. We have seen the cons operation that is one of the earliest examples of nondestructive, that is, functional, modification. This action prepends an element to the head of a list, and as we're dealing with the singly linked list, the original doesn't have to be updated: a new cons cell is added in front of it with its next pointer referencing the original list that becomes the new tail. This way, we can both preserve the pointer to the original head and add a new head. Such an approach is the basis for most of the functional data structures: the functional trees, for example, add a new head and a new route from the head to the newly added element, adding new nodes along the way—according to the same principle.

It is interesting, though, that lists can be used in destructive and nondestructive fashions likewise. There are both low- and high-level functions in Lisp that perform list modification, and their existence is justified by the use cases in many algorithms. Purely functional lists render many of the efficient list algorithms useless. One of the high-level list modification functions is nconc. It concatenates two lists together updating in the process the next pointer of the last cons cell of the first list:

```
CL-USER> (let ((l1 (list 1 2 3))
               (l2 (list 4 5 6)))
           (nconc l1 l2)  ; note no assignment to l1
           l1)            ; but it is still changed
(1 2 3 4 5 6)
```

There's a functional variant of this operation, append, and, in general, it is considered distasteful to use nconc as the risk of unwarranted modification outweighs the minor efficiency gains. Using append, we'll need to modify the previous piece of code because otherwise the newly created list will be garbage-collected immediately:

```
CL-USER> (let ((l1 (list 1 2 3))
               (l2 (list 4 5 6)))
           (setf l1 (append l1 l2))
           l1)
(1 2 3 4 5 6)
```

The low-level list modification operations are rplaca and rplacd. They can be combined with list-specific accessors nth and nthcdr that provide indexed access to list elements and tails, respectively. Here's, for example, how to add an element in the middle of a list:

```
CL-USER> (let ((l1 (list 1 2 3)))
           (rplacd (nthcdr 0 l1)
                   (cons 4 (nthcdr 1 l1)))
           l1)
(1 4 2 3)
```

Just to reiterate, although functional list operations are the default choice, for efficient implementation of some algorithms, you'll need to resort to the ugly destructive ones.

Different Kinds of Lists

We have, thus far, seen the most basic linked list variant—a singly linked one. It has a number of limitations: for instance, it's impossible to traverse it from the end to the beginning. Yet, there are many algorithms that require accessing the list from both sides or do other things with it that are inefficient or even impossible with the singly linked one; hence, other, more advanced list variants exist.

But first, let's consider an interesting tweak to the regular singly linked list—a circular list. It can be created from the normal one by making the last cons cell point to the first. It may seem like a problematic data structure to work with, but all the potential issues with infinite looping while traversing it are solved if we keep a pointer to any node and stop iteration when we encounter this node for the second time. What's the use for such structure? Well, not so many, but there's a prominent one: the ring buffer. A ring or circular buffer is a structure that can hold a predefined number of items, and each item is added to the next slot of the current item. This way, when the buffer is completely filled, it will wrap around to the first element, which will be overwritten at the next modification. By our buffer-filling algorithm, the element to be overwritten is the one that was written the earliest for the current item set. Using a circular linked list is one of the simplest ways to implement such a buffer. Another approach would be to use an array of a certain size moving the pointer to the next item by incrementing an index in the array. Obviously, when the index reaches array size, it should be reset to zero.

A more advanced list variant is a doubly linked one, in which all the elements have both the next and previous pointers. The following definition, using inheritance, extends our original list-cell with a pointer to the previous element. Thanks to the basic object-oriented capabilities of structs, it will work with the current definition of our-own-list as well and allow it to function as a doubly linked list:

```
(defstruct (list-cell2 (:include list-cell))
  prev)
```

Yet, we still haven't shown the implementation of the higher-level operations of adding and removing an element to/from our-own-list. Obviously, they will differ for singly and doubly linked lists, and that distinction will require us to differentiate the doubly linked list types. That, in turn, will demand invocation of a rather heavy OO machinery, which is beyond the subject of this book. Instead, for now, let's just examine the basic list addition function, for the doubly linked list:

```
(defun our-cons2 (data list)
  (when (null list) (setf list (make-our-own-list)))
  (let ((new-head (make-list-cell2
                      :data data
                      :next @list.head)))
    (when (rtl:? list 'head)
      (setf (rtl:? list 'head 'prev) new-head))
    (make-our-own-list
      :head new-head
      :tail (rtl:? list 'tail)
      :size (1+ (rtl:? list 'size)))))
```

The first thing to note is the use of the @ syntactic sugar, from RUTILS, that implements the mainstream dot notation for slot-value access. `@list.head.prev` refers to the `prev` field of the `head` field of the provided `list` structure of the assumed `our-own-list` type. The more standard Lisp variants (which are more cumbersome) may look like one of the following: `(our-cons2-prev (our-own-list-head list))` or `(slot-value (slot-value list 'head) 'prev)`.[2]

More important here is that, unlike for the singly linked list, this function requires an in-place modification of the head element of the original list: setting its `prev` pointer. This immediately makes doubly linked lists nonpersistent.

Finally, the first line is the protection against trying to access the null list (that will result in a much-feared, especially in Java land, null pointer exception class of error).

At first sight, it may seem that doubly linked lists are more useful than singly linked ones. But they also have higher overhead so, in practice, they are used quite sporadically. We may see just a couple of use cases on the pages of this book. One of them is presented in the next part—a double-ended queue.

Besides doubly linked list, there are also association lists that serve as a variant of key-value (kv) data structures. At least three types may be found in Common Lisp code, and we'll briefly discuss them in Chapter 7. Finally, a skip list is a probabilistic data structure based on singly linked lists that allows for faster search. Other more esoteric list variants, such as self-organized list and XOR-list, may also be found in the literature—but very rarely in practice.

FIFO and LIFO

The flexibility of lists allows them to serve as a common choice for implementing a number of popular abstract data structures.

Queue

A queue or FIFO (first-in-first-out) has the following interface:

- enqueue an item at the end.

- dequeue the first element: get it and remove it from the queue.

---

[2]Although, for structs, it is implementation-dependent if this will work. In all the current implementations, it will.

It imposes a first-in-first-out (FIFO) ordering on the elements. A queue can be implemented directly with a singly linked list like `our-own-list`. Obviously, it can also be built on top of a dynamic array but will require permanent expansion and contraction of the collection, which, as we already know, isn't the preferred scenario for its usage.

There are numerous uses for the queue structures for processing items in a certain order (some of which we'll see in further chapters of this book).

Stack

A stack or LIFO (last-in-first-out) is even simpler than a queue, and it is used even more widely. Its interface is as follows:

- `push` an item on top of the stack making it the first element.

- `pop` an item from the top: get it and remove it from the stack.

A simple Lisp list can serve as a stack, and you can see such uses in almost every file with Lisp code. The most common pattern is result accumulation during iteration—using the stack interface, we can rewrite `simple-mapcar` in an even simpler way (which is idiomatic Lisp):

```
(defun simple-mapcar (fn list)
  (let ((rez (list)))
    (dolist (item list)
      (push (funcall fn item) rez))
    (reverse rez)))
```

Stacks hold elements in reverse-chronological order and can thus be used to keep the history of changes to be able to undo them. This feature is used in procedure calling conventions by the compilers: there exists a separate segment of program memory called the stack segment, and when a function call happens (beginning from the program's entry point called the `main` function in C), all of its arguments and local variables are put on this stack as well as the return address in the program code segment where the call was initiated. Such an approach allows for the existence of local variables that last only for the duration of the call and are referenced relative to the current stack head and not bound to some absolute position in memory like the global ones. After the procedure call returns, the stack is "unwound," and all the local data is forgotten returning the context to the same state in which it was before the call. Such stack-based history-keeping is a very common and useful pattern that may be utilized in userland code likewise.

Lisp itself also uses this trick to implement global variables with a capability to have context-dependent values through the extent of let blocks: each such variable also has a stack of values associated with it. This is one of the most underappreciated features of the Lisp language used quite often by experienced lispers. Here is a small example with a standard global variable (they are called **special** in Lisp parlance due to this special property) *standard-output* that stores a reference to the current output stream:

```
CL-USER> (print 1)
1
1
CL-USER> (let ((*standard-output* (make-broadcast-stream)))
          (print 1))
1
```

In the first call to print, we see both the printed value and the returned one and, in the second, only the return value of the print-function, while its output is sent, effectively, to /dev/null.

Stacks can be also used to implement queues. We'll need two of them to do that: one will be used for enqueuing the items and the other for dequeuing. Here's the implementation:

```
(defstruct queue
  head
  tail)

(defun enqueue (item queue)
  (push item (rtl:? queue 'head)))

(defun dequeue (queue)
  ;; Here and in the next condition, we use the property that an empty list
  ;; is also logically false. This is discouraged by many Lisp
  ;; styleguides, yet in many cases such code is not only more compact
  ;; but also more clear.
  (unless @queue.tail
```

```
    (do ()
        ;; this loop continues until the head becomes empty
        ((null (rtl:? queue 'head)))
      (push (pop (rtl:? queue 'head)) (rtl:? queue 'tail))))
      ;; By pushing all the items from the head to the tail,
      ;; we reverse their order - this is the second reversing
      ;; that cancels the reversing performed when we push the items
      ;; onto the head, so it restores the original order.
  (when (rtl:? queue 'tail)
    (values (pop (rtl:? queue 'tail))
          t)))  ; this second value is used to indicate
              ; that the queue was not empty

CL-USER> (let ((q (make-queue)))
          (print q)
          (enqueue 1 q)
          (enqueue 2 q)
          (enqueue 3 q)
          (print q)
          (dequeue q)
          (print q)
          (enqueue 4 q)
          (print q)
          (dequeue q)
          (print q)
          (dequeue q)
          (print q)
          (dequeue q)
          (print q)
          (dequeue q))
#S(QUEUE :HEAD NIL :TAIL NIL)
#S(QUEUE :HEAD (3 2 1) :TAIL NIL)
#S(QUEUE :HEAD NIL :TAIL (2 3))
#S(QUEUE :HEAD (4) :TAIL (2 3))
#S(QUEUE :HEAD (4) :TAIL (3))
```

```
#S(QUEUE :HEAD (4) :TAIL NIL)
#S(QUEUE :HEAD NIL :TAIL NIL)
NIL  ; no second value indicates that the queue is now empty
```

Such queue implementation still has O(1) operation times for enqueue/dequeue. Each element will experience exactly four operations: two pushes and two pops (for the head and tail). However, for dequeue this will be the average (amortized) performance, while there may be occasional peaks in individual operation runtimes: specifically, after long uninterrupted series of enqueues.

Another stack-based structure is the stack with a minimum element, that is, some structure that not only holds elements in LIFO order but also keeps track of the minimum among them. The challenge is that if we just add the min slot that holds the current minimum, when this minimum is popped out of the stack, we'll need to examine all the remaining elements to find the new minimum. We can avoid this additional work by adding another stack—a stack of minimums. Now, each push and pop operation requires us to also check the head of this second stack and, in case the added/removed element is the minimum, push it to the stack of minimums or pop it from there, accordingly.

A well-known algorithm that illustrates stack usage is fully parenthesized arithmetic expression evaluation:

```
(defun arith-eval (expr)
  "EXPR is a list of symbols that may include:
   square brackets, arithmetic operations, and numbers."
  (let ((ops ())
        (vals ())
        (op nil)
        (val nil))
    (dolist (item expr)
      (case item
        ([ ) ; do nothing
        ((+ - * /) (push item ops))
        (] (setf op (pop ops)
                 val (pop vals))
           (case op
             (+ (incf val (pop vals)))
             (- (decf val (pop vals)))
```

88

```
         (* (setf val (* val (pop vals))))
         (/ (setf val (/ val (pop vals)))))
       (push val vals))
     (otherwise (push item vals))))
  (pop vals)))
CL-USER> (arith-eval '([ 1 + [ [ 2 + 3 ] * [ 4 * 5 ] ] ] ]))
101
```

Deque

A deque is a short name for a double-ended queue, which can be traversed in both orders: FIFO and LIFO. It has four operations: push-front and push-back (also called shift) and pop-front and pop-back (unshift). This structure may be implemented with a doubly linked list or likewise a simple queue with two stacks. The difference for the two-stack implementation is that now items may be pushed back and forth between head and tail depending on the direction we're popping from, which results in worst-case linear complexity of such operations: when there's constant alteration of front and back directions.

The use case for such structure is the algorithm that utilizes both direct and reverse ordering: a classic example being job-stealing algorithms, where the main worker is processing the queue from the front, while other workers, when idle, may steal the lowest-priority items from the back (to minimize the chance of a conflict for the same job).

Stacks in Action: SAX Parsing

Custom XML parsing is a common task for those who deal with different datasets, as many of them come in XML form, for example, Wikipedia and other Wikidata resources. There are two main approaches to XML parsing:

- DOM parsing reads the whole document and creates its tree representation in memory. This technique is handy for small documents, but, for huge ones, such as the dump of Wikipedia, it will quickly fill all available memory. Also, dealing with the deep tree structure, if you want to extract only some specific pieces from it, is not very convenient.

- SAX parsing is an alternative variant that uses the stream approach. The parser reads the document and, upon completing the processing of a particular part, invokes the relevant callback: what to do when an open tag is read, when a closing one is read, and with the contents of the current element. These actions happen for each tag, and we can think of the whole process as traversing the document tree utilizing the so-called "visitor pattern": when visiting each node, we have a chance to react after the beginning, in the middle, and in the end.

Once you get used to SAX parsing, due to its simplicity, it becomes a tool of choice for processing XML, as well as JSON and other formats that allow for a similar stream parsing approach. Often the simplest parsing pattern is enough: remember the tag we're looking at, and when it matches a set of interesting tags, process its contents. However, sometimes, we need to make decisions based on the broader context. For example, let's say we have the text marked up into paragraphs, which are split into sentences, which are, in turn, tokenized. To process such a three-level structure, with SAX parsing, we could use the following outline (utilizing the primitives from the CXML library):

```
(defclass text-sax (sax:sax-parser-mixin)
  ((parags :initform (list) :accessor sax-parags)
   (parag :initform (list) :accessor sax-parag)
   (sent :initform (list) :accessor sax-sent)
   (tag-stack :initform (list) :accessor sax-tag-stack)))

(defmethod sax:start-element ((sax text-sax)
                              namespace-uri local-name qname attrs)
  (declare (ignore namespace-uri qname attrs))
  (push (rtl:mkeyw local-name) (sax-tag-stack sax)))

(defmethod sax:end-element ((sax text-sax)
                            namespace-uri local-name qname)
  (declare (ignore namespace-uri qname))
  (with-slots (tag-stack sent parag parags) sax
    (case (pop tag-stack)
      (:paragraph (push (reverse parag) parags)
                  (setf parag nil))
      (:sentence (push (reverse sent) parag)
                 (setf sent nil)))))
```

```
(defmethod sax:characters ((sax text-sax) text)
  (when (eql :token (first (sax-tag-stack sax)))
    (push text (sax-sent sax))))

(defmethod sax:end-document ((sax text-sax))
  (reverse (sax-parags sax)))
```

It is our first encounter with the Common Lisp Object System (CLOS) that is based on the concepts of objects pertaining to certain classes and methods specialized on those classes. Objects are, basically, enhanced structs (with multiple inheritance capabilities), while methods allow the programmer to arrange overloaded behavior of the same operations (called "generic functions" in Lisp parlance) for different classes of inputs into separate self-contained code blocks. CLOS is a very substantial topic that is beyond the scope of this book.[3] Yet, for those familiar with the OOP paradigm and its implementation in any programming language, the idea behind the preceding code should be familiar. In fact, this is how SAX parsing is handled in similar Python or Java libraries: by extending the provided base class and implementing the specialized versions of its API functions.

This code returns the accumulated structure of paragraphs from the sax:end-document method. It uses two stacks—for the current sentence and the current paragraph—to accumulate intermediate data during the parsing process. In a similar fashion, another stack of encountered tags might have been used to exactly track our position in the document tree if there were such necessity. Overall, the more you'll be using SAX parsing, the more you'll realize that stacks are enough to address 99% of the arising challenges.

Here is an example of running the parser on a toy XML document:

```
CL-USER> (cxml:parse-octets
          ;; FLEXI-STREAMS library is used here
          (flex:string-to-octets "<text>
<paragraph>
  <sentence><token>A</token><token>test</token></sentence>
  <sentence><token>foo</token><token>bar</token><token>baz</token>
  </sentence>
</paragraph>
```

---

[3]To further learn about this topic, I would recommend reading the relevant chapters from the book *Practical Common Lisp*: Generic Functions and Classes.

```
<paragraph>
  <sentence><token>42</token></sentence>
</paragraph>
</text>")
            (make-instance 'text-sax))
(((("A" "test")
  ("foo" "bar" "baz"))
 (("42")))
```

Lists as Sets

Another very important abstract data structure is a set. It is a collection that holds each element only once no matter how many times we add it there. This structure may be used in a variety of cases: when we need to track the items we have already seen and processed, when we want to calculate some relations between groups of elements, and so forth.

Basically, its interface consists of set-theoretic operations:

- Add/remove an item.

- Check whether an item is in the set.

- Check whether a set is a subset of another set.

- Union, intersection, difference, and so on.

An interesting aspect of sets is that an efficient implementation of element-wise operations (add/remove/member) requires the use of different concrete data structures and than an implementation of set-wise operations (union/intersection/...), so a choice should be made depending on the main use case. One way to implement sets is by using linked lists. Lisp has standard library support for this with the following functions:

- `adjoin` to add an item to the list if it's not already there

- `member` to check for item presence in the set

- `subsetp` for subset relationship query

- `union`, `intersection`, `set-difference`, and `set-exclusive-or` for set operations

This approach works well for small sets (up to tens of elements), but it is rather inefficient in general. Adding an item to the set or checking for membership will require $O(n)$ operations, while, in the hash-set (which we'll discuss in Chapter 7), these are $O(1)$ operations. A naive implementation of union and other set-theoretic operations will require $O(n^2)$ as we'll have to compare each element from one set with each one from the other. However, if our set lists are in sorted order, set-theoretic operations can be implemented efficiently in just $O(n)$ where n is the total number of elements in all sets, by performing a single linear scan over each set in parallel. Using a hash-set will also result in the same complexity.

Here is a simplified implementation of union for sets of numbers built on sorted lists:

```
(defun sorted-union (s1 s2)
  (let ((rez ()))
    (do ()
        ((and (null s1) (null s2)))
      (let ((i1 (first s1))
            (i2 (first s2)))
        (cond ((null i1) (dolist (i2 s2)
                           (push i2 rez))
                         (return))
              ((null i2) (dolist (i1 s1)
                           (push i1 rez))
                         (return))
              ((= i1 i2) (push i1 rez)
                         (setf s1 (rest s1)
                               s2 (rest s2)))
              ((< i1 i2) (push i1 rez)
                         (setf s1 (rest s1)))
              ;; just T may be used instead
              ;; of the following condition
              ((> i1 i2) (push i2 rez)
                         (setf s2 (rest s2)))))))
    (reverse rez)))

CL-USER> (sorted-union '(1 2 3)
                       '(0 1 5 6))
(0 1 2 3 5 6)
```

This approach may be useful even for unsorted list-based sets as sorting is a merely O(n * log n) operation. Even better though, when the use case requires primarily set-theoretic operations on our sets and the number of changes/ membership queries is comparatively low, the most efficient technique may be to keep the lists sorted at all times.

Merge Sort

Speaking about sorting, the algorithms we discussed for array sorting in the previous chapter do not work as efficient for lists for they are based on swap operations, which are O(n), in the list case. Thus, another approach is required, and there exist a number of efficient list sorting algorithms, the most prominent of which is merge sort. It works by splitting the list into two equal parts until we get to trivial one-element lists and then merging the sorted lists into the bigger sorted ones. The merging procedure for sorted lists is efficient as we've seen in the previous example. A nice feature of such an approach is its stability, that is, preservation of the original order of the equal elements, given the proper implementation of the merge procedure:

```
(defun merge-sort (list comp)
  (if (null (rest list))
      list
      (let ((half (floor (length list) 2)))
        (merge-lists (merge-sort (subseq seq 0 half) comp)
                     (merge-sort (subseq seq half) comp)
                     comp))))

(defun merge-lists (l1 l2 comp)
  (let ((rez ()))
    (do ()
        ((and (null l1) (null l2)))
      (let ((i1 (first l1))
            (i2 (first l2)))
        (cond ((null i1) (dolist (i l2)
                           (push i rez))
                         (return))
```

```
            ((null i2) (dolist (i l1)
                          (push i rez))
                        (return))
            ((funcall comp i1 i2) (push i1 rez)
                                  (setf l1 (rest l1)))
            (t (push i2 rez)
               (setf l2 (rest l2))))))))
  (reverse rez)))
```

The same complexity analysis as for binary search applies to this algorithm. At each level of the recursion tree, we perform $O(n)$ operations. Each element is pushed into the resulting list once and reversed once, and there are at most four comparison operations: three null checks and one call of the comp function. We also need to perform one copy per element in the subseq operation and take the length of the list (although it can be memorized and passed down as the function call argument) on the recursive descent. This totals to not more than ten operations per element, which is a constant. And the height of the tree is, as we already know, (log n 2). So the total complexity is $O(n * log\ n)$.

Let's now measure the real time needed for such sorting, and let's compare it to the time of prod-sort (with optimal array accessors) from Chapter 5:

```
CL-USER> (rtl:with ((lst (random-list 10000))
                    (vec (make-array 10000 :initial-contents lst)))
           (print-sort-timings "Prod" 'prod-sort vec)
           (print-sort-timings "Merge " 'merge-sort lst))
= Prodsort of random vector =
Evaluation took:
  0.048 seconds of real time
= Prodsort of sorted vector =
Evaluation took:
  0.032 seconds of real time
= Prodsort of reverse sorted vector =
Evaluation took:
  0.044 seconds of real time
= Merge sort of random vector =
Evaluation took:
  0.007 seconds of real time
```

```
= Merge sort of sorted vector =
Evaluation took:
  0.007 seconds of real time
= Merge sort of reverse sorted vector =
Evaluation took:
  0.008 seconds of real time
```

Interestingly enough, merge sort turned out to be around five times faster, although it seems that the number of operations required at each level of recursion is at least two to three times bigger than for quicksort. Why we got such result is left as an exercise to the reader: I'd start from profiling the function calls and looking where most of the time is wasted...

It should be apparent that the merge-lists procedure works in a similar way to set-theoretic operations on sorted lists that we've discussed in the previous part. It is, in fact, provided in the Lisp standard library. Using the standard merge, merge sort may be written in a completely functional and also generic way to support any kind of sequences:

```
(defun merge-sort (seq comp)
  (if (or (null seq)  ; avoid expensive length calculation
          (<= (length seq) 1))
      seq
      (let ((half (floor (length seq) 2)))
        (merge (type-of seq)
               (merge-sort (subseq seq 0 half) comp)
               (merge-sort (subseq seq half) comp)
               comp))))
```

There's still one substantial difference of merge sort from the array sorting functions: it is not in-place. So it also requires the $O(n * \log n)$ additional space to hold the half sublists that are produced at each iteration. Sorting and merging them in-place is not possible. There are ways to somewhat reduce this extra space usage but not totally eliminate it.

Parallelization of Merge Sort

The extra space drawback of merge sort may, however, turn irrelevant if we consider the problem of parallelizing this procedure. The general idea of parallelized implementation of any algorithm is to split the work in a way that allows reducing the runtime proportional to the number of workers performing those jobs. In the ideal case, if we have m workers and are able to spread the work evenly, the running time should be reduced by a factor of m. For the merge sort, it will mean just $O(n/m * log\ n)$. Such ideal reduction is not always achievable, though, because often there are bottlenecks in the algorithm that require all or some workers to wait for one of them to complete its job.

Here's a trivial parallel merge sort implementation that uses the eager-future2 library, which adds high-level data parallelism capabilities based on the Lisp implementation's multithreading facilities:

```
(defun parallel-merge-sort (seq comp)
  (if (or (null seq) (<= (length seq) 1))
      seq
      (rtl:with ((half (floor (length seq) 2))
                 (thread1 (eager-future2:pexec
                            (merge-sort (subseq seq 0 half) comp)))
                 (thread2 (eager-future2:pexec
                            (merge-sort (subseq seq half) comp))))
        (merge (type-of seq)
               (eager-future2:yield thread1)
               (eager-future2:yield thread2)
               comp))))
```

The eager-future2:pexec procedure submits each merge-sort to the thread pool that manages multiple CPU threads available in the system and continues program execution not waiting for it to return, while eager-future2:yield pauses execution until the thread performing the appropriate merge-sort returns.

When I ran our testing function with both serial and parallel merge sorts on my machine, with four CPUs, I got the following result:

```
CL-USER> (rtl:with ((lst1 (random-list 10000))
                    (lst2 (copy-list lst1)))
          (print-sort-timings "Merge " 'merge-sort lst1)
          (print-sort-timings "Parallel Merge "
                                'parallel-merge-sort lst2))
= Merge sort of random vector =
Evaluation took:
  0.007 seconds of real time
  114.29% CPU
= Merge sort of sorted vector =
Evaluation took:
  0.006 seconds of real time
  116.67% CPU
= Merge sort of reverse sorted vector =
Evaluation took:
  0.007 seconds of real time
  114.29% CPU
= Parallel Merge sort of random vector =
Evaluation took:
  0.003 seconds of real time
  266.67% CPU
= Parallel Merge sort of sorted vector =
Evaluation took:
  0.003 seconds of real time
  266.67% CPU
= Parallel Merge sort of reverse sorted vector =
Evaluation took:
  0.005 seconds of real time
  220.00% CPU
```

A speedup of approximately 2x, which is also reflected by the rise in CPU utilization from around 100% (i.e., one CPU) to 250%. These are correct numbers as the merge procedure is still executed serially and remains the bottleneck. There are more sophisticated ways to achieve optimal m times speedup in merge sort parallelization, but we won't discuss them here due to their complexity.

Lists and Lisp

Historically, Lisp's name originated as an abbreviation of "List Processing," which points both to the significance that lists played in the language's early development and to the fact that flexibility (a major feature of lists) was always a cornerstone of its design. Why are lists important to Lisp? Maybe, originally, it was connected with the availability and the good support of this data structure in the language itself. But, quickly, the focus shifted to the fact that, unlike other languages, Lisp code is input in the compiler not in a custom string-based format but in the form of nested lists that directly represent the syntax tree. Coupled with superior support for the list data structure, it opens numerous possibilities for programmatic processing of the code itself, which are manifest in the macro system, code walkers and generators, and so on. So "List Processing" turns out to be not about lists of data, but about lists of code, which perfectly describes the main distinctive feature of this language...

Takeaways

In this chapter, we have seen the possibilities that the flexibility of linked structures opens: lists were used as sequences, sets, stacks, and queues. We'll continue utilizing this flexibility over and over in the following parts.

CHAPTER 7

Key-Values

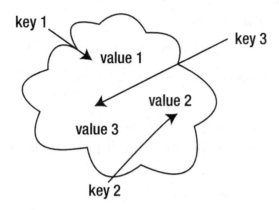

To conclude the description of essential data structures, we need to discuss key-values (kvs), which are the broadest family of structures one can imagine. Unlike arrays and lists, kvs are not concrete structures. In fact, they span, at least in some capacity, all of the popular concrete ones, as well as some obscure.

The main feature of kvs is efficient access to the values by some kind of keys that they are associated with. In other words, each element of such data structure is a key-value pair that can be easily retrieved if we know the key, and, on the other hand, if we ask for the key that is not in the structure, the null result is also returned efficiently. By "efficiently," we usually mean $O(1)$ or, at least, something sublinear (like $O(\log n)$), although, for some cases, even $O(n)$ retrieval time may be acceptable. See how broad this is! So a lot of different structures may play the role of key-values.

© Vsevolod Domkin 2021
V. Domkin, *Programming Algorithms in Lisp*, https://doi.org/10.1007/978-1-4842-6428-7_7

By the way, there isn't even a single widely adopted name for such structures. Besides key-values—which isn't such a popular term (I derived it from key-value stores)—in different languages, they are called maps, dictionaries, associative arrays, tables, objects, and so on.

In a sense, these are the most basic and essential data structures. They are so essential that some dynamic languages—for example, Lua, explicitly, and JavaScript, without a lot of advertisement—rely on them as the core (sometimes sole) language's data structure. Moreover, key-values are used almost everywhere. The following is a list of some of the most popular scenarios:

- Implementation of the object system in programming languages.

- Most of the key-value stores are, for the most part, glorified key-value structures.

- Internal tables in the operating system (running process tables or file descriptor tables in the Linux kernel), programming language environment, or application software.

- All kinds of memoization and caching.

- Efficient implementation of sets.

- Ad hoc or predefined records for returning aggregated data from function calls.

- Representing various dictionaries (in language processing and beyond).

Considering such a wide spread, it may be surprising that, historically, the programming language community only gradually realized the usefulness of key-values. For instance, such languages as C and C++ don't have the built-in support for general kvs (if we don't count structs and arrays, which may be considered significantly limited versions). Lisp, on the contrary, was to some extent pioneering their recognition with the concepts of alists and plists, as well as being one of the first languages to have hash-table support in the standard.

Concrete Key-values

Let's see what concrete structures can be considered key-values and in which cases it makes sense to use them.

Simple Arrays

Simple sequences, especially arrays, may be regarded as a particular variant of kvs that allows only numeric keys with efficient (and fastest) constant-time access. This restriction is serious. However, as we'll see in the following, it can often be worked around with clever algorithms. As a result, arrays actually play a major role in the key-value space, but not in the most straightforward form. However, if it is possible to be content with numeric keys and their number is known beforehand, vanilla arrays are the best possible implementation option. For example, OS kernels that have a predefined limit on the number of processes and a "process table" that is indexed by pid (process id) that lies in the range `0..MAX_PID`.

So let's note this curious fact that arrays are also a variant of key-values.

Associative Lists

The main drawback of using simple arrays for kvs is not even the restriction that all keys should somehow be reduced to numbers, but the static nature of arrays that do not lend themselves well to resizing. As an alternative, we could then use linked lists, which do not have this restriction. If the key-value contains many elements, linked lists are clearly not ideal in terms of efficiency. Many times, the key-value contains very few elements, perhaps only half a dozen or so. In this case, even a linear scan of the whole list may not be such an expensive operation. This is where various forms of associative lists enter the scene. They store pairs of keys and values and don't impose any restrictions, neither on the keys nor on the number of elements. But their performance quickly degrades below acceptable once the number of elements grows above several. Many flavors of associative lists can be invented. Historically, Lisp supported two variants in the standard library:

- **alists** (association lists) are lists of cons pairs. A cons pair is the original Lisp data structure, and it consists of two values called the `car` and the `cdr` (the names come from two IBM machine instructions). Association lists have dedicated operations to find a pair in the list (`assoc`) and to add an item to it (`pairlis`), although it may be easier to just push the new cons cell onto it. Modification may be performed simply by altering the `cdr` of the appropriate cons cell. ((:foo . "bar") (42 . "baz")) is an alist of two items with keys :foo and 42 and values "bar" and "baz". As you can see, it's heterogenous in a sense that it allows keys of arbitrary type.

- **plists** (property lists) are flat lists of alternating keys and values. They also have dedicated search (getf) and modify (setf getf) operations, while insertion may be performed by calling push twice (on the value and then the key). The plist with the same data as the previous alist will look like this: (:foo "bar" 42 "baz"). Plists are used in Lisp to represent the keyword function arguments as a whole.

Deleting an item from such lists is quite efficient if we already know the place that we want to clear, but tracking this place if we haven't found it yet is a bit cumbersome. In general, the procedure will be to iterate the list by tails until the relevant cons cell is found and then make the previous cell point to this one's tail. A destructive version for alists will look like this:

```
(defun alist-del (key alist)
  (loop :for tail := alist :then (rest tail) :while tail
        :for prev := alist :then tail
        ;; a more general version of the function will take
        ;; an additional :test argument instead of hardcoding EQL
        :when (eql key (car (first tail)))
        :do (return (if (eql prev alist)
                        ;; special case of the first item
                        (rest alist)
                        (progn (setf (rest prev) (rest tail))
                               alist)))
        :finally (return alist)))
```

However, the standard provides higher-level removal operations for plists (remf) and alists: (remove key alist :key 'car).

Both of these ad hoc list-based kvs have some historical baggage associated with them and are not very convenient to use. Nevertheless, they can be utilized for some simple scenarios, as well as for interoperability with the existing language machinery. And, however counterintuitive it may seem, if the number of items is small, alists may be the most efficient key-value data structure.

Another nonstandard but more convenient and slightly more efficient variant of associative lists was proposed by Ron Garret and is called **dlists** (dictionary lists). It is a cons pair of two lists: the list of keys and the list of values. The dlist for our example will look like this: `((:foo 42) . ("bar" "baz"))`.

As the interface of different associative lists is a thin wrapper over the standard list API, the general list processing knowledge can be applied to dealing with them, so we won't spend any more time describing how they work. Instead, I'd like to end the description of list-based kvs with this quote from a Scheme old-timer John Cowan posted as a comment to this chapter:

> *One thing to say about alists is that they are very much the simplest persistent key-value object; we can both have pointers to the same alist and I can cons things onto mine without affecting yours. In principle this is possible for plists also, but the standard functions for plists mutate them.*
>
> *In addition, the maximum size at which an alist's $O(n)$ behavior dominates the higher constant factor of a hash table has to be measured for a particular implementation: in Chicken Scheme, the threshold is about 30.*
>
> *The self-rearranging alist is not persistent but has other nice properties. Whenever you find something in the alist, you make sure you have kept the address of the previous pair as well. Then you splice the found item out of its existing place, cons it at the front of the alist, and return it. Your caller has to be sure to remember that the alist is now at a new location. If you want, you can also shorten the alist at any point as you search it to keep the list bounded, which makes it a LRU cache.*
>
> *An interesting hybrid structure is an alist whose last pair does not have () in the cdr but rather a hash table. So when you get down to the end, you look in the hash table. This is useful when a lot of the mappings are always the same but it is necessary to temporarily change a few. As long as the hash table is treated as immutable, this data structure is persistent.*
>
> *There's life in the old alist yet!*

Hash-Tables

Hash-tables are, probably, the most common way to do key-values, nowadays. They are dynamic and don't impose restrictions on keys while having an amortized $O(1)$ performance albeit with a rather high constant. The next chapter will be exclusively dedicated to hash-table implementation and usage. Here, it suffices to say that hash-tables come in many different flavors, including the ones that can be efficiently precomputed if we want to store a set of items that is known ahead of time. Hash-tables are, definitely, the most versatile key-value variant and thus the default choice for such a structure. However, they are not so simple and may pose a number of surprises that the programmer should understand in order to use them properly.

Structs

Speaking of structs, they may also be considered a special variant of key-values with a predefined set of keys. In this respect, structs are similar to arrays, which have a fixed set of keys (from 0 to MAX_KEY). As we already know, generally, structs internally map to arrays, so they may be considered a layer of syntactic sugar that provides names for the keys and handy accessors. Usually, the struct is pictured not as a key-value but rather a way to make the code more "semantic" and understandable. Yet, if we consider returning the aggregate value from a function call, as the possible set of keys is known beforehand, it's a good stylistic and implementation choice to define a special-purpose one-off struct for this instead of using an alist or a hash-table. Here is a small example—compare the clarity of the alternatives:

```
(defun foo-adhoc-list (arg)
  (let ((rez (list)))
    ...
    (push "hello" rez)
    ...
    (push arg rez)
    ...
    rez))

CL-USER> (foo-adhoc-list 42)
(42 "hello")

(defun foo-adhoc-hash (arg)
  (let ((rez (make-hash-table)))
    ...
    (setf (gethash :baz rez) "hello")
    ...
```

```
    (setf (gethash :quux rez) arg))
    ...
    rez))
CL-USER> (foo-adhoc-hash 42)
#<HASH-TABLE :TEST EQL :COUNT 2 {1040DBFE83}>

(defstruct foo-rez
  baz quux)
(defun foo-struct (&rest args)
  (let ((rez (make-foo-rez)))
    ...
    (setf (foo-baz rez) "hello")
    ...
    (setf (foo-quux rez) 42))
    ...
    rez))
CL-USER> (foo-struct 42)
#S(FOO-REZ :BAZ "hello" :QUUX 42)
```

Trees

Another versatile option for implementing kvs is by using trees. There are even
more tree variants than hash-tables, and we'll also have dedicated chapters to study
them. Generally, the main advantage of trees, compared to simple hash-tables, is the
possibility to impose some ordering on the keys (although linked hash-tables also allow
for that), while the disadvantage is less efficient operation: $O(\log n)$. Also, trees don't
require hashing. Another major direction that the usage of trees opens is the possibility
of persistent key-value implementation. Some languages, like Java, have standard library
support for tree-based kvs (TreeMap), but most languages delegate dealing with such
structures to library authors for there is a wide choice of specific trees and none may
serve as the default choice of a key-value structure. Trees and their usage as kvs will also
be discussed in more detail in a separate chapter.

Operations

The primary operation for a kv structure is access to its elements by key: to set, change, and remove. As there are so many different variants of concrete kvs, there are a number of different low-level access operations, some of which we have already discussed in the previous chapters and the others we will see in the next ones.

Yet, most of the algorithms don't necessarily require the efficiency of built-in accessors, while their clarity will seriously benefit from a uniform generic access operation. Such an operation, as we have already mentioned, is defined by RUTILS and is called generic-elt or ? , for short. We have already seen it in action in some of the preceding examples. And that's not an accident as kv access is among the most frequent operations. In the following chapter, we will stick to the rule of using the specific accessors like gethash when we are talking about some structure-specific operations and ? in all other cases—when clarity matters more than low-level considerations. ? is implemented using the CLOS generic function machinery that provides dynamic dispatch to a concrete retrieval operation and allows defining additional variants for new structures as the need arises. Another useful feature of generic-elt is chaining that allows expressing multiple accesses as a single call. This comes in very handy for nested structures. Consider an example of accessing the first element of the field of the struct that is the value in some hash-table: (? x :key 0 'field). If we were to use concrete operations, it would look like this: (slot-value (nth 0 (gethash :key x)) 'field).

The following is the backbone of the generic-elt function that handles chaining and error reporting:

```
(defgeneric generic-elt (obj key &rest keys)
  (:documentation
    "Generic element access in OBJ by KEY.
    Supports chaining with KEYS.")
  (:method :around (obj key &rest keys)
    (reduce #'generic-elt keys :initial-value (call-next-method obj key)))
  (:method (obj key &rest keys)
    (declare (ignore keys))
    (error 'generic-elt-error :obj obj :key key)))
```

And here are some methods for specific kvs (as well as sequences):

```
(defmethod generic-elt ((obj hash-table) key &rest keys)
  (declare (ignore keys))
  (gethash key obj))

(defmethod generic-elt ((obj vector) key &rest keys)
  (declare (ignore keys))
  ;; Python-like handling of negative indices as offsets from the end
  (when (minusp key) (setf key (- (length obj) key)))
  (aref obj key))

(defmethod generic-elt ((obj (eql nil)) key &rest keys)
  (declare (ignore key keys))
  (error "Can't access NIL with generic-elt!"))
```

generic-setf is a complement function that allows defining setter operations for generic-elt. There exists a built-in protocol to make Lisp aware that generic-setf should be called whenever setf is invoked for the value accessed with ? : (defsetf ? generic-setf).

It is also common to retrieve all keys or values of the kv, which is handled in a generic way by the keys and vals RUTILS functions.

Key-values are not sequences in a sense that they are not necessarily ordered, although some variants are. But even unordered kvs may be traversed in some random order. Iterating over kvs is another common and essential operation. In Lisp, as we already know, there are two complimentary iteration patterns: the functional map and the imperative do style. RUTILS provides both of them as mapkv and dokv, although I'd recommend to first consider the macro dotable that is specifically designed to operate on hash-tables.

Finally, another common necessity is the transformation between different kv representations, primarily between hash-tables and lists of pairs, which is also handled by RUTILS with its ht->pairs/ht->alist and pairs->ht/alist->ht functions.

As you see, the authors of the Lisp standard library hadn't envisioned the generic key-value access protocols, and so it is implemented completely in a third-party add-on. Yet, what's most important is that the building blocks for doing that were provided by the language, so this case shows the critical importance that these blocks (primarily, CLOS generic functions) have in future-proofing the language's design.

Memoization

One of the major use cases for key-values is memoization—storing the results of previous computations in a dedicated table (**cache**) to avoid recalculating them. Memoization is one of the main optimization techniques; I'd even say the default one. Essentially, it trades space for speed. And the main issue is that space is also limited, so memoization algorithms are geared toward optimizing its usage to retain the most relevant items, that is, maximize the probability that the items in the cache will be reused.

Memoization may be performed ad hoc or explicitly: just set up some key scheme and a table to store the results and add/retrieve/remove the items as needed. It can also be delegated to the compiler in the implicit form. For instance, Java or Python provides the @memoize decorator: once it is used with the function definition, each call to it will pass through the assigned cache using the call arguments as the cache keys. This is how the same feature may be implemented in Lisp, in the simplest fashion:

```
(defun start-memoizing (fn)
  (stop-memoizing fn)
  (setf (symbol-function fn)
        (let ((table (make-hash-table :test 'equal))
              (vanilla-fn (symbol-function fn)))
          (setf (get fn :cache) table
                (get fn :fn) vanilla-fn)
          (lambda (&rest args)
            (rtl:getsethash (format nil "~{~A~^|~}" args)
                            table
                            (apply vanilla-fn args))))))

(defun stop-memoizing (fn)
  ;; WHEN-IT is a so called anaphoric macro, from RUTILS, that assigns
  ;; the value of its first argument to an implicitly created variable IT
  ;; and evaluates the body when IT isn't null
  (rtl:when-it (get fn :fn)
    (setf (symbol-function fn) rtl:it
          (get fn :fn) nil)))

CL-USER> (defun foo (x)
           (sleep 5)
           x)
```

```
CL-USER> (start-memoizing 'foo)
CL-USER> (time (foo 1))
Evaluation took:
  5.000 seconds of real time
CL-USER> (time (foo 1))
Evaluation took:
  0.000 seconds of real time
CL-USER> (time (foo 2))
Evaluation took:
  5.001 seconds of real time
```

We use a hash-table to store the memoized results. The `getset#` macro from RUTILS tries to retrieve the item from the table by key and, if it's not present there, performs the calculation given as its last argument returning its result while also storing it in the table at key. Another useful Lisp feature utilized in this facility is called "symbol plist": every symbol has an associated key-value plist. Items in this plist can be retrieved using the `get` operator.[1]

This approach is rather primitive and has a number of drawbacks. First of all, the hash-table is not limited in capacity. Thus, if it is used carelessly, a memory leak is inevitable. Another possible issue may occur with the keys, which are determined by simply concatenating the string representations of the arguments—possibly nonunique. Such bug may be very subtle and hard to infer. Overall, memoization is the source of implicit behavior that always poses potential trouble but sometimes is just necessary. A more nuanced solution will allow us to configure both how the keys are calculated and various parameters of the cache, which we'll discuss next. One more possible decision to make might be about what to cache and what not: for example, we could add a time measurement around the call to the original function, and only when it exceeds a predefined limit the results will be cached.

---

[1] Symbol plists represent one of the unpleasant legacy features of the language in that the most obvious accessor name, namely, get, is reserved for working with symbols. Therefore, this name cannot be used for accessing other kinds of data. Historically, symbol plists were the first and only variant of key-values available in the language (at that time, the other languages didn't have the slightest idea of such a high-level concept).

111

Memoization in Action: Transposition Tables

Transposition tables are a characteristic example of the effective usage of memoization, which comes from classic game AI. But the same approach may be applied in numerous other areas with lots of computation paths that converge and diverge at times. We'll return to similar problems in the last third of this book.

In such games as chess, the same position may be reached in a great variety of moves. All possible sequences are called transpositions, and it is obvious that, regardless of how we reached a certain position, if we have already analyzed that situation previously, we don't need to repeat the analysis when it repeats. So caching the results allows avoiding a lot of redundant computation. However, the number of positions, in chess, that comes up during the analysis is huge, so we don't stand a chance of remembering all of them. In this case, a good predictor for the chance of a situation to occur is very likely the number of times it has occurred in the past. For that reason, an appropriate caching technique, in this context, is plain LFU (least frequently used). But there's more. Yet, another measure of the value of a certain position is how early it occurred in the game tree (since the number of possible developments, from it, is larger). So classic LFU should be mixed with this temporal information yielding a domain-specific caching approach. And the parameters of combining the two measures together are subject to empirical evaluation and research.

There's much more to transposition tables than mentioned in this short introduction. For instance, the keys describing the position may need to include additional information if the history of occurrence in it impacts the further game outcome (castling and repetition rules). Here's, also, a quote from Wikipedia on their additional use in another common chess-playing algorithm:

> *The transposition table can have other uses than finding transpositions. In alpha-beta pruning, the search is fastest (in fact, optimal) when the child of a node corresponding to the best move is always considered first. Of course, there is no way of knowing the best move beforehand, but when iterative deepening is used, the move that was found to be the best in a shallower search is a good approximation. Therefore this move is tried first. For storing the best child of a node, the entry corresponding to that node in the transposition table is used.*

Cache Invalidation

The problem of cache invalidation arises when we set some limit on the size of the cache. Once it is full—and a properly setup cache should be full, effectively, all the time—we have to decide which item to remove (evict) when we need to put a new one in the cache. I've already mentioned the saying that (alongside naming things) it is the hardest challenge in computer science. In fact, it's not; it's rather trivial, from the point of view of algorithms. The hard part is defining the notion of relevance. There are two general approximations which are used unless there are some specific considerations: frequency of access or time of last access. Let's see the algorithms built around these. Each approach uses some additional data stored with each key. The purpose of the data is to track one of the properties, that is, either frequency of access or time of last access.

Second Chance and Clock Algorithms

The simplest approach to cache invalidation except for random choice eviction may be utilized when we are severely limited in the amount of additional space we can use per key. Usually, this situation is typical for hardware caches. The minimal possible amount of information to store is 1 bit. If we have just as much space, the only option we have is to use it as a flag indicating whether the item was accessed again after it was put into the cache. This technique is very fast and very simple and improves cache performance to some extent. There may be two ways of tracking this bit efficiently:

1. Just use a bit-vector (usually called "bitmap," in such context) of the same length as the cache size. To select the item for eviction, find the first 0 from the left or right. With the help of one of the hardware instructions from the bit scan family (ffs, find first zero; clz, count trailing zeroes; etc.), this operation can be blazingly fast. In Lisp, we could use the high-level function position:

```
(defun find-candidate-second-chance (bitmap)
  (declare (type bit-vector bitmap))
  (position 0 bitmap))
```

The type declaration is necessary for the implementation to emit the appropriate machine instruction. If you're not confident in that, just disassemble the function and look at the generated machine code:

```
CL-USER> (disassemble 'find-candidate-second-chance)
; disassembly for FIND-CANDIDATE-SECOND-CHANCE
; Size: 228 bytes. Origin: #x103A8E42F0
...
; 340:      B878D53620       MOV EAX, #x2036D578
           ; #<FDEFN SB-KERNEL:%BIT-POSITION/0>
...
```

So SBCL uses `sb-kernel:%bit-position/0`. Nice. If you look inside this function, though, you'll find out that it's also pretty complicated. And, overall, there are lots of other assembler instructions in this piece, so if our goal is squeezing the last bit out of it, there's more we can do:

- Force the implementation to optimize for speed: put `(declaim (optimize (speed 3) (debug 0) (safety 1)))` at the top of the file with the function definition or use `proclaim` in the REPL with the same declarations.

- Use the low-level function `sb-kernel:%bit-position/0` directly. However, we should keep in mind that explicitly depending on such code might break our application, so this solution may be applied in limited contexts and is not future-proof. Yet, sometimes, when the only thing you need is a one-off solution for an immediate problem at hand and you don't care about supporting this code, it may be acceptable.

- Go even deeper and use the machine instruction directly—SBCL allows that as well: `(sb-vm::%primitive sb-vm::unsigned-word-find-first-bit x)`. But this will be truly context-dependent (on the endianness, hardware architecture, and the size of the bit-vector itself, which should fit into a machine word for this technique to work). However, there's one problem with the function `find-candidate-second-chance`: if all the bits are set, it will return nil.

By selecting the first element (or, even better, some random element), we can fix this problem. Still, eventually, we'll end up with all elements of the bitmap set to 1, so the method will degrade to simple random choice. It means that we need to periodically reset the bit-vector, either on every eviction—this is a good strategy if we happen to hit the cache more often than miss—or after some number of iterations, or after every bit is set to 1. Overall, such an approach falls into a category of "crazy hacks."

2. An alternative method for selecting a candidate to evict is known as the clock algorithm. It keeps examining the visited bit of each item, in a cycle: if it's equal to 1, reset it and move to the next item; if it's 0, select the item for eviction. Basically, it's yet another strategy for dealing with the saturation of the bit-vector. Here's how it may be implemented in Lisp with the help of the **closure pattern**: the function keeps track of its internal state, using a lexical variable that is only accessible from inside the function and that has a value that persists between calls to the function. The closure is created by the let block, and the variable closed over is i, here:

```
(let ((i 0))
  (defun find-candidate-clock (bitmap)
    (declare (type (vector bit) bitmap))
    (loop :with len := (length bitmap)
          :until (zerop (aref bitmap i))
          :do (setf (aref bitmap i) 0)
              (setf i (mod (1+ i) len)))
    i))
```

Our loop is guaranteed to find the zero bit at least after we cycle over all the elements and return to the first one that we have set to zero ourselves. Obviously, here and in other places where it is not stated explicitly, we're talking about single-threaded execution only.

LFU

So what if we don't have such a serious restriction on the size of the access counter? In this case, a similar algorithm that uses a counter instead of a flag will be called least frequently used (LFU) item eviction. There is one problem though: the access counter will only grow over time, so some items that were heavily used during some period will never be evicted from the cache, even though they may never be accessed again. To counteract this accumulation property, which is similar to bitmap saturation we've seen in the previous algorithm, a similar measure can be applied. Namely, we'll have to introduce some notion of epochs, which reset or diminish the value of all counters. The most common approach to epochs is to right shift each counter, that is, divide by 2. This strategy is called **aging**. An LFU cache with aging may be called LRFU—least recently/frequently used.

As usual, the question arises: How often to apply aging? The answer may be context-dependent and dependent on the size of the access counter. For instance, usually, a 1-byte counter, which can distinguish between 256 access operations, will be good enough, and it rarely makes sense to use a smaller one as most hardware operates in byte-sized units. The common strategies for aging may be

- Periodically with an arbitrarily chosen interval—which should be enough to accumulate some number of changes in the counters but not to overflow them.

- After a certain number of cache access operations. Such an approach may ensure that the counter doesn't overflow: say, if we use a 1-byte counter and age after each 128 access operations, the counter will never exceed 192. Or we could perform the shift after 256 operations and still ensure lack of overflows with high probability.

LRU

An alternative approach to LFU is LRU—evict the item that was used the longest time ago. LRU means that we need to store either last-access timestamps or some generation/epoch counters. Another possibility is to utilize access counters, similar to the ones that were used for LFU, except that we initialize them by setting all bits to 1, that is, to the maximum possible value (255 for a 1-byte counter). The counters are decremented, on each cache access, simultaneously for all items except for the item being accessed.

The benefit of such an approach is that it doesn't require accessing any external notion of time making the cache fully self-contained, which is necessary for some hardware implementations, for instance. The only thing to remember is not to decrement the counter beyond 0. :)

Unlike LFU, this strategy can't distinguish between a heavily accessed item and a sparingly accessed one. So, in the general case, I'd say that LFU with aging (LRFU) should be the default approach, although its implementation is slightly more complex.

Low-Level Caching

So memoization is the primary tool for algorithm optimization, and the lower we descend into our computing platform, the more this fact becomes apparent. For hardware, it is, basically, the only option. There are many caches in the platform that act behind the scenes, but which have a great impact on the actual performance of your code: the CPU caches, the disk cache, the page cache, and other OS caches. The main issue, here, is the lack of transparency into their operation and sometimes even the lack of awareness of their existence. This topic is, largely, beyond the scope of our book, so if you want to learn more, there's a well-known talk "A Crash Course in Modern Hardware" and an accompanying list of "Latency Numbers Every Programmer Should Know" that you can start with. Here, I can provide only a brief outline.

The most important cache in the system is the CPU cache—or, rather, in most of the modern architectures, a system of two or three caches. There's an infamous **von Neumann's bottleneck** of the conventional computer hardware design: the CPU works roughly two orders of magnitude faster than it can fetch data from memory. Last time I checked, the numbers were as follows: execution of one memory transfer took around 250–300 CPU cycles, that is, around 300 additions or other primitive instructions could be run during that time. And the problem is that CPUs operate only on data that they get from memory, so if the bottleneck didn't exist at all, theoretically, we could have two orders of magnitude faster execution. Fortunately, the degradation in performance is not so drastic, thanks to the use of CPU caches: only around an order of magnitude. The cache transfer numbers are the following: from L1 (the fastest and hence smallest) cache, around 5 cycles; from L2, 20–30 cycles; and from L3, 50–100 cycles (that's why L3 is not always used as it's almost on par with the main memory). Why do I say that fastest means smallest? Just because fast access memory is more expensive and requires more energy. Otherwise, we could just make all RAM as fast as the L1 cache.

How do these caches operate? This is one of the things that every algorithmic programmer should know, at least, in general. Even if some algorithm seems good on paper, a more cache-friendly one with worse theoretical properties may very well outperform it.

The CPU cache temporarily stores contents of the memory cells (memory words) indexed by their addresses. It is called set-associative as it operates not on single cells but on sequential blocks of those (in the so-called cache lines). The L1 cache of size 1 MB, usually, will store 64 such blocks, each one holding 16 words. This approach is oriented toward the normal sequential layout of executable code, structures, and arrays—the majority of the memory contents. And the corresponding to it sequential memory access pattern. That is, after reading one memory cell, usually, the processor will move on to the next: either because it's the next instruction to execute or the next item in the array being iterated over. That's why so much importance in program optimization folklore is given to **cache alignment**, that is, structuring the program's memory so that the things commonly accessed together will fit into the same cache line. One example of this principle is the padding of structures with zeroes to align their size to be a multiple of 32 or 64. The same applies to code padding with nops. And this is another reason why arrays are a preferred data structure compared to linked lists: when the whole contents fit in the same cache line, its processing performance is blazingly fast. The catch, though, is that it's, practically, impossible for normal programmers to directly observe how CPU cache interoperates with their programs. There are no tools to make it transparent, so what remains is to rely on the general principles, second-guessing, and trial and error.

Another interesting choice for hardware (and some software) caches is write-through vs. write-back behavior. The question is how the cache deals with cached data being modified:

- Either the modifications will be immediately stored to the main storage, effectively, making the whole operation longer.

- Or they may, first, be persisted to the cache only, while writing to the backing store (synchronization) will be performed on all data in the cache at configured intervals.

The second option is faster as there are a smaller number of expensive round-trips, but it is less resilient to failure. A good example of the write-back cache in action is the origin of the Windows "Safely remove hardware" option. The underlying assumption is that the data to be written to the flash drive passes through the OS cache, which may be configured in the write-back fashion. In this case, forced sync is required before disconnecting the device to ensure that the latest version of the cached data is saved to it.

Another example of caching drastically impacting performance, which everyone is familiar with, is paging or swapping—an operation performed by the operating system. When the executing programs together require more (virtual) memory than the size of the RAM that is physically available, the OS saves some of the pages of data that these programs use to a place on disk known as the swap section.

Takeaways

1. Key-values are very versatile and widely used data structures. Don't limit your understanding of them to a particular implementation choice made by the designers of the programming language you're currently using.

2. Trading space for time is, probably, the most widespread and impactful algorithmic technique.

3. Caching, which is a direct manifestation of this technique and one of the main applications of key-value data structures, is one of the principal factors impacting program performance, on a large scale. It may be utilized by the programmer in the form of memoization and will also inevitably be used by the underlying platform, in hard to control and predict ways. The area of program optimization for efficient hardware utilization represents a distinct set of techniques, requiring skills that are obscure and not fully systematized.

CHAPTER 8

Hash-Tables

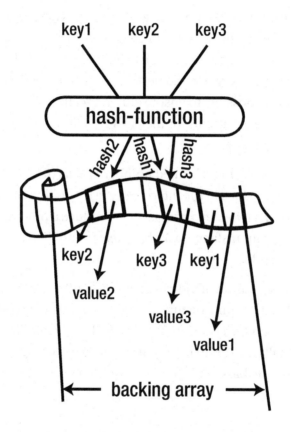

Now, we can move on to studying advanced data structures which are built on top of the basic ones such as arrays and lists, but may exhibit distinct properties and have different use cases and special algorithms. Many of them will combine the basic data structures to obtain new properties not accessible to the underlying structures. The first and most important of these advanced structures is, undoubtedly, the hash-table. However vast is the list of candidates to serve as key-values, hash-tables are the default choice for implementing them.

© Vsevolod Domkin 2021
V. Domkin, *Programming Algorithms in Lisp*, https://doi.org/10.1007/978-1-4842-6428-7_8

Also, hash-sets, in general, serve as the main representation for medium- and large-sized sets as they ensure $O(1)$ membership test, as well as optimal set-theoretic operation complexity. A simple version of a hash-set can be created using a normal hash-table with t for all values.

Implementation

The basic properties of hash-tables are average $O(1)$ access and support for arbitrary keys. These features can be realized by storing the items in an array at indices determined by a specialized function that maps the keys in a pseudo-random way—hashes them. Technically, the keys should pertain to the domain that allows hashing, but, in practice, it is always possible to ensure either directly or by using an intermediate transformation. The choice of variants for the hash-function is rather big, but there are some limitations to keep in mind:

1. As the backing array has a limited number of cells (n), the function should produce values in the interval [0, n). This limitation can be respected by a two-step process: first, produce a number in an arbitrary range (for instance, a 32-bit integer) and then take the remainder of its division by n.

2. Ideally, the distribution of indices should be uniform, but similar keys should map to quite distinct indices. That is, hashing should turn things which are close into things which are distant. This way, even very small changes to the input will yield sweeping changes in the value of the hash. This property is called the "avalanche effect."

Dealing with Collisions

Even better would be if there were no collisions—situations when two or more keys are mapped to the same index. Is that, at all, possible? Theoretically, yes, but all the practical implementations that we have found so far are too slow and not feasible for a hash-table that is dynamically updated. However, such approaches may be used if the keyset is static and known beforehand. They will be covered in the discussion of perfect hash-tables.

For dynamic hash-tables, we have to accept that collisions are inevitable. The probability of collisions is governed by an interesting phenomenon called "the Birthday Paradox." Let's say we have a group of people of some size, for instance, 20. What is the probability that two of them have birthdays on the same date? It may seem quite improbable, considering that there are 365 days in a year and we are talking just about a handful of people. But if you take into account that we need to examine each pair of people to learn about their possible birthday collision, that will give us (/ (* 20 19) 2), that is, 190 pairs. We can calculate the exact probability by taking the complement to the probability that no one has a birthday collision, which is easier to reason about. The probability that two people don't share their birthday is (/ (- 365 1) 365): there's only one chance in 365 that they do. For three people, we can use the chain rule and state that the probability that they don't have a birthday collision is a product of the probability that any two of them don't have it and that the third person also doesn't share a birthday with any of them. This results in (* (/ 364 365) (/ (- 365 2) 365)). The value (- 365 2) refers to the third person not having a birthday intersection with neither the first nor the second individually, and those are distinct, as we have already asserted in the first term. Continuing in such fashion, we can count the number for 20 persons:

```
(defun birthday-collision-prob (n)
  (let ((rez 1))
    (dotimes (i n)
      (setf rez (* rez (/ (- 365 i) 365))))
    ;; don't forget that we want the complement of the probability
    ;; of no collisions, hence (- 1.0 ...)
    (- 1.0 rez)))
```

```
CL-USER> (birthday-collision-prob 20)
0.4114384
```

So, among 20 people, there's already a 40% chance of observing a coinciding birthday. And this number grows quickly: it will become 50% at 23, 70% at 30, and 99.9% at just 70!

But why on Earth, you could ask, have we started to discuss birthdays? Well, if you substitute keys for persons and the array size for the number of days in a year, you'll get the formula of the probability of at least one collision among the hashed keys in an array, provided the hash-function produces perfectly uniform output. (It will be even higher if the distribution is nonuniform).

```
(defun hash-collision-prob (n size)
  (let ((rez 1))
    (dotimes (i n)
      (setf rez (* rez (/ (- size i) size))))
    (- 1.0 rez)))
```

Let's say we have ten keys. What should be the array size to be safe against collisions?

```
CL-USER> (hash-collision-prob 10 10)
0.9996371
```

99.9%. OK, we don't stand a chance to accidentally get a perfect layout. :(What if we double the array size?

```
CL-USER> (hash-collision-prob 10 20)
0.9345271
```

93%. Still, pretty high.

```
CL-USER> (hash-collision-prob 10 100)
0.37184352
CL-USER> (hash-collision-prob 10 10000)
0.004491329
```

So, if we were to use a 10000-element array to store ten items, the chance of a collision would fall below 1%. Not practical...

Note that the number depends on both arguments, so (hash-collision-prob 10 100) (0.37) is not the same as (hash-collision-prob 20 200) (0.63).

We did this exercise to completely abandon any hope of avoiding collisions and accept that they are inevitable. Such mind/coding experiments may be an effective smoke test of our novel algorithmic ideas: before we go full speed and implement them, it makes sense to perform some back-of-the-envelope feasibility calculations.

Now, let's discuss what difference the presence of these collisions makes to our hash-table idea and how to deal with this issue. The obvious solution is to have a fallback option: when two keys hash to the same index, store both of the items in a list. The retrieval operation, in this case, will require a sequential scan to find the requested key and return the corresponding value. Such an approach is called "chaining," and it is used by some implementations. Yet, it has a number of drawbacks:

- It complicates the implementation: we now have to deal with both a static array and a dynamic list/array/tree. This change opens a possibility for some hard-to-catch bugs, especially, in the concurrent settings.

- It requires more memory than the hash-table backing array, so we will be in a situation when some of the slots of the array are empty while others chain several elements.

- It will have poor performance due to the necessity of dealing with a linked structure and, what's worse, not respecting cache locality: the chain will not fit in the original array so at least one additional RAM round-trip will be required.

One upside of this approach is that it can store more elements than the size of the backing array. And, in the extreme case, it degrades to bucketing: when a small number of buckets point to long chains of randomly shuffled elements.

The more widely used alternative to chaining is called "open addressing" or "closed hashing." With it, the chains are, basically, stored in the same backing array. The algorithm is simple: when the calculated hash is pointing at an already occupied slot in the array, find the next vacant slot by cycling over the array. If the table isn't full, we're guaranteed to find one. If it is full, we need to resize it first. Now, when the element is retrieved by key, we need to perform the same procedure: calculate the hash, and then compare the key of the item at the returned index. If the keys are the same, we've found the desired element; otherwise, we need to cycle over the array comparing keys until we encounter the item we need.

Here's an implementation of the simple open addressing hash-table using `eql` for key comparison:

```
(defstruct ht
  array
  (count 0))
```

```
(defun ht (&rest kvs)
  (let ((rez (make-ht :array (make-array 16 :initial-element (list)))))
    (loop :for (k v) :in kvs :do
      (add-ht k v rez))
    rez))

(defun ht-get (key ht)
  (rtl:with ((size (length (rtl:? ht 'array)))
             (start (rem (hash key) size)))
    (do ((count 0 (1+ count))
         (i start (rem (1+ i) size))
         (item (rtl:? ht 'array start)
               (rtl:? ht 'array i)))
        ((or (null item)
             (= count size)))
      (when (eql key (car item))
        (return
          (values (cdr item)
                  ;; the second value is an index, at which the item
                  ;; was found
                  ;; (also used to distinguish the value nil from not found,
                  ;; which is also represented by nil
                  ;; but with no second value)
                  i)))))))

(defun ht-add (key val ht)
  (rtl:with ((array (ht-array ht))
             (size (length array)))
    ;; flet defines a local function that has access
    ;; to the local variables defined in HT-ADD
    (flet ((add-item (k v)
             (do ((i (rem (hash k) size)
                     (rem (1+ i) size)))
                 ((null (rtl:? ht 'array i))
                  (setf (rtl:? ht 'array i) (cons k v)))
               ;; this do-loop doesn't have a body
               )))
```

```
(when (= (hash-table-count ht) size)
  ;; when the backing array is full
  ;; expand it to have the length equal to the next power of 2
  (setf size (expt 2 (ceiling (log (1+ count) 2)))
        (rtl:? ht 'array) (make-array size :initial-element nil))
  ;; and re-add its contents
  (rtl:dovec (item array)
    (add-item (car item) (cdr item)))
  ;; finally, add the new item
  (incf (rtl:? ht 'count))
  (add-item key val)))

(defun ht-rem (key ht)
  ;; here, we use the index of the item returned as the 2nd value of HT-GET
  (rtl:when-it (nth-value 1 (ht-get key ht))
    (setf (rtl:? ht 'array rtl:it) nil)
    ;; return the index to indicate that the item was found
    it))
```

To avoid constant resizing of the hash-table, just as with dynamic arrays, the backing array is, usually, allocated to have the size equal to a power of 2: 16 elements, to begin with. When it is filled up to a certain capacity, it is resized to the next power of 2: 32, in this case. Usually, around 70–80% is considered peak occupancy as too many collisions may happen afterward and the table access performance may severely degrade. In practice, this means that normal open addressing hash-tables also waste 20% to 50% of allocated space. This inefficiency becomes a serious problem with large tables, so other implementation strategies become preferable when the size of data reaches tens and hundreds of megabytes. Note that, in our preceding trivial implementation, we have, effectively, used the threshold of 100% to simplify the code. Adding a configurable threshold is just a matter of introducing a parameter and initiating resizing not when (= (hash-table-count ht) size) but upon (= (hash-table-count ht) (floor size threshold)). As we've seen, resizing the hash-table requires calculating the new indices for all stored elements and adding them anew into the resized array.

Analyzing the complexity of the access function of the hash-table and proving that it is amortized O(1) isn't trivial. It depends on the properties of the hash-function, which should ensure good uniformity. Besides, the resizing threshold also matters: the more elements are in the table, the higher the chance of collisions. Also, you should keep in mind that if the keys possess some strange qualities that prevent them from being hashed uniformly, the theoretical results will not hold.

In short, if we consider a hash-table with 60% occupancy (which should be the average number, for a common table), we end up with the following probabilities:

- Probability that we'll need just one operation to access the item (i.e., the initially indexed slot is empty): 0.4

- Probability that we'll need two operations (the current slot is occupied; the next one is empty): (* 0.6 0.4)—0.24

- Probability that we'll need three operations: (* (expt 0.6 2) 0.4)—0.14

- Probability that we'll need four operations: (* (expt 0.6 3) 0.4)—0.09

Actually, these calculations are slightly off, and the correct probability of finding an empty slot should be somewhat lower, although the larger the table is, the smaller the deviation in the numbers. Finding out why is left as an exercise for the reader. :)

As you see, there's a progression here. With probability around 0.87, we'll need no more than four operations. Without continuing with the arithmetic, I think it should be obvious that we'll need, on average, around three operations to access each item and the probability that we'll need twice as many (6) is quite low (below 5%). So we can say that the number of access operations is constant (i.e., independent of the number of elements in the table) and is determined only by the occupancy percentage. So, if we keep the occupancy in the reasonable bounds, named earlier, on average, one hash-code calculation/lookup and a couple of retrievals and equality comparisons will be needed to access an item in our hash-table.

Hash-Code

So we can conclude that a hash-table is primarily parametrized by two things: the hash-function and the equality predicate. In Lisp, in particular, there's a choice of just the four standard equality predicates: eq, eql, equal, and equalp. It's somewhat of a legacy that you can't use other comparison functions, so some implementations, as an extension, allow the programmer to specify other predicates. However, in practice, the following approach is sufficient for the majority of the hash-table use cases:

- Use the `eql` predicate if the keys are numbers, characters, or symbols.

- Use `equal` if the keys are strings or lists of the mentioned items.

- Use `equalp` if the keys are vectors, structs, or anything else containing one of those (however, there is no standard function to compare CLOS objects by value).

But I'd recommend trying your best to avoid using the complex keys requiring `equalp`. Besides the performance penalty of using the heaviest equality predicate that performs deep structural comparison, structs, and vectors, in particular, will most likely hash to the same index. Here is a quote from one of the implementers describing why this happens:

> *Structs have no extra space to store a unique hash code within them. The decision was made to implement this because automatic inclusion of a hashing slot in all structure objects would have made all structs an average of one word longer. For small structs this is unacceptable. Instead, the user may define a struct with an extra slot, and the constructor for that struct type could store a unique value into that slot (either a random value or a value gotten by incrementing a counter each time the constructor is run). Also, create a hash generating function which accesses this hash-slot to generate its value. If the structs to be hashed are buried inside a list, then this hash function would need to know how to traverse these keys to obtain a unique value. Finally, then, build your hash-table using the :hash-function argument to make-hash-table (still using the equal test argument), to create a hash-table which will be well-distributed. Alternatively, and if you can guarantee that none of the slots in your structures will be changed after they are used as keys in the hash-table, you can use the equalp test function in your make-hash-table call, rather than equal. If you do, however, make sure that these struct objects don't change, because then they may not be found in the hash-table.*

But what if you still need to use a struct or a CLOS object as a hash key (for instance, if you want to put them in a set)? There are three possible workarounds:

- Choose one of their slots as a key (if you can guarantee its uniqueness).

- Add a special slot to hold a unique value that will serve as a key.

- Use the literal representation obtained by calling the print-function of the object (provided there is a custom print-function defined for you object). Still, you'll need to ensure that it will be unique and constant. Using an item that changes while being the hash key is a source of very nasty bugs, so avoid it at all cost.

These considerations are also applicable to the question of why Java requires defining both `equals` and `hashCode` methods for objects that are used as keys in the hash-table or hash-set.

Advanced Hashing Techniques

Beyond the direct implementation of open addressing, called "linear probing" (for it tries to resolve collisions by performing a linear scan for an empty slot), a number of approaches were proposed to improve hash distribution and reduce the collision rate. However, for the general case, their superiority remains questionable, and so the utility of a particular approach has to be tested in the context of the situations when linear probing demonstrates suboptimal behavior. One type of such situations occurs when the hash-codes become clustered near some locations due to deficiencies of either the hash-function or the keyset.

The simplest modification of linear probing is called "quadratic probing." It operates by performing the search for the next vacant slot using the linear probing offsets (or some other sequence of offsets) that are just raised to the power 2. That is, if, with linear probing, the offset sequence was 1,2,3, and so on, with the quadratic one, it is 1,4,9,... "Double hashing" is another simple alternative, which, instead of a linear sequence of offsets, calculates the offsets using another hash-function. This approach makes the sequence specific to each key, so the keys that map to the same location will have different possible variants of collision resolution. "2-choice hashing" also uses two hash-functions but selects the particular one for each key based on the distance from the original index it has to be moved for collision resolution.

More elaborate changes to the original idea are proposed in cuckoo, hopscotch, and Robin Hood caching, to name some of the popular alternatives. We won't discuss them now, but if the need arises to implement a nonstandard hash-table, it's worth studying all of those before proceeding with an idea of your own. However, who knows, someday you might come up with a viable alternative technique, as well...

Hash-Functions

The class of possible hash-functions is very diverse: any function that sufficiently randomizes the key hashes will do. But what does "good enough" mean? One of the ways to find out is to look at the pictures of the distribution of hashes. Yet, there are other factors that may condition the choice: speed, complexity of implementation, and collision resistance (important for cryptographic hashes that we won't discuss in this book).

The good news is that, for most practical purposes, there's a single function that is both fast and easy to implement and understand. It is called **FNV-1a**:

```
(defparameter *fnv-primes*
  '((32 . 16777619)
    (64 . 1099511628211)
    (128 . 309485009821345068724781371)
    (256 . 374144419156711147060143317175368453031918731002211)))

(defparameter *fnv-offsets*
  '((32 . 2166136261)
    (64 . 14695981039346656037)
    (128 . 144066263297769815596495629667062367629)
    (256 . 100029257958052580907070968620625704837092796014241193945225284501741471925557)))

(defun fnv-1a (x &key (bits 32))
  (assert (member bits '(32 64 128 256)))
  (let ((rez (rtl:assoc1 bits *fnv-offsets*))
        (prime (rtl:assoc1 bits *fnv-primes*)))
    (dotimes (i (/ bits 8))
      (setf rez (ldb (byte bits 0)
                     (* (logxor rez (ldb (byte 8 (* i 8)) x))
                        prime))))
    rez))
```

The constants *fnv-primes* and *fnv-offsets* are pre-calculated up to 1024 bits (here, I used just a portion of the tables).

Note that, in this implementation, we use normal Lisp multiplication (*) that is not limited to fixed-size numbers (32-bit, 64-bit, etc.), so we need to extract only the first bits with ldb.

Also note that if you were to calculate FNV-1a with some online hash calculator, you'd, probably, get a different result. Experimenting with it, I noticed that it is the same if we use only the nonzero bytes from the input number. This observation aligns well with calculating the hash for simple strings when each character is a single byte. For them, the hash-function would look like the following:

```
(defun fnv-1a-str (str)
  (let ((rez (assoc1 32 *fnv-offsets*))
        (prime (assoc1 32 *fnv-primes*)))
    (rtl:dovec (char str)
      (setf rez (ldb (byte 32 0)
                     (* (logxor rez (char-code char))
                        prime))))
    rez))
```

So even such a simple hash-function has nuances in its implementation, and it should be meticulously checked against some reference implementation or a set of expected results.

Alongside FNV-1a, there's also FNV-1, which is a slightly worse variation, but it may be used if we need to apply two different hash-functions at once (like in two-way or double hashing).

What is the source of the hashing property of FNV-1a? XORs and modulos. Combining these simple and efficient operations is enough to create a desired level of randomization. Most of the other hash-functions use the same building blocks as FNV-1a. They all perform arithmetic (usually, addition and multiplication as division is slow) and XORing, adding into the mix some prime numbers. For instance, here's what the code for another popular hash-function "djb2" approximately looks like:

```
(defun djb2-str (str)
  (let ((rez 5381))  ; a DJB2 prime number
    (rtl:dovec (char str)
      (setf rez (ldb 32 (+ (char-code char)
                           (ldb (byte 32 0)
                                (+ (ash rez 5)
                                   rez))))))
    rez))
```

Operations

The generic key-value operations we have discussed in the previous chapter obviously also apply to hash-tables. There are also specific low-level ones, defined by the Lisp standard. And it's worth mentioning that, in regard to hash-tables, I find the standard quite lacking so a lot of utilities were added as part of RUTILS. The reason for the deficiency in the standard is, I believe, that when hash-tables had been added to Lisp, they were still pretty novel technology not widely adopted in the programming language community. So there had been neither any significant experience using them nor a good understanding of the important role they would play. Languages such as Python or Clojure as well as the ones that were designed even later were developed with this knowledge already in mind. Yet, this situation doesn't pose insurmountable difficulty for Lisp users as the language provides advanced extension tools such as macros and reader macros, so the necessary parts can be added and, in fact, exist as third-party extensions. Using them becomes just a question of changing your habits and adapting to more efficient approaches. The situation is different for the users of many other languages, such as Java users, who had to wait for the new major version of the language to get access to such things as literal hash-table initialization—the feature I consider to be crucially important to improving the level of code clarity, in the declarative paradigm.

Initialization

Normally, the hash-table can be created with `make-hash-table`, which has a number of configuration options, including `:test` (default: `eql`). Most of the implementations allow the programmer to make synchronized (thread-safe) hash-tables via another configuration parameter, but the variants of concurrency control will differ.

Yet, it is important to have a way to define hash-tables already pre-initialized with a number of key-value pairs, and `make-hash-table` can't handle this. Pre-initialized hash-tables represent a common necessity for tables serving as dictionaries, and such pre-initialization greatly simplifies many code patterns. Thus, RUTILS provides such a syntax (in fact, in two flavors) with the help of reader macros:

```
#{equal "foo" :bar "baz" 42}
#h(equal "foo" :bar "baz" 42)
```

Both of these expressions will expand into a call to make-hash-table with equal test and two calls to set operation to populate the table with the kv pairs "foo" :bar and "baz" 42 . For this stuff to work, you need to switch to the appropriate readtable by executing (named-readtables:in-readtable rutils-readtable).

The reader macro to parse #h()-style literal readtables isn't very complicated. As all reader macros, it operates on the character stream of the program text, processing one character at a time. Here is its implementation:

```
(defun |#h-reader| (stream char arg)
  (read-char stream)  ; skip the open paren
  ;; we can also add a sanity check to ensure that this character
  ;; is indeed a #\(
  (rtl:with (;; read-delimited-list is a standard library function
             ;; that reads items until a delimiter is encountered
             ;; and then returns them as a list of parsed Lisp objects
             (sexp (read-delimited-list #\) stream t))
             ;; the idea is that the first element may be a hash-table
             ;; test function; in this case, the number of items in the
             ;; definition will be odd as each key-value pair should have
             ;; an even number of elements
             (test (when (oddp (length sexp))
                     (first sexp)))
             ;; the rest of the values, after the possible test function,
             ;; are key-value pairs
             (kvs (rtl:group 2 (if test (rest sexp) sexp)))
             (ht (gensym)))
    `(let ((,ht (make-hash-table :test ',(or test 'eql))))
       ;; iterate the tail of the KVS list (:on loop clause)
       ;; and, for each key-value pair, generate an expression
       ;; to add the value for the key in the resulting hash-table
       ,@(mapcar (lambda (kv)
                   `(setf (rtl:? ,ht ,(first kv)) ,(second kv)))
                 ,kvs)
       ,ht)))
```

After such a function is defined, it can be plugged into the standard readtable:

```
(set-dispatch-macro-character #\# #\h '|#h-reader|)
```

Or it may be used in a named readtable (you can learn how to do that, from the docs).

`print-hash-table` is the utility to perform the reverse operation—display hash-tables in the similar manner:

```
CL-USER> (print-hash-table #h(equal "foo" :bar "baz" 42))
#{EQUAL
  "foo" :BAR
  "baz" 42
 }
#<HASH-TABLE :TEST EQUAL :COUNT 2 {10127C0003}>
```

The last line of the output is the default Lisp printed representation of the hash-table. As you see, it is opaque and doesn't display the elements of the table. RUTILS also allows switching to printing the literal representation instead of the standard one with the help of `toggle-print-hash-table`. However, this extension is intended only for debugging purposes as it is not fully standard-conforming.

Access

Accessing the hash-table elements is performed with `gethash`, which returns two things: the value at key and `t` when the key was found in the table, or two nils otherwise. By using `(setf (gethash key ht) val)` (or `(setf (rtl:? ht key) val)`), we can modify the stored value. Notice the reverse order of arguments of `gethash` compared to the usual order in most accessor functions, when the structure is placed first and the key second. However, `gethash` differs from generic `?` in that it accepts an optional argument that is used as the default value if the requested key is not present in the table. An alternative approach can be found in such languages as Python, where there's a notion of "default hash-tables" that may be initialized with a common default element. Lisp doesn't provide such capability out of the box; however, it's possible to easily implement default hash-tables and plug them into the `generic-elt` mechanism:

```
(defstruct default-hash-table
  table
  default-value)
```

```
(defun gethash-default (key ht)
  (gethash key (rtl:? ht 'table) (rtl:? ht 'default-value)))

(defmethod generic-elt ((kv default-hash-table) key &rest keys)
  (gethash-default key kv))
```

RUTILS also defines a number of aliases/shorthands for hash-table operations. As the # symbol is etymologically associated with hashes, it is used in the names of all these functions:

- get# is a shorthand and a more distinctive alias for gethash.

- set# is an alias for (setf (gethash ....

- getset# is an implementation of the common pattern: this operation either retrieves the value if the key is found in the table or calculates its third argument, returns it, and also sets it for the given key for future retrieval.

- rem# is an alias for remhash (remove the element from the table).

- take# both returns the key and removes it (unlike rem# that only removes).

- in# tests for the presence of the key in the table.

- also, p# is an abbreviated version of print-hash-table.

Iteration

Hash-tables are unordered collections, in principle. But, still, there is always a way to iterate over them in some (unspecified) order. The standard utility for that is either maphash, which unlike map doesn't populate the resulting collection and is called just for the side effects, or the special loop syntax. Both are suboptimal, from several points of view, so RUTILS defines a couple of alternative options:

- dotable functions in the same manner as dolist except that it uses two variables: for the key and the value.

- mapkv, mentioned in the previous chapter, works just like mapcar by creating a new result table with the same configuration as the hash-table it iterates over and assigns the results of invoking the first argument—the function of two elements—with each of the kv pairs.

Despite the absence of a predefined ordering, there are ways in which some order may be introduced. For example, in SBCL, the order in which the elements are added is preserved by using additional vectors called index-vector and next-vector that store this information. Another option which allows forcing arbitrary ordering is to use the so-called **linked hash-table**. It is a combination of a hash-table and a linked list: each key-value pair also has the next pointer, which links it to some other item in the table. This way, it is possible to have ordered key-values without resorting to tree-based structures. A poor man's linked hash-table can be created on top of the normal one with the following trick: substitute values by pairs containing a value plus a pointer to the next pair and keep track of the pointer to the first pair in a special slot:

```
(defstruct linked-hash-table-item
  key
  val
  next)

(defstruct linked-hash-table
  (table (make-hash-table))
  head
  tail)

(defun gethash-linked (key ht)
  ;; we use GETHASH instead of a shorter (rtl:? ht 'table key 'val)
  ;; to preserve the second return value
  (gethash key (rtl:? ht 'table)))

(defun sethash-linked (key ht val)
  ;; The initial order of items is the order of addition.
  ;; If we'd like to impose a different order, we'll have to perform
     reordering
  ;; after each addition or implement a custom sethash function.
  (with-slots (table head tail) ht
    (rtl:if-it (gethash key table)
               (setf (rtl:? rtl:it 'val) val)
               (let ((new (make-linked-hash-table-item
                           :key key :val val)))
                 (rtl:sethash key table new)
```

```
            (when (null head)
              (setf (rtl:? ht 'head) new))
            (setf (rtl:? ht 'tail)
                  (if tail
                      (setf (rtl:? ht 'tail 'next) new)
                      new))))))

(defmethod mapkv (fn (ht linked-hash-table))
  (let ((rez (make-linked-hash-table
              :table (make-hash-table
                      :test (hash-table-test (rtl:? ht 'table))))))
    (do ((item (rtl:? ht 'head) (rtl:? item 'next)))
        ((null item))
      (let ((k (rtl:? item 'key)))
        (sethash-linked k rez (funcall fn k (rtl:? item 'val)))))
    rez))
```

The issue with this approach, as you can see from the code, is that we also need to store the key, and it duplicates the data also stored in the backing hash-table itself. So an efficient linked hash-table has to be implemented from scratch using an array as a base instead of a hash-table.

Perfect Hashing

In the previous exposition, we have concluded that using hash-tables implies a significant level of reserved unused space (up to 30%) and inevitable collisions. Yet, if the keyset is static and known beforehand, we can do better: find a hash-function, which will exclude collisions (simple perfect hashing) and even totally get rid of reserved space (minimal perfect hashing, MPH). Although the last variant will still need extra space to store the additional information about the hash-functions, it may be much smaller: in some methods, down to ~3–4 bits per key, so just 5–10% overhead. Statistically speaking, constructing such a hash-function is possible. But the search for its parameters may require some trial and error.

Implementation

The general idea is simple, but how to find the appropriate hash-function? There are several approaches described in sometimes hard-to-follow scientific papers and a number of cryptic programs in low-level C libraries. At a certain point in time, I needed to implement some variant of an MPH, so I read those papers and studied the libraries to some extent. Not the most pleasant process, I should confess. One of my Twitter pals once wrote: "Looks like it's easier for people to read 40 blog posts than a single whitepaper." And, although he was putting a negative connotation to it, I recognized the statement as a very precise description of what a research engineer does: read a whitepaper (or a dozen, for what it's worth) and transform it into working code and—as a possible byproduct—into an explanation ("blog post") that other engineers will understand and be able to reproduce. And it's not a skill every software developer should be easily capable of. Not all papers can even be reproduced because the experiment was not set up correctly, some parts of the description are missing, the data is not available, and so on. Of those, which, in principle, can be, only some are presented in the form that is clear enough to be reliably programmed.

Here is one of the variants of minimal perfect hashing that possesses such qualities. It works for datasets of any size as a three-step process:

1. At the first stage, by the use of a common hash-function (in particular, the Jenkins hash), all keys are near-uniformly distributed into buckets, so that the number of keys in each bucket doesn't exceed 256. It can be achieved with very high probability if the hash divisor is set to (ceiling (length keyset) 200). This allows the algorithm to work for datasets of arbitrary size, thereby reducing the problem to a simpler one that already has a known solution.

2. Next, for each bucket, the perfect hash-function is constructed. This function is a table (and it's an important mathematical fact that each discrete function is equivalent to a table, albeit, potentially, of unlimited length). The table contains byte-sized offsets for each hash-code, calculated by another application of the Jenkins hash, which produces two values in one go (actually, three, but one of them is not used). The divisor of the hash-function, this time,

equals to double the number of elements in the bucket. And the uniqueness requirement is that the sum of offsets corresponding, in the table, to the two values produced by the Jenkins hash is unique, for each key. To check if the constraint is satisfied, the hashes are treated as vertices of a graph, and if it happens to be acyclic (the probability of this event is quite high if the parameters are chosen properly), the requirement can be satisfied, and it is possible to construct the perfect hash-function, by the process described as the next step. Otherwise, we change the seed of the Jenkins hash and try again until the resulting graph is acyclic. In practice, just a couple of tries are needed.

3. Finally, the hash-function for the current bucket may be constructed from the graph by the CHM92 algorithm (named after the authors and the year of the paper), which is another version of perfect hashing but suitable only for limited keysets. Here, you can see the CHM92 formula implemented in code:

```
(deftype octet () '(unsigned-byte 8))
(deftype quad () '(unsigned-byte 32))

(defstruct mpht
  (data #() :type simple-vector)
  (offsets (make-array 0 :element-type 'octet) :type (simple-array octet))
  (meta (make-array 0 :element-type 'quad) :type (simple-array quad))
  (div nil))

;; div is the divisor of the top-level hash, which is calculated as:
;; (/ (1- (length meta)) 2)

(defun mpht-index (item mpht)
  (with-slots (offsets meta div) mpht
    (rtl:with ((bucket-id (* (mod (jenkins-hash item) div) 2))
               (bucket-offset (aref meta bucket-id))
               (bucket-seed (aref meta (+ 1 bucket-id)))
               ;; the number of items in the bucket is calculated
               ;; by subtracting the offset of the next bucket
               ;; from the offset of the current one
```

```
        (bucket-count (- (aref meta (+ 2 bucket-id))
                         bucket-offset))
        (hash1 hash2 (jenkins-hash2
                      item bucket-div))
        (base (* bucket-offset 2)))
  (+ bucket-offset (mod (+ (aref offsets (+ base hash1))
                           (aref offsets (+ base hash2)))
                        bucket-count)))))
```

The jenkins-hash function is not provided here for the sake of space conservation: apart from FNV-1, most hash-functions require a page or two of code to implement, and Jenkins hash is no exception. The actual implementation can be found in the const-table repository.

This algorithm guarantees exactly $O(1)$ hash-table access and uses 2 bytes per key, that is, it will result in a constant 25% overhead on the table's size (in a 64-bit system): two byte-sized offsets for the hashes plus negligible 8 bytes per bucket (each bucket contains ~200 elements) for meta-information. Better space utilization solutions (up to four times more efficient) exist, but they are harder to implement and explain.

The Jenkins hash-function was chosen for two reasons:

- Primarily, because, being a relatively good-quality hash, it has a configurable parameter seed that is used for probabilistic probing (searching for an acyclic graph). On the contrary, FNV-1a doesn't work well with an arbitrary prime, hence the usage of a pre-calculated one that isn't subject to change.

- Also, it produces three pseudo-random numbers right away, and we need two for the second stage of the algorithm.

The CHM92 Algorithm

The CHM92 algorithm operates by performing a depth-first search (DFS) on the graph, in the process labeling the edges with unique numbers and calculating the corresponding offset for each of the Jenkins hash values. In the picture, you can see one of the possible labelings: each vertex is the value of one of the two hash-codes returned by jenkins-hash2 for each key, and every edge, connecting them, corresponds to a key that produced the hashes. The unique indices of the edges were obtained during

DFS. Now, each hash-code is mapped iteratively to the number that is (- edge-index other-vertex-index). So some codes will map to the same number, but it is guaranteed that, for each key, the sum of two corresponding numbers will be unique (as the edge indices are unique).

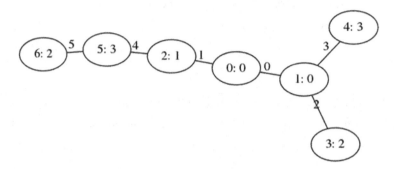

Let's say we have implemented the described scheme like I did in the const-table library. Now, we need to perform the measurements to validate that we have, in fact, achieved the desired improvement over the standard hash-table implementation. In this case, we are interested not only in speed measurements, which we already know how to perform, but also in calculating the space occupied.

The latter goal is harder to achieve. Usually, most of the programming languages will provide the analog of a sizeof function that returns the space occupied by an array, a structure, or an object. Here, we're interested not in "shallow" sizeof but in a "deep" one that will descend into the structure's slots and add their sizes recursively.

First, let's create functions to populate the tables with a significant number of random string key-value pairs:

```
(defun random-string (size)
  (coerce (loop :repeat size :collect (code-char (+ 32 (random 100))))
          'string))

(defun random-hash-table (&key (n 100000))
  (let ((rez (make-hash-table :test 'equal)))
    (loop :repeat n :do
      (setf (gethash (random-string (+ 3 (random 4))) rez)
            (random-string (+ 3 (random 4)))))
    rez))

(defun random-const-table (&key (n 100000))
  (let ((rez (make-const-table :test 'equal)))
```

```
(loop :repeat n :do
  (setf (gethash (random-string (+ 3 (random 4))) rez)
        (random-string (+ 3 (random 4)))))
rez))
```

A very approximate space measurement may be performed using the standard operator room. But it doesn't provide detailed per-object statistics. Here's a result of the room measurement, in SBCL (the format of the report will be somewhat different, for each implementation):

```
CL-USER> (room)
Dynamic space usage is:    45,076,224 bytes.
Immobile space usage is:   18,998,832 bytes (64,672 bytes overhead).
Read-only space usage is:           0 bytes.
Static space usage is:          1,264 bytes.
Control stack usage is:         9,048 bytes.
Binding stack usage is:           640 bytes.
Control and binding stack usage is for the current thread only.
Garbage collection is currently enabled.

Breakdown for dynamic space:
  11,369,232 bytes for   76,040 simple-vector objects
   9,095,952 bytes for  160,669 instance objects
   8,289,568 bytes for  518,098 cons objects
   3,105,920 bytes for   54,655 simple-array-unsigned-byte-8 objects
   2,789,168 bytes for   54,537 simple-base-string objects
   2,344,672 bytes for    9,217 simple-character-string objects
   6,973,472 bytes for  115,152 other objects

  43,967,984 bytes for  988,368 dynamic objects (space total)


Breakdown for immobile space:
  16,197,840 bytes for 24,269 code objects
   1,286,496 bytes for 26,789 symbol objects
   1,041,936 bytes for 27,922 other objects

  18,526,272 bytes for 78,980 immobile objects (space total)
```

```
CL-USER> (defparameter *ht* (random-hash-table))
*HT*
CL-USER> (room)
...
Breakdown for dynamic space:
  13,349,920 bytes for    77,984 simple-vector objects
  11,127,008 bytes for   208,576 simple-character-string objects
   9,147,824 bytes for   161,469 instance objects
   8,419,360 bytes for   526,210 cons objects
   3,517,792 bytes for     2,997 simple-array-unsigned-byte-32 objects
   3,106,288 bytes for    54,661 simple-array-unsigned-byte-8 objects
   7,671,168 bytes for   166,882 other objects

  56,339,360 bytes for 1,198,779 dynamic objects (space total)
```

So it seems like we added roughly 10 megabytes by creating a hash-table with 100,000 random five- to nine-character keys and values. Almost all of that space went into the keys and values themselves—9 MB ("11,127,008 bytes for 208,576 simple-character-string objects" vs. "2,344,672 bytes for 9,217 simple-character-string objects"—a bit less than when 200,000 new strings were added).

Also, if we examine the hash-table, we can see that its occupancy is rather high—around 90%! (The number of keys, 99706 instead of 100000, tells us that there was a small portion of duplicate keys among the randomly generated ones.)

```
CL-USER> (describe *ht*)
#<HASH-TABLE :TEST EQUAL :COUNT 99706 {1002162EF3}>  [hash-table]

Occupancy: 0.9
Rehash-threshold: 1.0
Rehash-size: 1.5
Size: 111411
```

And now, a simple time measurement:

```
CL-USER> (let ((keys (keys *ht*)))
           (time (loop :repeat 100 :do
                   (dolist (k keys)
                     (gethash k *ht*)))))
```

```
Evaluation took:
  0.029 seconds of real time
  0.032000 seconds of total run time (0.032000 user, 0.000000 system)
  110.34% CPU
  72,079,880 processor cycles
  0 bytes consed
```

Now, let's try the const-tables that are the MPHT implementation:

```
CL-USER> (time (defparameter *ct* (cstab:build-const-table *ht*)))
...............................................................................
Evaluation took:
  0.864 seconds of real time
...
CL-USER> (room)
...
Breakdown for dynamic space:
  14,179,584 bytes for     78,624 simple-vector objects
  11,128,464 bytes for    208,582 simple-character-string objects
   9,169,120 bytes for    161,815 instance objects
   8,481,536 bytes for    530,096 cons objects
   3,521,808 bytes for      2,998 simple-array-unsigned-byte-32 objects
   3,305,984 bytes for     54,668 simple-array-unsigned-byte-8 objects
   7,678,064 bytes for    166,992 other objects

  57,464,560 bytes for 1,203,775 dynamic objects (space total)
```

Another megabyte was added for the metadata of the new table, which doesn't seem significantly different from the hash-table version. Surely, often we'd like to be much more precise in space measurements. For this, SBCL recently added an allocation profiler sb-aprof, but we won't go into the details of its usage in this chapter.

And now, time measurement:

```
CL-USER> (let ((keys (rtl:keys *ht*)))
           (time (loop :repeat 100 :do
                   (dolist (k keys)
                     (cstab:csget k *ct*)))))
Evaluation took:
  3.561 seconds of real time
```

Oops, a two-orders-of-magnitude slowdown! It has to do with many factors: the lack of optimization in my implementation compared to the one in SBCL, the need to calculate more hashes and with a slower hash-function, and others. I'm sure that the implementation may be sped up at least an order of magnitude, but, even then, what's the benefit of using it over the default hash-tables? Especially considering that MPHTs have a lot of moving parts and rely on a number of "low-level" algorithms like graph traversal or efficient membership testing, most of which need a custom efficient implementation...

Still, there's one dimension in which MPHTs may provide an advantage: significantly reduce space usage by not storing the keys. However, it becomes problematic if we need to distinguish the keys that are in the table from the unknown ones as those will also hash to some index, that is, overlap with an existing key. So, either the keyspace should be known beforehand and exhaustively covered in the table or some precursory membership test is necessary when we anticipate the possibility of unseen keys. Yet, there are ways to perform the test efficiently (exactly or probabilistically), which require much less storage space than would be needed to store the keys themselves. Some of them we'll see in the following chapters.

If the keys are omitted, the whole table may be reduced to a **jump-table**. Jump-tables are a low-level trick possible when all the keys are integers in the interval [0, n). It removes the necessity to perform sequential equality comparisons for every possible branch until one of the conditions matches: instead, the numbers are used directly as an offset. That is, the table is represented by a vector, each hash-code being the index in that vector.

A jump-table for the MPHT will be simply a data array, but sometimes evaluation of different code is required for different keys. Such more complex behavior may be implemented in Lisp using the lowest-level operators tagbody and go (and a bit of macrology if we need to generate a huge table). This implementation will be a complete analog of the C switch statement. The skeleton for such "executable" table will look like this, where 0, 1, ... are goto labels:

```
(block nil
  (tagbody (go key)
    0 (return (do-something0))
    1 (return (do-something1))
    ...))
```

Distributed Hash-Tables

Another active area of hash-table-related research is algorithms for distributing them over the network. This is a natural way to represent a lot of datasets, and thus there are numerous storage systems (both general- and special-purpose) which are built as distributed hash-tables. Among them are, for instance, Amazon DynamoDB and an influential open source project Kademlia. We will discuss in more detail, in Chapter 15, some of the technologies developed for this use case, and here I wanted to mention just one concept.

Consistent hashing addresses the problem of distributing the hash-codes among k storage nodes under the real-world limitations that some of them may become temporarily unavailable or new peers may be added into the system. The changes result in changes of the value of k. The straightforward approach would just divide the space of all codes into k equal portions and select the node into whose portion the particular key maps. Yet, if k is changed, all the keys need to be rehashed, which we'd like to avoid at all cost as rehashing the whole database and moving the majority of the keys between the nodes, at once, will saturate the network and bring the system to a complete halt.

The idea or rather the tweak behind consistent hashing is simple: we also hash the node ids and store the keys on the node that has the next hash-code larger than the hash of the key (modulo n, i.e., wrap around 0). Now, when a new node is added, it is placed on this so-called "hash ring" between two other peers, so only part of the keys from a single node (the next on the ring) require being redistributed to it. Likewise, when the node is removed, only its keys need to be reassigned to the next peer on the ring (it is supposed that the data is stored in multiple copies on different nodes, so when one of the nodes disappears, the data doesn't become totally lost).

The only problem with applying this approach directly is the uneven distribution of keys originating from uneven placement of the hash-codes of the nodes on the hash ring. This problem can be solved with another simple tweak: have multiple ids for each node that will be hashed to different locations, effectively emulating a larger number of virtual nodes, each storing a smaller portion of the keys. Due to the randomization property of hashes, not so many virtual nodes will be needed, to obtain a nearly uniform distribution of keys over the nodes.

A more general version of this approach is called **rendezvous hashing**. In it, the key for the item is combined with the node id for each node and then hashed. The largest value of the hash determines the designated node to store the item.

Hashing in Action: Content Addressing

Hash-tables are so ubiquitous that it's, actually, difficult to single out some peculiar use case. Instead, let's talk about hash-functions. They can find numerous uses beyond determining the positions of the items in the hash-table, and one of them is called "content addressing": globally identify a piece of data by its fingerprint instead of using external meta-information like name or path. This is one of the suggested building blocks for large-scale distributed storage systems, but it works locally, as well: your git SCM system silently uses it behind the scenes to identify the changesets it operates upon.

The advantages of content addressing are the following:

- Its potential for space economy: if the system has a chance of operating on repeated items (like git does, although it's not the only reason for choosing such naming scheme for blobs: the other being the lack of a better variant), content addressing will make it possible to avoid storing them multiple times.

- It guarantees that the links will always return the same content, regardless of where it is retrieved from, who added it to the network, how, and when. This enables such distributed protocols as BitTorrent that split the original file into multiple pieces, each one identified by its hash. These pieces can be distributed in an untrusted network.

- As mentioned in the preceding text, content addressing also results in a conflict-free naming scheme (provided that the hash has enough bits—usually, cryptographic hashes such as SHA1 are used for this purpose, although, in many cases, such powerful hash-functions are an overkill).

The trivial implementation of content addressing (using the sha1 library for hash calculations—a de facto standard hash for such purposes) could look something like this:

```
(defun content-address (object)
  (sha1:sha1-hex (with-output-to-string (out)
                   (format out "~A:" (class-of object))
                   (print-object object out))))

(defun ca-get-object (address repo)
  (gethash address repo))
```

```
(defun ca-add-object (object repo)
  (let ((addr (content-address object)))
    (values (rtl:set# addr repo object)
            addr)))

(defun ca-rem-object (object repo)
  (remhash (content-address object) repo))
```

Once again, we'll be relying on the CLOS `print-object` generic function that may need extension for some particular object types we'd like to store in our repository:

```
CL-USER> (defparameter *repo* (make-hash-table :test 'equal))

CL-USER> (ca-add-object "test" *repo*)
"test"
"514BE1254CC9825EE125651650B5F9F6CF5C55D9"

CL-USER> (rtl:print-hash-table *repo*)
#{EQUAL
  "514BE1254CC9825EE125651650B5F9F6CF5C55D9" "test"
 }
```

However, there are some additional considerations that usually come into play when such a system is implemented on a large scale. The primary one of them is that maintaining a flat mapping for zillions of keys becomes prohibitively resource demanding. That's why the keyspace is usually split into two or more parts that define a hierarchy of tables. For instance, in git which has to deal with the limitations of the deteriorating performance of filesystems when the number of files in a single directory exceeds a certain limit, the original 40-character object name (obtained from an SHA1 hash) is split into a two-character directory name and a 38-character filename. We could implement the same scheme for our content addressing code in the following manner:

```
(defun content-address2 (object)
  ;; here, we use SHA1-DIGEST to get the numeric
  ;; value (as a sequence of bytes) of the hash
  ;; instead of its string representation
  ;; that was previously obtained from SHA1-HEX
  (let ((hash (sha1:sha1-digest
```

```
                (with-output-to-string (out)
                  (format out "~A:" (class-of object))
                  (print-object object out)))))
   (rtl:pair (elt hash 0)
                ;; the cryptic format ~{~2,'0X~} is used
                ;; to print numbers in hex (X) with a fixed length
                ;; of 2 chars padded by zeroes from the left
                (format nil "~{~2,'0X~}" (subseq hash 1)))))

(defun ca-get-object2 (address2 repo)
  (apply 'rtl:? repo address2))

(defun ca-add-object2 (object repo)
  (rtl:with (((top addr) (content-address2 object))
             (subrepo (rtl:getset# top repo
                                    (make-hash-table :test 'equal))))
    (values (rtl:set# addr subrepo object)
            (rtl:pair top addr))))

(defun ca-rem-object2 (object repo)
  (rtl:with (((top addr) (content-address2 object)))
    (rtl:when-it (gethash top repo)
      (remhash addr rtl:it))))

CL-USER> (defparameter *repo2* (make-hash-table))
(ca-add-object2 "foo" *repo2*)
(ca-add-object2 "bar" *repo2*)
"bar"
(195 "F50F210FA56B285C6DA1B09C72782791BBB15A")
CL-USER> (rtl:print-hash-table *repo2*)
#{
  138 #{EQUAL
        "8AB31BA5528396616249FCA3879C734FF3440D" "foo"
        }
  195 #{EQUAL
        "F50F210FA56B285C6DA1B09C72782791BBB15A" "bar"
        }
}
```

Such a hierarchy facilitates sharding (distributed storage). However, making this system distributed over the network raises many more concerns, and we'll return to discussing them in Chapter 15 of the book.

Takeaways

This chapter presented a number of complex approaches that require a lot of attention to detail to be implemented efficiently. On the surface, the hash-table concept may seem rather simple, but, as we have seen, the production-grade implementations are not that straightforward. What general conclusions can we make?

1. In such mathematically loaded areas as hash-function and hash-table implementation, rigorous testing is critically important, for there are a number of unexpected sources of errors: incorrect implementation, integer overflow, concurrency issues, and so on. A good testing strategy is to use an already existing trusted implementation and perform a large-scale comparison testing with a lot of random inputs.

2. Besides, a correct implementation doesn't necessarily mean a fast one. Low-level optimization techniques play a crucial role here.

3. In the implementation of MPHT, we have seen in action another important approach to solving algorithmic and, more generally, mathematical problems: reducing them to a problem that has a known solution. Namely, we have turned a problem of efficiently finding a perfect hash-table for an unlimited number of keys into finding it for a limited number of keys.

4. Space measurement is another important area of algorithm evaluation that is somewhat harder to accomplish than runtime profiling. We'll also see more usage of both of these tools throughout the book.

CHAPTER 9

Trees

Balancing a binary tree is the infamous interview problem that has all that folklore and debate associated with it. To tell you the truth, like the other 99% of programmers, I never had to perform this task for some work-related project. And not even due to the existence of ready-made libraries, but because self-balancing binary trees are, actually, pretty rarely used. But trees, in general, are ubiquitous even if you may not recognize their presence. The source code we operate with, at some stage of its life, is represented as a tree (a popular term here is Abstract Syntax Tree or AST, but the abstract variant is not the only one the compilers process). The directory structure of the filesystem is the tree. The object-oriented class hierarchy is likewise. And so on. So, returning to interview questions, trees indeed are a good area as they allow to cover a number of basic points: linked data structures, recursion, and complexity. But there's a much better task, which I have encountered a lot in practice and also used quite successfully in the interview process: breadth-first tree traversal. We'll talk about it a bit later.

Similar to how hash-tables can be thought of as more sophisticated arrays (they are sometimes even called "associative arrays"), trees may be considered an expansion of linked lists. Although, technically, a few specific trees are implemented not as a linked data structure but are based on arrays, the majority of trees are linked. Like hash-tables, some trees also allow for efficient access to the element by key, representing an alternative key-value implementation option.

© Vsevolod Domkin 2021
V. Domkin, *Programming Algorithms in Lisp*, https://doi.org/10.1007/978-1-4842-6428-7_9

Basically, a tree is a recursive data structure that consists of nodes. Each node may have zero or more children. If the node doesn't have a parent, it is called the **root** of the tree. And the constraint on trees is that the root is always single. Graphs may be considered a generalization of trees that don't impose this constraint, and we'll discuss them in a separate chapter. In graph terms, a tree is an acyclic directed single-component graph. Directed means that there's a one-way parent-child relation. And acyclic means that a child can't have a connection to the parent either directly or through some other nodes (in the opposite case, what will be the parent and what the child?). The recursive nature of trees manifests in the fact that if we extract an arbitrary node of the tree with all of its descendants, the resulting part will remain a tree. We can call it a **subtree**. Besides parent-child or, more generally, ancestor-descendant "vertical" relationships that apply to all the nodes in the tree, we can also talk about horizontal siblings—the set of nodes that have the same parent/ancestor.

Another important tree concept is the distinction between terminal (leaf) and nonterminal (branch) nodes. Leaf nodes don't have any children. In some trees, the data is stored only in the leaves with branch nodes serving to structure the tree in a certain manner. In other trees, the data is stored in all nodes without any distinction.

Implementation Variants

As we said, the default tree implementation is a linked structure. A linked list may be considered a degenerate tree with all nodes having a single child. A tree node may have more than one child, and so, in a linked representation, each tree root or subroot is the origin of a number of linked lists (sometimes, they are called "paths"):

```
Tree:  a
      / \
     b   c
    / \   \
   d   e   f

Lists:
a -> b -> d
a -> b -> e
a -> c -> f
```

```
b -> d
b -> e
c -> f
```

So a simple linked tree implementation will look a lot like a linked list one:

```
(defstruct (tree-node (:conc-name nil))
  key
  children)  ; instead of linked list's next

CL-USER> (rtl:with ((f (make-tree-node :key "f"))
                    (e (make-tree-node :key "e"))
                    (d (make-tree-node :key "d"))
                    (c (make-tree-node :key "c" :children (list f)))
                    (b (make-tree-node :key "b" :children (list d e))))
           (make-tree-node :key "a"
                           :children (list b c)))
#S(TREE-NODE
   :KEY "a"
   :CHILDREN (#S(TREE-NODE
                :KEY "b"
                :CHILDREN (#S(TREE-NODE :KEY "d" :CHILDREN NIL)
                           #S(TREE-NODE :KEY "e" :CHILDREN NIL)))
              #S(TREE-NODE
                :KEY "c"
                :CHILDREN (#S(TREE-NODE :KEY "f" :CHILDREN NIL)))))
```

Similar to lists that had to be constructed from tail to head, we had to populate the tree in reverse order: from leaves to root. With lists, we could, as an alternative, use push and reverse the result, in the end. But, for trees, there's no such operation as reverse.

Obviously, not only lists can be used as a data structure to hold the children. When the number of children is fixed (e.g., in a binary tree), they may be defined as separate slots: for example, left and right. Another option will be to use a key-value, which allows assigning labels to tree edges (as the keys of the kv), but the downside is that the ordering isn't defined (unless we use an ordered kv like a linked hash-table). We may also want to assign weights or other properties to the edges, and, in this case, either an additional collection (say child-weights) or a separate edge struct should be defined to store all those properties. In the latter case, the node structure will contain edges instead of children. In fact, the tree can also be represented as a list of such edge structures, although this approach is quite inefficient, for most of the use cases.

Another tree representation utilizes the available linked list implementation directly instead of reimplementing it. Let's consider the following simple Lisp form:

```
(defun foo (bar)
  "Foo function."
  (baz bar))
```

It is a tree with the root containing the symbol defun and four children:

- The terminal symbol foo

- The tree containing the function arguments ((bar))

- The terminal string (the docstring "Foo function.")

- The tree containing the form to evaluate ((baz bar))

By default, in the list-based tree, the first element is the head, and the rest are the leaves. This representation is very compact and convenient for humans, so it is used not only for source code. For example, you can see a similar representation for the constituency trees, in linguistics:

```
(TOP (S (NP (DT This)) (VP (VBZ is) (NP (DT a) (NN test))) (. .)))
;; if we'd like to use the above form as Lisp code,
;; we'd have to shield the symbol "." with ||: (|.| |.|) instead of (. .)
```

It is equivalent to the following parse tree:

```
    TOP
   /  |      \
   |  VP      |
   |  |  \    |
  NP  |  NP   |
   |  |  / \  |
  DT VBZ DT  NN   .
This is  a  test  .
```

Another, more specific alternative is when we are interested only in the terminal nodes. In that case, there will be no explicit root, and each list item will be a subtree. The following trees are equivalent:

```
(((a b (c d)) e) (f (g h)))
<root>
      /        \
    / \      / \
  / | \ e    f    /\
 a  b /\        g  h
    c  d
```

A tree that has all terminals at the same depth and all nonterminal nodes present—a complete tree—with a specified number of children may be stored in a vector. This is a very efficient implementation that we'll have a glance at when we talk about heaps.

Finally, a tree may be also represented, although quite inefficiently, with a matrix (only one-half is necessary).

Tree Traversal

It should be noted that, unlike with other structures, basic operations, such as tree construction, modification, and element search and retrieval, work differently for different tree variants. Thus, we'll discuss them further when describing those variants.

Yet, one tree-specific operation is common to all tree representations: traversal. Traversing a tree means iterating over its subtrees or nodes in a certain order. The most direct traversal is called depth-first search or **DFS**. It is the recursive traversal from parent to child and then to the next child after we return from the recursion. The simplest DFS for our tree-node -based tree may be coded in the following manner:

```
(defun dfs-node (fn root)
  (funcall fn (key root))
  (dolist (child (children root))
    (dfs-node fn child)))
```

```
;; Here, *tree* is taken from the previous example
CL-USER> (dfs-node 'print *tree*)
"a"
"b"
"d"
"e"
"c"
"f"
```

In the spirit of Lisp, we could also define a convenience macro:

```
(defmacro dotree-dfs ((value root) &body body)
  (let ((node (gensym)))  ; GENSYM is a fresh symbol
                          ; used to prevent possible symbol
                          ; collisions for NODE
    `(dfs-node (lambda (,node)
                 (let ((,value (key ,node)))
                   ,@body))
               ,root)))
```

And if we'd like to traverse a tree represented as a list, the changes are minor:

```
(defun dfs-list (fn tree)
  ;; we need to handle both subtrees (lists) and
  ;; leaves (atoms) - so, we'll just convert
  ;; everything to a list
  (let ((tree (rtl:mklist tree)))
    (funcall fn (first tree))
    (dolist (child (rest tree))
      (dfs-list fn child))))

CL-USER> (dfs-list 'print '(defun foo (bar)
                             "Foo function."
                             (baz bar)))
DEFUN
FOO
BAR
```

```
"Foo function."
BAZ
BAR
```

Recursion is very natural in tree traversal: we could even say that trees are recursion realized in a data structure. And the good news here is that, very rarely, there's a chance to hit recursion limits as the majority of trees are not infinite, and also the height of the tree, which conditions the depth of recursion, grows proportionally to the logarithm of the tree size,[1] and that's pretty slow.

These simple DFS implementations apply the function before descending down the tree. This style is called **preorder** traversal. There are alternative styles: **inorder** and **postorder**. With postorder, the call is executed after the recursion returns, that is, on the recursive ascent:

```
(defun post-dfs (fn node)
  (dolist (child (children node))
    (post-dfs fn child))
  (funcall fn (key node)))

CL-USER> (post-dfs 'print *tree*)
"d"
"e"
"b"
"f"
"c"
"a"
```

Inorder traversal is applicable only to binary trees: first, traverse the left side, then call fn, and then descend into the right side.

An alternative traversal approach is breadth-first search (**BFS**). It isn't so natural as DFS as it traverses the tree layer by layer, that is, it has to, first, accumulate all the nodes that have the same depth and then integrate them. In the general case, it isn't justified, but there are a number of algorithms where exactly such ordering is required.

---

[1]This statement is strictly true for balanced trees, but, even for imbalanced trees, such estimation is usually correct.

Here is an implementation of BFS (preorder) for our tree-nodes:

```
(defun bfs (fn nodes)
  (let ((next-level (list)))
    (dolist (node (rtl:mklist nodes))
      (funcall fn (key node))
      (dolist (child (children node))
        (push child next-level)))
    (when next-level
      (bfs fn (reverse next-level)))))
```

```
CL-USER> (bfs 'print *tree*)
"a"
"b"
"c"
"d"
"e"
"f"
```

An advantage of BFS traversal is that it can handle potentially unbounded trees, that is, it is suitable for processing trees in a streamed manner, layer by layer.

In object orientation, tree traversal is usually accomplished by means of the so-called **visitor pattern**. Basically, it's the same approach of passing a function to the traversal procedure but in disguise of additional (and excessive) OO-related machinery. Here is a visitor pattern example in Java:

```
interface ITreeVisitor {
    List<ITreeNode> children;
    void visit(ITreeNode node);
}

interface ITreeNode {
    void accept(ITreeVisitor visitor);
}

interface IFn {
    void call(ITreeNode);
}
```

```java
class TreeNode implements ITreeNode {
    public void accept(ITreeVisitor visitor) {
        visitor.visit(this);
    }
}

class PreOrderTreeVisitor implements ITreeVisitor {
    private IFn fn;

    public PreOrderTreeVisitor(IFn fn) {
        this.fn = fn;
    }

    public void visit(ITreeNode node) {
        fn.call(node);
        for (ITreeeNode child : node.children())
            child.visit(this);
    }
}
```

The zest of this example is the implementation of the method `visit` that calls the function with the current node and iterates over its children by recursively applying the same visitor. You can see that it's exactly the same as our `dfs-node`.

One of the interesting tree traversal tasks is tree printing. There are many ways in which trees can be displayed. The simplest one is directory style (like the one used by the Unix tree utility):

```
$ tree /etc/acpi
/etc/acpi
├── asus-wireless.sh
├── events
│   ├── asus-keyboard-backlight-down
│   ├── asus-keyboard-backlight-up
│   ├── asus-wireless-off
│   └── asus-wireless-on
└── undock.sh
```

It may be implemented with DFS and only requires tracking of the current level in the tree:

```
(defun pprint-tree-dfs (node &optional (level 0)
                             (skip-levels (make-hash-table)))
  (when (= 0 level)
    (format t "~A~%" (key node)))
  (let ((last-index (1- (length (children node)))))
    (rtl:doindex (i child (children node))
      (let ((last-child-p (= i last-index)))
        (dotimes (j level)
          (format t "~C     "
                  (if (rtl:? skip-levels j) #\Space #\|)))
        (format t "~C── ~A~%"
                (if last-child-p #\└ #\├)
                (key child))
        (setf (rtl:? skip-levels level) last-child-p)
        (pprint-tree-dfs child
                         (1+ level)
                         skip-levels)))))
```

```
CL-USER> (pprint-tree-dfs *tree*)
a
├── b
│   ├── d
│   └── e
└── c
    └── f
```

1+ and 1- are standard Lisp shortcuts for adding/subtracting 1 to/from a number. The skip-levels argument is used for the last elements to not print the excess |.

A more complicated variant is top-to-bottom printing:

```
;; example from CL-NLP library
CL-USER> (nlp:pprint-tree
          '(TOP (S (NP (NN "This"))
                   (VP (VBZ "is")
```

```
                (NP (DT "a")
                    (JJ "simple")
                    (NN "test")))
            (|.| ".")))
        TOP
         :
         S
   .-----------:---------.
   :              VP      :
   :        .---------.   :
  NP   :         NP        :
   :   :    .----:-----.   :
  NN  VBZ  DT   JJ     NN   .
   :   :    :    :      :   :
 This  is   a  simple  test .
```

This style, most probably, will need a BFS and a careful calculation of spans of each node to properly align everything. Implementing such a function is left as an exercise to the reader, and a very enlightening one, I should say.

Binary Search Trees

Now, we can return to the topic of basic operations on tree elements. The advantage of trees is that, when built properly, they guarantee O(log n) for all the main operations: search, insertion, modification, and deletion.

This quality is achieved by keeping the leaves sorted and the trees in a balanced state. "Balanced" means that any pair of paths from the root to the leaves have lengths that may differ by at most some predefined quantity: ideally, just 1 (AVL trees), or, as in the case of Red-Black (RB) trees, the longest path can be at most twice as long as the shortest. Yet, such situations when all the elements align along a single path, effectively, turning the tree into a list, should be completely ruled out. We have already seen, with binary search and quicksort (remember the justification for the three-median rule), why this constraint guarantees logarithmic complexity.

The classic example of balanced trees are binary search trees (BSTs), of which AVL and Red-Black trees are the most popular variants. All the properties of BSTs may be trivially extended to n-ary trees, so we'll discuss the topic using the binary tree examples.

Just to reiterate the general intuition for the logarithmic complexity of tree operations, let's examine a complete binary tree: a tree that has all levels completely filled with elements, except maybe for the last one. In it, we have n elements, and each level contains twice as many nodes as the previous. This property means that n is not greater than `(+ 1 2 4 ... (/ k 2) k)`, where k is the capacity of the last level. This formula is nothing but the sum of a geometric progression with the number of items equal to h, which is, by the textbook

```
(/ (* 1 (- 1 (expt 2 h)))
   (- 1 2))
```

In turn, this expression may be reduced to `(- (expt 2 h) 1)`. So `(+ n 1)` equals `(expt 2 h)`, that is, the height of the tree (h) equals `(log (+ n 1) 2)`.

BSTs have the ordering property: if some element is to the right of another in the tree, it should consistently be greater (or smaller—depending on the ordering direction). This constraint means that after the tree is built, just extracting its elements by performing an inorder DFS produces a sorted sequence. The treesort algorithm utilizes this approach directly to achieve the same `O(n * log n)` complexity as other efficient sorting algorithms. This `n * log n` is the complexity of each insertion (`O(log n)`) multiplied by the number of times it should be performed (n). So treesort operates by taking a sequence and adding its elements to the BST, then traversing the tree, and putting the encountered elements into the resulting array, in a proper order.

Besides, the ordering property also means that, after adding a new element to the tree, in the general case, it should be rebalanced as the newly added element may not be placed in an arbitrary spot, but has just two admissible locations, and choosing either of those may violate the balance constraint. The specific balance invariants and approaches to tree rebalancing are the distinctive properties of each variant of BSTs that we will see in the following.

Splay Trees

A splay tree represents a kind of BST that is one of the simplest to understand and to implement. It is also quite useful in practice. It has the least strict constraints and a nice property that recently accessed elements occur near the root. Thus, a splay tree can naturally act as an LRU cache. However, there are degraded scenarios that result in $O(n)$ access performance, although the average complexity of splay tree operations is $O(\log n)$ due to amortization (we'll talk about it in a bit).

The approach to balancing a splay tree is to move the element we have accessed/inserted into the root position. The movement is performed by a series of operations that are called tree rotations. A certain pattern of rotations forms a step of the algorithm. For all BSTs, there are just two possible tree rotations, and they serve as the basic block, in all balancing algorithms. A rotation may be either a left or a right one. Their purpose is to put the left or the right child into the position of its parent, preserving the order of all the other child elements. The rotations can be illustrated by the following diagrams in which x is the parent node, y is the target child node that will become the new parent, and A, B, and C are subtrees. It is said that the rotation is performed around the edge x -> y.

Left rotation:

```
    x               y
   / \             / \
  y   C   ->      A   x
 / \                 / \
A   B               B   C
```

Right rotation:

```
    x                   y
   / \                 / \
  A   y     ->        x   C
     / \             / \
    B   C           A   B
```

As you see, the left and right rotations are complementary operations, that is, performing one after the other will return the tree to the original state. During the rotation, the inner subtree (B) has its parent changed from y to x.

Here's an implementation of rotations:

```
(defstruct (bst-node (:conc-name nil)
                     (:print-object (lambda (node out)
                                     (format out "[~a-~@[~a~]-~@[~a~]]"
                                            (key node)
                                            (lt node)
                                            (rt node)))))
  key
  val  ; we won't use this slot in the examples,
       ; but without it, in real-world use cases,
       ; such a tree doesn't have any value ;)
  lt   ; left child
  rt)  ; right child

(defun tree-rotate (node parent grandparent)
  (cond
    ((eql node (lt parent)) (setf (lt parent) (rt node)
                                  (rt node) parent))
    ((eql node (rt parent)) (setf (rt parent) (lt node)
                                  (lt node) parent))
    (t (error "NODE (~A) is not the child of PARENT (~A)"
              node parent)))
  (cond
    ((null grandparent) (return-from tree-rotate node))
    ((eql parent (lt grandparent)) (setf (lt grandparent) node))
    ((eql parent (rt grandparent)) (setf (rt grandparent) node))
    (t (error "PARENT (~A) is not the child of GRANDPARENT (~A)"
              parent grandparent))))
```

You have probably noticed that we need to pass to this function not only the nodes on the edge around which the rotation is executed but also the grandparent node of the target to link the changes to the tree. If grandparent is not supplied, it is assumed that parent is the root, and we need to separately reassign the variable holding the reference to the tree to child, after the rotation.

Splay trees combine rotations into three possible actions:

- The **zig** step is used to make the node the new root when it's already the direct child of the root. It is accomplished by a single left/right rotation(depending on whether the target is to the left or to the right of the root) followed by an assignment.

- The **zig-zig** step is a combination of two zig steps that is performed when both the target node and its parent are left/right nodes. The first rotation is around the edge between the target node and its parent and the second around the target and its former grandparent that has become its new parent, after the first rotation.

- The **zig-zag** step is performed when the target and its parent are not in the same direction: either one is left while the other is right or vice versa. In this case, correspondingly, first, a left rotation around the parent is needed and then a right one around its former grandparent (that has now become the new parent of the target). Or vice versa.

However, with our implementation of tree rotations, we don't have to distinguish the three different steps as they are all handled at once, and so the implementation of the operation splay becomes really trivial:

```
(defun splay (node &rest chain)
  (loop :for (parent grandparent) :on chain :do
    (tree-rotate node parent grandparent))
  node)
```

The key point here and in the implementation of splay tree operations is the use of reverse chains of nodes from the child to the root which will allow performing chains of splay operations in an end-to-end manner and also custom modifications of the tree structure.

From the code, it is clear that splaying requires at maximum the same number of steps as the height of the tree because each rotation brings the target element one level up. Now, let's discuss why all splay tree operations are O(log n). Element access requires binary search for the element in the tree, which is O(log n) provided the tree is balanced, and then splaying it to root—also O(log n). Deletion requires searching, then swapping the element either with the rightmost child of its left subtree or the leftmost child of its right subtree (direct predecessor/successor)—to make it childless—removing it, and, finally, splaying the parent of the removed node. And update is, at worst, deletion followed by insertion.

Here is the implementation of the splay tree built of bst-nodes and restricted to only arithmetic comparison operations. All of the high-level functions, such as st-search, st-insert, or st-delete, return the new tree root obtained after that should substitute the previous one in the caller code:

```
(defun node-chain (item root &optional chain)
  "Return as the values the node equal to ITEM or the closest one to it
   and the chain of nodes leading to it, in the splay tree based in ROOT."
  (if root
      (with-slots (key lt rt) root
        (let ((chain (cons root chain)))
          (cond ((= item key) (values root
                                       chain))
                ((< item key) (st-search item lt chain))
                ((> item key) (st-search item rt chain)))))
      (values nil
              chain)))

(defun st-search (item root)
  (rtl:with ((node chain (node-chain item root)))
    (when node
      (apply 'splay chain))))

(defun st-insert (item root)
  (assert root nil "Can't insert item into a null tree")
  (rtl:with ((node chain (st-search item root)))
    (unless node
      (let ((parent (first chain)))
        ;; here, we use the property of the := expression
        ;; that it returns the item being set
```

```
          (push (setf (rtl:? parent (if (> (key parent) item)
                                       'lt
                                       'rt))
                  (make-bst-node :key item))
                chain)))
    (apply 'splay chain)))

(defun idir (dir)
  (case dir
    (rtl:lt 'rt)
    (rtl:rt 'lt)))

(defun closest-child (node)
  (dolist (dir '(lt rt))
    (let ((parent nil)
          (current nil))
      (do ((child (funcall dir node) (funcall (idir dir) child)))
          ((null child) (when current
                          (return-from closest-child
                            (values dir
                                    current
                                    parent))))
        (setf parent current
              current child)))))

(defun st-delete (item root)
  (rtl:with ((node chain (st-search item root))
             (parent (second chain)))
    (if (null node)
        root  ; ITEM was not found
        (rtl:with ((dir child child-parent (closest-child node))
                   (idir (idir dir)))
          (when parent
            (setf (rtl:? parent (if (eql (lt parent) node)
                                    'lt
                                    'rt))
                  child))
```

```
    (when child
      (setf (rtl:? child idir) (rtl:? node idir))
      (when child-parent
        (setf (rtl:? child-parent idir) (rtl:? child dir))))
    (if parent
        (apply 'splay (rest chain))
        child)))))

(defun st-update (old new root)
  (st-insert new (st-delete old root)))
```

The deletion is somewhat tricky due to the need to account for different cases: when removing the root, the direct child of the root, or the other node.

Let's test the splay tree operation in the REPL (coding pprint-bst as a slight modification of pprint-tree-dfs is left as an exercise to the reader):

```
CL-USER> (defparameter *st* (make-bst-node :key 5))
CL-USER> *st*
[5--]
CL-USER> (pprint-bst (setf *st* (st-insert 1 *st*)))
1
├──.
└── 5
CL-USER> (pprint-bst (setf *st* (st-insert 10 *st*)))
10
├── 1
│   ├── .
│   └── 5
└── .
CL-USER> (pprint-bst (setf *st* (st-insert 3 *st*)))
3
├── 1
└── 10
    ├── .
    └── 5
CL-USER> (pprint-bst (setf *st* (st-insert 7 *st*)))
7
```

```
├── 3
│       ├── 1
│       └── 5
└── 10
CL-USER> (pprint-bst (setf *st* (st-insert 8 *st*)))
8
├── 7
│       ├── 3
│       │       ├── 1
│       │       └── 5
│       └── .
└── 10
CL-USER> (pprint-bst (setf *st* (st-insert 2 *st*)))
2
├── 1
└── 8
        ├── 7
        │       ├── 3
        │       │       ├── .
        │       │       └── 5
        │       └── .
        └── 10
CL-USER> (pprint-bst (setf *st* (st-insert 4 *st*)))
4
├── 2
│       ├── 1
│       └── 3
└── 8
        ├── 7
        │       ├── 5
        │       └── .
        └── 10
CL-USER> *st*
[4-[2-[1--]-[3--]]-[8-[7-[5--]-]-[10--]]]
```

As you can see, the tree gets constantly rearranged at every insertion.

Accessing an element, when it's found in the tree, also triggers tree restructuring:

```
CL-USER> (pprint-bst (st-search 5 *st*))
5
├── 4
│   ├── 2
│   │   ├── 1
│   │   └── 3
│   └── .
└── 8
    ├── 7
    └── 10
```

The insertion and deletion operations, for the splay tree, also may have an alternative implementation: first, split the tree in two at the place of the element to be added/removed and then combine them. For insertion, the combination is performed by making the new element the root and linking the previously split subtrees to its left and right. As for deletion, splitting the splay tree requires splaying the target element and then breaking the two subtrees apart (removing the target that has become the root). The combination is also $O(\log n)$, and it is performed by splaying the rightmost node of the left subtree (the largest element) so that it doesn't have the right child. Then the right subtree can be linked to this vacant slot.

Although regular access to the splay tree requires splaying of the element we have touched, tree traversal should be implemented without splaying. Or rather, just the normal DFS/BFS procedures should be used. First of all, this approach will keep the complexity of the operation at $O(n)$ without the unnecessary $\log n$ multiplier added by the splaying operations. Besides, accessing all the elements inorder will trigger the edge-case scenario and turn the splay tree into a list—exactly the situation we want to avoid.

Complexity Analysis

All of those considerations apply under the assumption that all the tree operations are $O(\log n)$. But we haven't proven it yet. Turns out that, for splay trees, it isn't a trivial task and requires **amortized analysis**. Basically, this approach averages the cost of all operations over all tree elements. Amortized analysis allows us to confidently use many advanced data structures for which it isn't possible to prove the required time bounds for individual operations, but the general performance over the lifetime of the data structure is in those bounds.

The principal tool of amortized analysis is the **potential method**. Its idea is to combine, for each operation, not only its direct cost but also the change to the *potential* cost of other operations that it brings. For splay trees, we can observe that only zig-zig and zig-zag steps are important for the analysis, as the zig step happens only once for each splay operation and changes the height of the tree by at most 1. Also, both zig-zig and zig-zag have the same potential.

Rigorously calculating the exact potential requires a number of mathematical proofs that we don't have space to show here, so let's just list the main results:

1. The potential of the whole splay tree is the sum of the ranks of all nodes, where rank is the logarithm of the number of elements in the subtree rooted at node:

    ```
    (defun rank (node)
      (let ((size 0))
        (dotree-dfs (_ node)
          (incf size))
        (log size 2)))
    ```

2. The change of potential produced by a single zig-zig/zig-zag step can be calculated in the following manner:

    ```
    (+ (- (rank grandparent-new) (rank grandparent-old))
       (- (rank parent-new) (rank parent-old))
       (- (rank node-new) (rank node-old)))
    ```

    Since `(= (rank node-new) (rank grandparent-old))` it can be reduced to:

    ```
    (- (+ (rank grandparent-new) (rank parent-new))
       (+ (rank parent-old) (rank node-old)))
    ```

Which is not larger than:

```
(- (+ (rank grandparent-new) (rank node-new))
   (* 2 (rank node-old)))
```

Which, in turn, due to the concavity of the log function, may be reduced to:

```
(- (* 3 (- (rank node-new) (rank node-old))) 2)
```

The amortized cost of any step is 2 operations larger than the change in potential as we need to perform 2 tree rotations, so it's not larger than:

```
(* 3 (- (rank node-new) (rank node-old)))
```

3. When summed over the entire splay operation, this expression "telescopes" to `(* 3 (- (rank root) (rank node)))` which is `O(log n)`. Telescoping means that when we calculate the sum of the cost of all zig-zag/zig-zig steps, the inner terms cancel each other out and only the boundary ones remain. The difference in ranks is, in the worst case, `log n` as the rank of the root is `(log n 2)` and the rank of the arbitrary node is between that value and `(log 1 2)` (0).

4. Finally, the total cost for `m` splay operations is `O(m log n + n log n)`, where the `m log n` term represents the total amortized cost of a sequence of `m` operations and `n log n` is the change in potential that it brings.

As mentioned, the preceding exposition is just a cursory look at the application of the potential method that skips some important details. If you want to learn more, you can start with the discussion on CS Theory StackExchange.

To conclude, similar to hash-tables, the performance of splay tree operations for a concrete element depends on the order of the insertion/removal of all the elements of the tree, that is, it has an unpredictable (random) nature. This property is a disadvantage compared to some other BST variants that provide precise performance guarantees. Another disadvantage, in some situations, is that the tree is constantly restructured, which makes it mostly unfit for usage as a persistent data structure and also may not play well with many storage options. Yet, splay trees are simple and, in many situations, due to their LRU property, may be preferable over other BSTs.

Red-Black and AVL Trees

Another BST that has similar complexity characteristics to splay trees and, in general, a somewhat similar approach to rebalancing is the scapegoat tree. Both of these BSTs don't require storing any additional information about the current state of the tree, which results in the random aspect of their operation. And although it is smoothed over all the tree accesses, it may not be acceptable in some usage scenarios.

An alternative approach, if we want to exclude the random factor, is to track the tree state. Tracking may be achieved by adding just 1 bit to each tree node (as with Red-Black trees) or 2 bits, the so-called balance factors (AVL trees).[2] However, for most of the high-level languages, including Lisp, we'll need to go to great lengths or even perform low-level non-portable hacking to, actually, ensure that exactly 1 or 2 bits is spent for this data, as the standard structure implementation will allocate a whole word even for a bit-sized slot. Moreover, in C likewise, due to cache alignment, the structure will also have the size aligned to memory word boundaries. So, by and large, usually we don't really care whether the data we'll need to track is a single bit flag or a full integer counter.

---

[2]Although it was shown that this value may also be reduced to a single bit if the tree is implemented as a rank balanced tree with delta ranks allowed of 1 or 2 meaning "when going upward there is an additional increment in height of one or two."

The balance guarantee of an RB tree is that, for each node, the height of the left and right subtrees may differ by at most a factor of 2. Such boundary condition occurs when the longer path contains alternating red and black nodes and the shorter only black nodes. Balancing is ensured by the requirement to satisfy the following invariants:

1. Each tree node is assigned a label: red or black (basically, a 1-bit flag: 0 or 1).

2. The root should be black (0).

3. All the leaves are also black (0). And the leaves don't hold any data. A good implementation strategy to satisfy this property is to have a constant singleton terminal node that all preterminals will link to: (defparameter *rb-leaf* (make-rb-node)).

4. If a parent node is red (1), then both its children should be black (0). Due to mock leaves, each node has exactly two children.

5. Every path from a given node to any of its descendant leaf nodes should contain the same number of black nodes.

So, to keep the tree in a balanced state, the insert/update/delete operations should perform rebalancing when the constraints are violated. Robert Sedgewick has proposed the simplest version of the Red-Black tree called the Left-Leaning Red-Black (LLRB) tree. The LLRB tree maintains an additional invariant that all red links must lean left except during inserts and deletes, which makes for the simplest implementation of the operations. In the following, we can see the outline of the insert operation:

```
(defstruct (rb-node (:include bst-node) (:conc-name nil))
  (red nil :type boolean))

(defun rb-insert (item root &optional parent)
  (let ((node (make-rb-node :key item)))
    (when (null root)
      (return-from rb-insert node))
    (when (and (red (lt root))
               (red (rt root)))
      (setf (red root) (not (red root))
            (red (lt root)) nil
            (red (rt root)) nil))
```

```
(cond ((< (key root) value)
       (setf (lt root) (rb-insert node (lt root) root)))
      ((> (key root) value)
       (setf (rt root) (rb-insert node (rt root) root))))
(when (and (red (rt root))
           (not (red (lt root))))
  (setf (red (lt root)) (red root)
        root (tree-rotate (lt root) root parent)
        (red root) t))
(when (and (red (lt root))
           (not (red (rt root))))
  (setf (red (rt root)) (red root)
        root (tree-rotate (rt root) root parent)
        (red root) t)))
root)
```

This code is more of an outline. You can easily find the complete implementation of the RB tree on the Internet. The key here is to understand the principle of their operation. Also, we won't discuss AVL trees in detail. Suffice to say that they are based on the same principles but use a different set of balancing operations.

Both Red-Black and AVL trees may be used when worst-case performance guarantees are required, for example, in real-time systems. Besides, they serve as a basis for implementing persistent data structures that we'll talk about later. The Java TreeMap and similar data structures from the standard libraries of many languages are implemented with one of these BSTs. And the implementations of them both are present in the Linux kernel and are used as data structures for various queues.

OK, now you know how to balance a binary tree. :D

B-Trees

A B-tree is a generalization of a BST that allows for more than two children. The number of children is not unbounded and should be in a predefined range. For instance, the simplest B-tree—2-3 tree—allows for two or three children. Such trees combine the main advantage of self-balanced trees—logarithmic access time—with the benefit of arrays—locality—the property which allows for faster cache access or retrieval from the storage. That's why B-trees are mainly used in data storage systems. Overall, B-tree implementations perform the same trick as we saw in prod-sort: switching to sequential search when the sequence becomes small enough to fit into the cache line of the CPU.

Each internal node of a B-tree contains a number of keys. For a 2-3 tree, the number is either 1 or 2. The keys act as separation values which divide the subtrees. For example, if the keys are x and y, all the values in the leftmost subtree will be less than x, all values in the middle subtree will be between x and y, and all values in the rightmost subtree will be greater than y. Here is an example:

```
              [ 7 . 18 ]
          /       |        \
[ 1 . 3 ]     [ 10 . 15 ]     [ 20 . _ ]
```

This tree has four nodes. Each node has two key slots and may have zero (in the case of the leaf nodes), two, or three children. The node structure for it might look like this:

```
(defstruct 23-node
  key1
  key2
  val1
  val2
  lt
  md
  rt)
```

Yet, a more general B-tree node would, probably, contain arrays for keys/values and children links:

```
(defstruct bt-node
  (keys (make-array *max-keys*))
  (vals (make-array *max-keys*))
  (children (make-array (1+ *max-keys*))))
```

The element search in a B-tree is very similar to that of a BST. Except that there will be up to *max-keys* comparisons instead of one, in each node. Insertion is more tricky as it may require rearranging the tree items to satisfy its invariants. A B-tree is kept balanced after insertion by the procedure of splitting a would-be overfilled node, of (1+ n) keys, into two (/ n 2) key siblings and inserting the mid-value key into the parent. That's why, usually, the range of the number of keys in the node in the B-tree is chosen to be between k and (* 2 k). Also, in practice, k will be pretty large: an order of 10s or even 100. Depth only increases when the root is split, maintaining balance. Similarly, a B-tree is kept balanced after deletion by merging or redistributing keys among siblings to maintain the minimum number of keys for non-root nodes. A merger reduces the number of keys in the parent potentially forcing it to merge or redistribute keys with its siblings and so on. The depth of the tree will increase slowly as elements are added to it, but an increase in the overall depth is infrequent and results in all leaf nodes being one more node farther away from the root.

A version of B-trees that is particularly developed for storage systems and is used in a number of filesystems, such as NTFS and ext4, and databases, such as Oracle and SQLite, is B+ trees. A B+ tree can be viewed as a B-tree in which each node contains only keys (not key-value pairs) and to which an additional level is added at the bottom with linked leaves. The leaves of the B+ tree are linked to one another in a linked list, making range queries or an (ordered) iteration through the blocks simpler and more efficient. Such a property could not be achieved in a B-tree, since not all keys are present in the leaves: some are stored in the root or intermediate nodes.

However, a newer Linux filesystem, developed specifically for use on the SSDs and called btrfs, uses plain B-trees instead of B+ trees because the former allows implementing copy-on-write, which is needed for efficient snapshots. The issue with B+ trees is that their leaf nodes are interlinked, so if a leaf were copy-on-write, its siblings and parents would have to be as well, as would their siblings and parents, and so on until the entire tree was copied. We can recall the same situation pertaining to the doubly linked lists compared to singly linked ones. So a modified B-tree without leaf linkage is used in btrfs, with a refcount associated with each tree node but stored in an ad hoc free map structure.

Overall, B-trees are a very natural continuation of BSTs, so we won't spend more time with them here. I believe it should be clear how to deal with them overall. Surely, there are a lot of B-tree variants that have their nuances, but those should be studied in the context of a particular problem they are considered for.

Heaps

A different variant of a binary tree is a binary heap. Heaps are used in many different algorithms, such as pathfinding, encoding, minimum spanning tree, and so on. They even have their own $O(\log n)$ sorting algorithm—the elegant heapsort. In a heap, each element is either the smallest (min-heap) or the largest (max-heap) element of its subtree. It is also a complete tree, and the last layer should be filled left to right. This invariant makes the heap well suited for keeping track of element priorities. So priority queues are, usually, based on heaps. Thus, it's beneficial to be aware of the existence of this peculiar data structure.

The constraints on the heap allow representing it in a compact and efficient manner—as a simple vector. Its first element is the heap root, the second and third are its left and right children (if present), and so on, by recursion. This arrangement permits access to the parent and children of any element using the simple offset-based formulas (in which the element is identified by its index):

```
(defun hparent (i)
  "Calculate the index of the parent of the heap element with an index I."
  (floor (- i 1) 2))

(defun hrt (i)
  "Calculate the index of the right child of the heap element with an index I."
  (* (+ i 1) 2))

(defun hlt (i)
  "Calculate the index of the left child of the heap element with an index I."
  (- (hrt i) 1))
```

So, to implement a heap, we don't need to define a custom node structure and, besides, can get to any element in $O(1)$! Here is the utility to rearrange an arbitrary array in a min-heap formation (in other words, we can consider a binary heap to be a special arrangement of array elements). It works by iteratively placing each element in its proper place by swapping with children until it's larger than both of the children:

```
(defun heapify (vec)
  (let ((mid (floor (length vec) 2)))
    (dotimes (i mid)
      (heap-down vec (- mid i 1))))
  vec)
```

```
(defun heap-down (vec beg &optional (end (length vec)))
  (let ((l (hlt beg))
        (r (hrt beg)))
    (when (< l end)
      (let ((child (if (or (>= r end)
                           (> (aref vec l)
                              (aref vec r)))
                       l r)))
        (when (> (aref vec child)
                 (aref vec beg))
          (rotatef (aref vec beg)
                   (aref vec child))
          (heap-down vec child end)))))
  vec)
```

And here is the reverse operation to pop the item up the heap:

```
(defun heap-up (vec i)
  (when (> (aref vec i)
           (aref vec (hparent i)))
    (rotatef (aref vec i)
             (aref vec (hparent i)))
    (heap-up vec (hparent i)))
  vec)
```

Also, as with other data structures, it's essential to be able to visualize the content of the heap in a convenient form, as well as to check the invariants. These tasks may be accomplished with the help of the following functions:

```
(defun draw-heap (vec)
  (format t "~%")
  (rtl:with ((size (length vec))
             (h (+ 1 (floor (log size 2)))))
    (dotimes (i h)
      (let ((spaces (make-list (- (expt 2 (- h i)) 1)
                               :initial-element #\Space)))
        (dotimes (j (expt 2 i))
```

```
            (let ((k (+ (expt 2 i) j -1)))
               (when (= k size) (return))
               (format t "~{~C~}~2D~{~C~}"
                         spaces (aref vec k) spaces)))
          (format t "~%"))))
     (format t "~%")
     vec)

(defun check-heap (vec)
  (dotimes (i (floor (length vec) 2))
    (when (= (hlt i) (length vec)) (return))
    (assert (not (> (aref vec (hlt i)) (aref vec i)))
            () "Left child (~A) is > parent at position ~A (~A)."
            (aref vec (hlt i)) i (aref vec i))
    (when (= (hrt i) (length vec)) (return))
    (assert (not (> (aref vec (hrt i)) (aref vec i)))
            () "Right child (~A) is > than parent at position ~A (~A)."
            (aref vec (hrt i)) i (aref vec i)))
  vec)
CL-USER> (check-heap #(10 5 8 2 3 7 1 9))
Left child (9) is > parent at position 3 (2).
   [Condition of type SIMPLE-ERROR]

CL-USER> (check-heap (draw-heap (heapify #(1 22 10 5 3 7 8 9 7 13))))
               22
       13               10
     9       3       7       8
   5   7   1

#(22 13 10 9 3 7 8 5 7 1)
```

Due to the regular nature of the heap, drawing it with BFS is much simpler than for most other trees.

As with ordered trees, heap element insertion and deletion require repositioning of some of the elements:

```
(defun heap-push (node vec)
  (vector-push-extend node vec)
  (heap-up vec (1- (length vec))))

(defun heap-pop (vec)
  (rotatef (aref vec 0) (aref vec (- (length vec) 1)))
  ;; PROG1 is used to return the result of the first form
  ;; instead of the last, like it happens with PROGN
  (prog1 (vector-pop vec)
    (heap-down vec 0)))
```

Now, we can implement heapsort. The idea is to iteratively arrange the array in heap order element by element. Each arrangement will take log n time as we're pushing the item down a complete binary tree, the height of which is log n. And we'll need to perform n such iterations:

```
(defun heapsort (vec)
  (heapify vec)
  (dotimes (i (length vec))
    (let ((last (- (length vec) i 1)))
      (rotatef (aref vec 0)
               (aref vec last))
      (heap-down vec 0 last)))
  vec)

CL-USER> (heapsort #(1 22 10 5 3 7 8 9 7 13))
#(1 3 5 7 7 8 9 10 13 22)
```

There are so many sorting algorithms, so why invent yet another one? That's a totally valid point, but the advantage of heaps is that they keep the maximum/minimum element constantly at the top so you don't have to perform a full sort or even descend into the tree if you need just the top element. This simplification is especially relevant if we constantly need to access such elements as with priority queues.

Actually, a heap should not necessarily be a tree. Besides the binary heap, there are also binomial, Fibonacci, and other kinds of heaps that may even not necessarily be trees, but even collections of trees (**forests**). We'll discuss some of them in more detail in the next chapters, in the context of the algorithms for which their use makes a notable difference in performance.

Tries

If I were to answer the question "What's the most underappreciated data structure?" I'd probably say, a trie. For me, tries are a gift that keeps on giving, and they have already saved me program performance in a couple of situations that seemed hopeless. Besides, they are very simple to understand and implement.

A trie is also called a prefix tree. It is, usually, used to optimize dictionary storage and lookup when the dictionary has a lot of entries and there is some overlap between them. The most obvious example is a normal English language dictionary. A lot of words have common stems ("work," "word," "worry" all share the same beginning "wor"), and there are many wordforms of the same word ("word," "words," "wording," "worded").

There are many approaches to trie implementation. Let's discuss the most straightforward and, so to say, primitive one. Here is a trie for representing a string dictionary that is character-based and uses an alist to store children pointers:

```
(defstruct (tr-node (:conc-name nil))
  val
  (children (list)))

(defun tr-lookup (key root)
  (rtl:dovec (ch key
                 ;; when iteration terminates normally
                 ;; we have found the node we were looking for
                 (val root))
    (rtl:if-it (rtl:assoc1 ch (children root))
               (setf root rtl:it)
               (return))))

(defun tr-add (key val root)
  (let ((i 0))
```

```
    (rtl:dovec (ch key)
      (rtl:if-it (rtl:assoc1 ch (children root))
                 (setf root rtl:it
                       i (1+ i))
                 (return)))
    (if (= i (length key))
        ;; something has already being stored at key -
        ;; so we signal a continuable error that
        ;; gives the user two options: overwrite or abort
        (cerror "Assign a new value"
                "There was already a value at key: ~A" (val root))
        (rtl:dovec (ch (rtl:slice key i))
          (let ((child (make-tr-node)))
            (push (cons ch child) (children root))
            (setf root child))))
    (setf (val root) val)))
```

```
CL-USER> (defparameter *trie* (make-tr-node))
*TRIE*
CL-USER> *trie*
#S(TR-NODE :VAL NIL :CHILDREN NIL)
```

For the sake of brevity, we won't define a special print-function for our trie and will use a default one. In a real setting, though, it is highly advisable:

```
CL-USER> (tr-lookup "word" *trie*)
NIL
CL-USER> (tr-add "word" 42 *trie*)
42
CL-USER> *trie*
#S(TR-NODE
   :VAL NIL
   :CHILDREN
   ((#\w
     . #S(TR-NODE
          :VAL NIL
          :CHILDREN
```

```
          ((#\o
            . #S(TR-NODE
                 :VAL NIL
                 :CHILDREN
                 ((#\r
                   . #S(TR-NODE
                        :VAL NIL
                        :CHILDREN
                        ((#\d
                          . #S(TR-NODE
                               :VAL 42
                               :CHILDREN NIL)))))))))))))
CL-USER> (tr-lookup "word" *trie*)
42
CL-USER> (tr-add "word" :foo *trie*)

There was already a value at key: 42
   [Condition of type SIMPLE-ERROR]

Restarts:
 0: [CONTINUE] Assign a new value
 1: [RETRY] Retry SLIME REPL evaluation request.
 2: [*ABORT] Return to SLIME's top level.
 3: [ABORT] abort thread (#<THREAD "repl-thread" RUNNING>)

Backtrace:
  0: (TR-ADD "word" :FOO #S(TR-NODE :VAL 42 :CHILDREN NIL))
  1: (SB-INT:SIMPLE-EVAL-IN-LEXENV (TR-ADD "word" :FOO *TRIE*) #<NULL-
LEXENV>)
  2: (EVAL (TR-ADD "word" :FOO *TRIE*))
  --more--

;;; Take the restart 0

:FOO
CL-USER> (tr-add "we" :baz *trie*)
:BAZ
CL-USER> *trie*
```

```
#S(TR-NODE
    :VAL NIL
    :CHILDREN
    ((#\w
      . #S(TR-NODE
            :VAL NIL
            :CHILDREN
            ((#\e . #S(TR-NODE
                        :VAL :BAZ
                        :CHILDREN NIL))
             (#\o . #S(TR-NODE
                        :VAL NIL
                        :CHILDREN
                        ((#\r
                          . #S(TR-NODE
                                :VAL NIL
                                :CHILDREN
                                ((#\k
                                  . #S(TR-NODE
                                        :VAL :BAR
                                        :CHILDREN NIL))
                                 (#\d
                                  . #S(TR-NODE
                                        :VAL :FOO
                                        :CHILDREN NIL)))))))))))))))
```

There are many ways to optimize this trie implementation. First of all, you can see that some space is wasted on intermediate nodes with no values. This is mended by **radix trees** (also known as Patricia trees) that merge all intermediate nodes. That is, our trie would change into the following more compact structure:

```
#S(TR-NODE
    :VAL NIL
    :CHILDREN
    ((#\w
      . #S(TR-NODE
            :VAL NIL
```

```
:CHILDREN
((#\e . #S(TR-NODE
            :VAL :BAZ
            :CHILDREN NIL))
  ("or" . #S(TR-NODE
            :VAL NIL
            :CHILDREN ((#\k . #S(TR-NODE
                                  :VAL :BAR
                                  :CHILDREN NIL))
                        (#\d . #S(TR-NODE
                                  :VAL :FOO
                                  :CHILDREN NIL)))))))))))
```

Besides, there are ways to utilize the array to store trie offsets (similar to heaps), instead of using a linked backbone for it. Such variant is called a **succinct** trie. Also, there are compressed (C-tries), hash-array mapped (HAMTs), and other kinds of tries.

The main advantage of tries is efficient space usage, thanks to the elimination of repetition in key storage. In many scenarios, usage of tries also improves the speed of access. Consider the task of matching against a dictionary of phrases, for example, biological or medical terms, names of companies, works of art, and so on. These are usually two- to three-word-long phrases, but, occasionally, there may be an outlier of ten or more words. The straightforward approach would be to put the dictionary into a hash-table and then iterate over the input string trying to find the phrases in the table, starting from each word. The only question is: Where do we put an end of the phrase? As we said, the phrase may be from one to, say, ten words in length. With a hash-table, we have to check every variant: a single-word phrase, a two-word one, and so on up to the maximum length. Moreover, if there are phrases with the same beginning, which is often the case, we'd do duplicate work of hashing that beginning, for each variant (unless we use an additive hash, but this isn't advised for hash-tables). With a trie, all the duplication is not necessary: we can iteratively match each word until we either find the match in the tree or discover that there is no continuation of the current subphrase.

Trees in Action: Efficient Mapping

Finally, the last family of tree data structures I had to mention is trees for representing spatial relations. Overall, mapping and pathfinding is an area that prompted the creation of a wide range of useful algorithms and data structures. There are two fundamental operations for processing spatial data: nearest neighbor search and range queries. Given the points on the plane, how do we determine the closest points to a particular one? How do we retrieve all points inside a rectangle or a circle? A primitive approach is to loop through all the points and collect the relevant information, which results in at least $O(n)$ complexity—prohibitively expensive if the number of points is beyond several tens or hundreds. And such problems, by the way, arise not only in the field of processing geospatial data (they are at the core of such systems as PostGIS, mapping libraries, etc.) but also in machine learning (for instance, the k-NN algorithm directly requires such calculations) and other areas.

A more efficient solution has a $O(\log\ n)$ complexity and is, as you might expect, based on indexing the data in a special-purpose tree. The changes to the tree will also have $O(\log\ n)$ complexity, while the initial indexing is $O(n\ \log\ n)$. However, in most of the applications that use this technique, changes are much less frequent than read operations, so the upfront cost pays off.

There are a number of trees that allow efficient storage of spatial data: segment trees, interval trees, k-d trees, R-trees, and so on. The most common spatial data structure is an **R-tree** (rectangle tree). It distributes all the points in an n-dimensional space (usually, n will be two or three) among the leaves of the tree by recursively dividing the space into k rectangles holding roughly the same number of points until each tree node has at most k points.

Let's say we have started from 1000 points on the plane and chosen k to be 10. In this case, the first level of the tree (i.e., children of the root) will contain ten nodes, each one having as the value the dimensions of the rectangle that bounds approximately 100 points. Every node like that will have ten more children, each one having around ten points. Maybe some will have more, and, in this case, we'll give those nodes ten children each with, probably, one or two points in the rectangles they will command. Now, we can perform a range search with the obtained tree by selecting only the nodes that intersect the query rectangle. For a small query box, this approach will result in the discarding of the majority of the nodes at each level of the tree. So a range search over an R-tree has $O(k\ \log\ n)$ where k is the number of intersecting rectangles.

Now, let's consider neighbor search. Obviously, the closest points to a particular one we are examining lie either in the same rectangle as the point or in the closest ones to it. So we need to, first, find the smallest bounding rectangle, which contains our point, perform the search in it, and then, if we haven't got enough points yet, process the siblings of the current tree node in the order of their proximity to it.

There are many other spatial problems that may be efficiently solved with this approach. One thing to note is that the described procedures require the tree to store, in the leaf nodes, references to every point contained in their rectangles.

Takeaways

So balancing a tree isn't such a unique and interesting task. On the contrary, it's quite simple yet boring due to the number of edge cases you have to account for. Yet, we have just scratched the surface of the general topic of trees. It is vast: the Wikipedia section for tree data structures contains almost 100 of them, and it's, definitely, not complete. Moreover, new tree variants will surely be invented in the future. But you will hardly deal with more than just a few variants during the course of your career, spending the majority of time with the simple "unconstrained" trees. And we have seen, in action, the basic principles of tree operation that will be helpful in the process.

There are a couple of other general observations about programming algorithms we can draw from this chapter:

1. Trees are very versatile data structures that are a default choice when you need to represent some hierarchy. They are also one of a few data structures for which recursive processing is not only admissible but also natural and efficient.

2. Visualization is key to efficient debugging of complex data structures. Unfortunately, it's hard to show in the book how I have spent several hours on the code for the splay tree, but without an efficient way to display the trees coupled with dynamic tracing, I would probably have spent twice as much. And both the `print-function` for individual node and `pprint-bst` were helpful here.

CHAPTER 10

Graphs

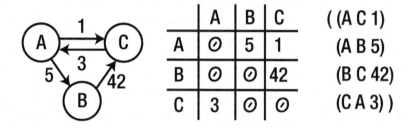

$$
\begin{array}{c|c|c|c}
 & A & B & C \\
\hline
A & \oslash & 5 & 1 \\
\hline
B & \oslash & \oslash & 42 \\
\hline
C & 3 & \oslash & \oslash \\
\end{array}
$$

```
( (A C 1)
  (A B 5)
  (B C 42)
  (C A 3) )
```

Graphs have already been mentioned several times in the book, in quite diverse contexts. Actually, if you are familiar with graphs, you can spot opportunities to use them in quite different areas for problems that aren't explicitly formulated with graphs in mind. So, in this chapter, we'll discuss how to handle graphs to develop such intuition to some degree.

But first, let's list the most prominent examples of the direct graph applications, some of which we'll see here in action:

- Pathfinding

- Network analysis

- Dependency analysis in planning, compilers, and so on

- Various optimization problems

- Distributing and optimizing computations

- Knowledge representation and reasoning with it

- Meaning representation in natural language processing

Graphs may be thought of as a generalization of trees: indeed, trees are, as we said earlier, connected directed acyclic graphs (DAGs). But there's an important distinction in the patterns of the usage of graphs and trees. Graphs, much more frequently than trees, have weights associated with the edges, which adds a whole new dimension both to

© Vsevolod Domkin 2021
V. Domkin, *Programming Algorithms in Lisp*, https://doi.org/10.1007/978-1-4842-6428-7_10

algorithms for processing them and to possible data that can be represented in the graph form. So, while the main application of trees is reflecting some hierarchy, for graphs, it is often more about determining connectedness and its magnitude, based on the weights.

Graph Representations

A graph is, basically, a set of nodes (called "vertices," V) and an enumeration of connections between two nodes ("edges," E). The edges may be directed or undirected (i.e., bidirectional) and also weighted or unweighted. There are many ways that may be used to represent these sets, which have varied utility for different situations. Here are the most common ones:

- As a linked structure: (defstruct node data links) where links may be either a list of other nodes, possibly paired with weights, or a list of edge structures represented as (defsturct edge source destination weight). For directed graphs, this representation will be similar to a singly linked list, but for undirected, to a heavier doubly linked one.

- As an adjacency matrix (V x V): This matrix is indexed by vertices and has zeroes when there's no connection between them and some nonzero number for the weight (1—in the case of unweighted graphs) when there is a connection. Undirected graphs have a symmetric adjacency matrix and so need to store only the above diagonal half of it.

- As an adjacency list that enumerates for each vertex the other vertices it's connected to and the weights of connections.

- As an incidence matrix (V x E): This matrix is similar to the adjacency list representation but with much more wasted space. The adjacency list may be thought of as a sparse representation of the incidence matrix. The matrix representation may be more useful for hypergraphs (that have more than two vertices for each edge), though.

- Just as a list of edges.

Topological Sort

Graphs may be divided into several kinds according to the different properties they have and specific algorithms which work on them:

- Disjoint (with several unconnected subgraphs), connected, and fully connected (every vertex is linked to all the others)

- Cyclic and acyclic, including directed acyclic (DAG)

- Bipartite, when there are two groups of vertices and each vertex from one group is connected only to the vertices from the other

In practice, **directed acyclic graphs** are quite important. These are directed graphs, in which there's no vertex that you can start a path from and return back to it. They find applications in optimizing scheduling and computation, determining historical and other types of dependencies (e.g., in dataflow programming and even spreadsheets), and so on. In particular, every compiler would use one, and even make will when building the operational plan. The basic algorithm on DAGs is **topological sort**. It creates a partial ordering of the vertices of the graph which ensures that every child vertex is always preceding all of its ancestors.

Here is an example. This is a DAG:

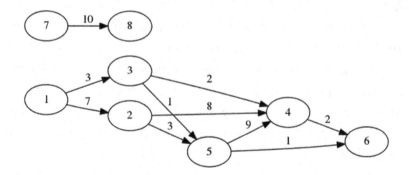

And these are the variants of its topological ordering:

```
6 4 5 3 2 1 8 7
6 4 5 2 3 1 8 7
8 7 6 4 5 3 2 1
8 7 6 4 5 2 3 1
```

There are several variants as the graph is disjoint, and also the order in which the vertices are traversed is not fully deterministic. There are two common approaches to topological sort: the Kahn's algorithm and the DFS-based one. Here is the DFS version:

1. Choose an arbitrary vertex and perform the DFS from it until a vertex is found without children that wasn't visited during the DFS.

2. While performing the DFS, add each vertex to the set of visited ones. Also check that the vertex hasn't been visited already, or else the graph is not acyclic.

3. Then, add the vertex we have found to the resulting sorted array.

4. Return to the previous vertex and repeat searching for the next descendant that doesn't have children and add it.

5. Finally, when all of the current vertex's children are visited, add it to the result array.

6. Repeat this for the next unvisited vertex until no unvisited ones remain.

Why does the algorithm satisfy the desired constraints? First of all, it is obvious that it will visit all the vertices. Next, when we add the vertex, we have already added all of its descendants—satisfying the main requirement. Finally, there's a consistency check during the execution of the algorithm that ensures there are no cycles.

Before proceeding to the implementation, as with other graph algorithms, it makes sense to ponder what representation will work the best for this problem. The default one—a linked structure—suits it quite well as we'll have to iterate all the outgoing edges of each node. If we had to traverse by incoming edges, then it wouldn't have worked, but a matrix one would have:

```
(defstruct node
  id edges)

(defstruct edge
  src dst label)

(defstruct (graph (:conc-name nil) (:print-object pprint-graph))
  (nodes (make-hash-table)))  ; mapping of node ids to nodes
```

As usual, we'll need a more visual way to display the graph than the default print-function. But that is pretty tricky considering that graphs may have an arbitrary structure with possibly intersecting edges. The simplest approach for small graphs would be to just draw the adjacency matrix. We'll utilize it for our examples (relying on the fact that we have control over the set of node ids):

```
(defun pprint-graph (graph stream)
  (let ((ids (sort (rtl:keys (nodes graph)) '<)))
    (format stream "~{    ~A~}~%" ids)  ; here, Tab is used for space
    (dolist (id1 ids)
      (let ((node (rtl:? graph 'nodes id1)))
        (format stream "~A" id1)
        (dolist (id2 ids)
          (format stream "    ~:[~;x~]"   ; here, Tab as well
                  (find id2 (rtl:? node 'edges) :key 'edge-dst)))
        (terpri stream)))))
```

Also, let's create a function to simplify graph initialization:

```
(defun init-graph (edges)
  (rtl:with ((rez (make-graph))
             (nodes (nodes rez)))
    (loop :for (src dst) :in edges :do
      (let ((src-node (rtl:getsethash src nodes (make-node :id src))))
        (rtl:getset# dst nodes (make-node :id dst))
        (push (make-edge :src src :dst dst)
              (rtl:? src-node 'edges))))
    rez))

CL-USER> (init-graph '((7 8)
                       (1 3)
                       (1 2)
                       (3 4)
                       (3 5)
                       (2 4)
                       (2 5)
```

```
                    (5 4)
                    (5 6)
                    (4 6)))
```

	1	2	3	4	5	6	7	8
1		x	x					
2				x	x			
3				x	x			
4						x		
5				x		x		
6								
7							x	
8								

So we already see in action three different ways of graph representation: linked, matrix, and edge lists. Now, we can implement and test topological sort:

```
(defun topo-sort (graph)
  (let ((nodes (nodes graph))
        (visited (make-hash-table))
        (rez (rtl:vec)))
    (rtl:dokv (id node nodes)
      (unless (gethash id visited)
        (visit node nodes visited rez)))
    rez))

(defun visit (node nodes visited rez)
  (dolist (edge (node-edges node))
    (rtl:with ((id (edge-dst edge))
               (child (elt nodes id)))
      (unless (find id rez)
        (assert (not (gethash id visited)) nil
                "The graph isn't acyclic for vertex: ~A" id)
        (setf (gethash id visited) t)
        (visit child nodes visited rez))))
  (vector-push-extend (node-id node) rez)
  rez)
```

```
CL-USER> (topo-sort (init-graph '((7 8)
                                  (1 3)
                                  (1 2)
                                  (3 4)
                                  (3 5)
                                  (2 4)
                                  (2 5)
                                  (5 4)
                                  (5 6)
                                  (4 6))))
#(8 7 6 4 5 2 3 1)
```

This technique of tracking the visited nodes is used in almost every graph algorithm. As noted previously, it can be implemented either by using an additional hash-table (like in the example) or by adding a Boolean flag to the vertex/edge structure itself.

MST

Now, we can move to algorithms that work with weighted graphs. They represent the majority of the interesting graph-based solutions. One of the most basic of them is determining the minimum spanning tree. Its purpose is to select only those graph edges that form a tree with the lowest total sum of weights. Spanning trees play an important role in network routing where there are a number of protocols that directly use them: STP (Spanning Tree Protocol), RSTP (Rapid STP), MSTP (Multiple STP), and so on.

If we consider the graph from the previous picture, its MST will include the edges 1-2, 1-3, 3-4, 3-5, 5-6, and 7-8. Its total weight will be 24.

Although there are quite a few MST algorithms, the most well-known are Prim's and Kruskal's. Both of them rely on some interesting solutions and are worth studying.

Prim's Algorithm

Prim's algorithm grows the tree one edge at a time, starting from an arbitrary vertex. At each step, the least-weight edge that has one of the vertices already in the MST and the other one outside is added to the tree. This algorithm always has an MST of the already processed subgraph, and when all the vertices are visited, the MST of the whole graph is completed. The most interesting property of Prim's algorithm is that its time complexity depends on the choice of the data structure for ordering the edges by weight. The straightforward approach that searches for the shortest edge will have $O(V^2)$ complexity, but if we use a priority queue, it can be reduced to $O(E\ logV)$ with a binary heap or even $O(E + V\ logV)$ with a Fibonacci heap. Obviously, $V\ logV$ is significantly smaller than $E\ logV$ for the majority of graphs: up to $E = V^2$ for fully connected graphs.

Here's the implementation of Prim's algorithm with an abstract heap:

```
(defvar *heap-indices*)

(defun prim-mst (graph)
  (let ((initial-weights (list))
        (mst (list))
        (total 0)
        (*heap-indices* (make-hash-table))
        weights
        edges
        cur)
    (rtl:dokv (id node (nodes graph))
      (if cur
          (push (rtl:pair id (or (elt edges id)
                                 ;; a standard constant that is
                                 ;; a good enough substitute for infinity
                                 most-positive-fixnum))
                initial-weights)
          (setf cur id
                edges (node-edges node))))
    (setf weights (heapify initial-weights))
    (loop
      (rtl:with (((id weight) (heap-pop weights)))
        (unless id (return))
        (when (elt edges id)
          ;; if not, we have moved to the new connected component
          ;; so there's no edge connecting it to the previous one
          (push (rtl:pair cur id) mst)
          (incf total weight))
```

```
    (rtl:dokv (id w edges)
      (when (< w weight)
        (heap-decrease-key weights id w)))
    (setf cur id
          edges (rtl:? graph 'nodes id 'edges)))))
  (values mst
          total)))
```

To make it work, we need to perform several modifications:

- First of all, the list of all node edges should be changed to a hash-table to ensure O(1) access by child id.

- We need to implement another fundamental heap operation heap-decrease-key, which we haven't mentioned in the previous chapter. For the binary heap, it's actually just a matter of executing heap-up after the value of a particular key is decremented. The tricky part is that it requires an initial search for the key in the heap. To ensure constant-time search and subsequently O(log n) total complexity, we need to store the pointers to heap elements in a separate hash-table. This is where a special variable *heap-indices* comes into play. All the heap operations will need to update the key positions tracked in it. Using a special variable may be very handy in such situations when we need to extend an existing API without breaking all the code that is already using it. Surely, we could also define a new set of heap operations (let's call them heapify-with-tracking, heap-pop-with-tracking, etc.) with an updated argument list, and we'll have to pass the tracking hash-table around with each call. That is a more standard and "proper" solution. Yet, sometimes it is not possible to do that, and in such situations, special variables provide a viable solution for retrofitting your code with new features. I won't list here the updated code for all the heap operations that uses the new variable (you can develop it on your own as an exercise); instead, we'll just take a look at the new version of the essential heap-down and heap-up, as well as the newly defined decrease-key operation:

```
(defun heap-down (vec beg &optional (end (length vec)))
    (let ((l (hlt beg))
          (r (hrt beg)))
      (when (< l end)
        (let ((child (if (or (>= r end)
                             (> (aref vec l)
                                (aref vec r)))
                         l r)))
          (when (> (aref vec child)
                   (aref vec beg))
            (rotatef (gethash (aref vec beg) *heap-indices*)
                     (gethash (aref vec child) *heap-indices*))
            (rotatef (aref vec beg)
                     (aref vec child))
            (heap-down vec child end)))))
    vec)

(defun heap-up (vec i)
  (let ((parent (hparent i)))
    (when (> (aref vec i)
             (aref vec parent))
      (rotatef (gethash (aref vec i) *heap-indices*)
               (gethash (aref vec parent) *heap-indices*)))
      (rotatef (aref vec i)
               (aref vec parent))
    (heap-up vec parent))
  vec)

(defun heap-decrease-key (vec key decrement)
  (let ((i (gethash key *heap-indices*)))
    (unless i (error "No key ~A found in the heap: ~A" key vec))
    (remhash key *heap-indices*)
    (setf (gethash (- key decrement) *heap-indices*) i)
    (decf (aref vec i) decrement)
    (heap-up vec i)))
```

Wait a minute. This may look fine except that we forgot to account for the possibility of duplicate keys in the heap! The hash-table will not support such duplicates out of the box. What can be done to rescue our approach? A straightforward solution (which will uglify our code even more, but that's a reality of the practical implementation of nicely looking theoretical ideas that we have to accept) is to keep a stack of indices for each key in the *heap-indices*. We don't really care what item we'd like to retrieve as long as it has the proper key. Here is the updated version of our functions:

```
(defun heap-decrease-key (vec key decrement)
    (let ((i (pop (gethash key *heap-indices*))))
      (unless i (error "No key ~A found in the heap: ~A" key vec))
      (when (null (gethash key *heap-indices*))
        (remhash key *heap-indices*))
      (push i (gethash (- key decrement) *heap-indices*))
      (decf (aref vec i) decrement)
      (heap-up vec i)))
  (defun heap-up (vec i)
    (rtl:with ((i-key (aref vec i))
               (parent (hparent i))
               (parent-key (aref vec parent)))
      (when (> i-key parent-key)
        (rtl:removef i (gethash i-key *heap-indices*))
        (rtl:removef parent (gethash parent-key *heap-indices*))
        (push i (gethash parent-key *heap-indices*))
        (push parent (gethash i-key *heap-indices*))
        (rotatef (aref vec i)
                 (aref vec parent))
      (heap-up vec parent))
    vec)
  ;; and so on and so forth
```

- The heap should store not only the keys but also values: another trivial but rather tedious change that will further complicate the code as, this time, we'll have to pass around a pair or a struct instead of an index and remember to always access the key of an item instead of the item itself. Something along these lines:

```
(defstruct heap-item
      key val)

(defun heap-up (vec i)
      (rtl:with ((i-key (heap-item-key (aref vec i)))
                 (parent (hparent i))
                 (parent-key (heap-item-key (aref vec parent))))
        (when (> i-key parent-key)
          (rtl:removef i (gethash i-key *heap-indices*))
          (rtl:removef parent (gethash parent-key *heap-indices*))
          (push i (gethash parent-key *heap-indices*))
          (push parent (gethash i-key *heap-indices*))
          (rotatef (aref vec i)
                   (aref vec parent))
        (heap-up vec parent))
      vec)
```

Let's confirm the stated complexity of this implementation. First, the outer loop operates for each vertex, so it has V iterations. Each iteration has an inner loop that involves a heap-pop (O(log V)) and a heap-update (also O(log V)) for a number of vertices, plus a small number of constant-time operations. heap-pop will be invoked exactly once per vertex, so it will need O(V logV) total operations, and heap-update will be called at most once for each edge (O(E logV)). Considering that E is usually greater than V, this is how we can arrive at the final complexity estimate.

Also, it's worth noting that adding the index-bookkeeping operations to each fundamental heap reordering doesn't change its basic logarithmic execution complexity, although it increases the hidden constant factor. Hash-table accesses are O(1); and, although rtl:removef performs a linear scan, we can be sure that the number of duplicate keys over the whole execution of the algorithm will not be comparable to the number of all keys as we're constantly performing the decrease-key operation, so even when a batch of duplicates stochastically accumulate, such state will not persist for a long time.

The Fibonacci heap may be used to further improve the complexity characteristics of this algorithm. Its decrease-key operation is O(1) instead of O(log V), so we are left with just O(V logV) for heap-pops and E heap-decrease-keys. Unlike the binary heap, the Fibonacci one is not just a single tree but a set of trees. And this property is used in decrease-key: instead of popping an item up the heap and rearranging the vector in the process, a new tree rooted at this element is cut from the current one. This is not always possible in constant time as there are some invariants that might be violated, which will in turn trigger some updates to the newly created two trees. Yet, using amortized cost analysis, it is possible to prove that the average operation complexity is still O(1).

Here's a brief description of the principle behind the Fibonacci heap adapted from Wikipedia:

> *A Fibonacci heap is a collection of heaps. The trees do not have a prescribed shape and, in the extreme case, every element may be its own separate tree. This flexibility allows some operations to be executed in a lazy manner, postponing the work for later operations. For example, merging heaps is done simply by concatenating the two lists of trees, and operation decrease key sometimes cuts a node from its parent and forms a new tree. However, at some point order needs to be introduced to the heap to achieve the desired running time. In particular, every node can have at most O(log n) children and the size of a subtree rooted in a node with k children is at least F(k+2), where F(k) is the k-th Fibonacci number. This is achieved by the rule that we can cut at most one child of each non-root node. When a second child is cut, the node itself needs to be cut from its parent and becomes the root of a new tree. The number of trees is decreased in the operation delete minimum, where trees are linked together.*

Here's an example Fibonacci heap that consists of three trees:

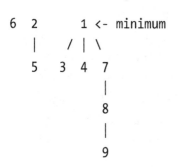

```
6   2       1 <- minimum
    |     / | \
    5   3  4  7
               |
               8
               |
               9
```

Kruskal's Algorithm

Kruskal's algorithm operates not from the point of view of vertices but of edges. At each step, it adds to the tree the current smallest edge unless it will produce a cycle. Obviously, the biggest challenge here is to efficiently find the cycle. Yet, the good news is that, like with the Prim's algorithm, we also have already access to an efficient solution for this problem—Union-Find. Isn't it great that we have already built a library of techniques that may be reused in creating more advanced algorithms? Actually, this is the goal of developing as an algorithm programmer—to be able to see a way to reduce the problem, at least partially, to some already known and proven solution.

Like Prim's algorithm, Kruskal's approach also has $O(E \ logV)$ complexity: for each vertex, it needs to find the minimum edge not forming a cycle with the already built partial MST. With Union-Find, this search requires $O(logE)$, but, as E is at most V^2, $logE$ is at most $logV^2$ that is equal to $2 \ logV$. Unlike Prim's algorithm, the partial MST built by Kruskal's algorithm isn't necessarily a tree for the already processed part of the graph.

The implementation of the algorithm, using the existing code for Union-Find, is trivial and left as an exercise to the reader.

Pathfinding

So far, we have only looked at problems with unweighted graphs. Now, we can move to weighted ones. Pathfinding in graphs is a huge topic that is crucial in many domains: maps, games, networks, and so on. Usually, the goal is to find the shortest path between two nodes in a directed weighted graph. Yet, there may be variations like finding shortest paths from a selected node to all other nodes, finding the shortest path in a maze (which may be represented as a grid graph with all edges of weight 1), and so on.

Once again, there are two classic pathfinding algorithms, each one with a certain feature that makes it interesting and notable. Dijkstra's algorithm (DA) is a classic example of greedy algorithms as its alternative name suggests—shortest path first (SPF). The A* builds upon it by adding the notion of a heuristic. Dijkstra's approach is the basis of many computer network routing algorithms, such as IS-IS and OSPF, while A* and modifications are often used in games, as well as in pathfinding on the maps.

Dijkstra's Algorithm

The idea of Dijkstra's pathfinding is to perform a limited BFS on the graph only looking at the edges that don't lead us "away" from the target. Dijkstra's approach is very similar to Prim's MST algorithm: it also uses a heap (binary or Fibonacci) to store the shortest paths from the origin to each node with their weights (lengths). At each step, it selects the minimum from the heap, expands it to the neighbor nodes, and updates the weights of the neighbors if they become smaller (the weights start from infinity).

For our SPF implementation, we'll need to use the same trick that was shown in the Union-Find implementation—extend the node structure to hold its weight and the path leading to it:

```
(defstruct (spf-node (:include node))
  (weight most-positive-fixnum)
  (path (list)))
```

Here is the main algorithm:

```
(defun spf (graph src dst)
  (rtl:with ((nodes (graph-nodes graph))
             (spf (list))
             ;; the following code should express initialize the heap
             ;; with a single node of weight 0 and all other nodes
             ;; of weight MOST-POSITIVE-FIXNUM
             ;; (instead of running a O(n*log n) HEAPIFY)
             (weights (init-weights-heap nodes src)))
    (loop
      (rtl:with (((id weight) (heap-pop weights)))
        (cond ((eql id dst)
               (let ((dst (elt nodes dst)))
                 ;; we return two values: the path and its length
                 (return (values (cons dst (spf-node-path dst))
                                 (spf-node-weight dst)))))
              ((= most-positive-fixnum weight)
               (return))) ; no path exists
```

```
(dolist (edge (rtl:? nodes id 'edges))
  (rtl:with ((cur (edge-dst edge))
             (node (elt nodes cur))
             (w (+ weight (spf-node-weight cur))))
    (when (< w (spf-node-weight node))
      (heap-decrease-key weights cur w)
      (setf (spf-node-weight node) w
            (spf-node-path node) (cons (rtl:? nodes id)
                                       (rtl:? nodes id
                                        'path)))))))))))))
```

A* Algorithm

There are many ways to improve the vanilla SPF. One of them is to move in parallel from both sides: the source and the destination.

A* algorithm (also called best-first search) improves upon Dijkstra's method by changing how the weight of the path is estimated. Initially, it was just the distance we've already traveled in the search, which is known exactly. But we don't know for sure the length of the remaining part. However, in Euclidian and similar spaces, where the triangle inequality holds (that the direct distance between two points is not greater than the distance between them through any other point), it's not an unreasonable assumption that the direct path will be shorter than the circuitous ones. This premise does not always hold as there may be obstacles, but quite often it does. So we add a second term to the weight, which is the direct distance between the current node and the destination. This simple idea underpins the A* search and allows it to perform much faster in many real-world scenarios, although its theoretical complexity is the same as for simple SPF. The exact guesstimate of the remaining distance is called the heuristic of the algorithm and should be specified for each domain separately: for maps, it is the linear distance, but there are clever ways to invent similar estimates where distances can't be calculated directly.

Overall, this algorithm is one of the simplest examples of the **heuristic** approach. Basically, the idea of heuristics lies in finding patterns that may significantly improve the performance of the algorithm for the common cases, although their efficiency can't be proven for the general case. Isn't it the same approach as, for example, hash-tables or splay trees that also don't guarantee the same optimal performance for each operation? The difference is that, although those techniques have possible local cases of suboptimality, they provide global probabilistic guarantees. For heuristic algorithms, usually, even such estimations are not available, although they may be performed for some of them. For instance, the performance of A* algorithm will suffer if there is an "obstacle" on the direct path to the destination, and it's not possible to predict, for the general case, what will be the configuration of the graph and where the obstacles will be. Yet, even in the worst case, A* will still have at least the same speed as the basic SPF.

The changes to the SPF algorithm needed for A* are the following:

- `init-weights-heap` will use the value of the heuristic instead of `most-positive-fixnum` as the initial weight. This approach will also require us to change the loop termination criteria from (= `most-positive-fixnum weight`) by adding some notion of visited nodes.

- There will be an additional term added to the weight of the node formula: (+ `weight (spf-node-weight node) (heuristic node)`).

A good comparison of the benefits A* brings over simple SPF may be shown with this picture of pathfinding on a rectangular grid without diagonal connections, where each node is labeled with its 2D coordinates. To find the path from node (0 0) to (2 2) (length 4) using Dijkstra's algorithm, we'll need to visit all of the points in the grid:

```
  0 1 2
0 + .
1 .
2
```

```
  0 1 2
0 + . .
1 . .
2 .
```

```
  0 1 2
0 + . .
1 . . .
2 . .
```

```
  0 1 2
0 + > v
1 . . v
2 . . +
```

With A*, however, we'll move straight to the point:

```
  0 1 2
0 + .
1 .
2
```

```
  0 1 2
0 + .
1 . .
2
```

```
  0 1 2
0 + .
1 . . .
2   .
```

```
  0 1 2
0 + v
1 . > v
2   . +
```

The final path, in these pictures, is selected by the rule to always open the left neighbor first.

Maximum Flow

Weighted directed graphs are often used to represent different kinds of networks. And one of the main tasks on such networks is efficient capacity planning. The main algorithm for that is maximum flow calculation. It works on so-called transport networks containing three kinds of vertices: a source, a sink, and intermediate nodes. The source has only outgoing edges, the sink has only incoming, and all the other nodes obey the balance condition: the total weights (flow) of all incoming and outgoing edges are equal. The task of determining maximum flow is to estimate the largest amount that can flow through the whole net from the source to the sink. Besides knowing the actual capacity of the network, it also allows finding the bottlenecks and edges that are not fully utilized. From this point of view, the problem is called minimum cut estimation.

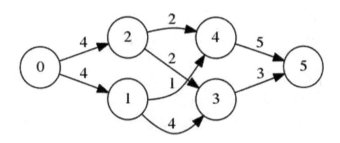

There are many approaches to solving this problem. The most direct and intuitive of them is the Ford-Fulkerson method. Once again, it is a greedy algorithm that computes the maximum flow by trying all the paths from source to sink until there is some residual capacity available. These paths are called "augmented paths" as they augment the network flow. And, to track the residual capacity, a copy of the initial weight graph called the "residual graph" is maintained. With each new path added to the total flow, its flow is subtracted from the weights of all of its edges in the residual graph. Besides—and this is the key point in the algorithm that allows it to be optimal despite its greediness—the same amount is added to the backward edges in the residual graph. The backward edges don't exist in the original graph, and they are added to the residual graph in order to let the subsequent iterations reduce the flow along some edge, but not below zero. Why may this restriction be necessary? Each graph node has a maximum input and output capacity. It is possible to saturate the output capacity by different input edges, and the optimal edge to use depends on the whole graph, so, in a single greedy step, it's not possible to determine over which edges more incoming flow should be directed. The backward edges virtually increase the output capacity by the value of the seized input capacity, thus allowing the algorithm to redistribute the flow later on if necessary.

We'll implement the Ford-Fulkerson algorithm using the matrix graph representation—first of all, to show it in action and also as it's easy to deal with backward edges in a matrix as they are already present, just with zero initial capacity. However, as this matrix will be sparse in the majority of the cases, to achieve optimal efficiency, just like with most other graph algorithms, we'll need to use a better way to store the edges: for instance, an edge list. With it, we could implement the addition of backward edges directly but lazily during the processing of each augmented path:

```
(defstruct mf-edge
  beg end capacity)

(defun max-flow (g)
  (let ((rg (copy-array g))  ; residual graph
        (rez 0))
    (loop :for path := (aug-path rg) :while path :do
      (let ((flow most-positive-fixnum))
        ;; the flow along the path is the residual capacity of the thinnest
           edge
        (dolist (edge path)
          (let ((cap (mf-edge-capacity edge)))
            (when (< (abs cap) flow)
              (setf flow (abs cap)))))
        (dolist (edge path)
          (with-slots (beg end) edge
            (decf (aref rg beg end) flow)
            (incf (aref rg end beg) flow)))
        (incf rez flow)))
    rez))

(defun aug-path (g)
  (rtl:with ((sink (1- (array-dimension g 0)))
             (visited (make-array (1+ sink) :initial-element nil)))
    (labels ((dfs (g i)
               (if (zerop (aref g i sink))
                   (dotimes (j sink)
                     (unless (or (zerop (aref g i j))
                                 (aref visited j))
                       (rtl:when-it (dfs g j)
                         (setf (aref visited j) t)
                         (return (cons (make-mf-edge
                                        :beg i :end j
```

```
                               :capacity (aref g i j))
                          rtl:it)))))
               (list (make-mf-edge
                      :beg i :end sink
                      :capacity (aref g i sink)))))))
    (dfs g 0))))
CL-USER> (max-flow #2A((0 4 4 0 0 0)
                       (0 0 0 4 2 0)
                       (0 0 0 1 2 0)
                       (0 0 0 0 0 3)
                       (0 0 0 0 0 5))))
7
```

So, as you can see from the code, to find an augmented path, we need to perform DFS on the graph from the source, sequentially examining the edges with some residual capacity to find a path to the sink.

A peculiarity of this algorithm is that there is no certainty that we'll eventually reach the state when there will be no augmented paths left. The FFA works correctly for integer and rational weights, but when they are irrational, it is not guaranteed to terminate. (The Lisp numeric tower provides the programmer with a chance to use rational-only arithmetic in place of floating-point numbers, therefore ensuring algorithm termination.) When the capacities are integers, the runtime of Ford-Fulkerson is bounded by $O(E\ f)$ where f is the maximum flow in the graph. This is because each augmented path can be found in $O(E)$ time, and it increases the flow by an integer amount of at least 1. A variation of the Ford-Fulkerson algorithm with guaranteed termination and a runtime independent of the maximum flow value is the Edmonds-Karp algorithm, which runs in $O(V\ E^2)$.

Graphs in Action: PageRank

Another important set of problems from the field of network analysis is determining "centers of influence," densely and sparsely populated parts, and "cliques." PageRank is the well-known algorithm for ranking the nodes in terms of influence (i.e., the number and weight of incoming connections they have), which was the secret sauce behind Google's initial success as a search engine. It will be the last of the graph algorithms we'll discuss in this chapter, so many more will remain untouched. We'll be returning to some of them in the following chapters, and you'll be seeing them in many problems once you develop an eye for spotting the graphs hidden in many domains.

The PageRank algorithm outputs a probability distribution of the likelihood that a person randomly clicking links will arrive at any particular page. This distribution ranks the relative importance of all pages. The probability is expressed as a numeric value between 0 and 1, but Google used to multiply it by 10 and round to the greater integer, so PR of 10 corresponded to the probability of 0.9 and more and PR of 1 to the interval from 0 to 0.1. In the context of PageRank, all web pages are the nodes in the so-called web graph, and the links between them are the edges, originally, weighted equally.

PageRank is an iterative algorithm that may be considered an instance of the very popular, in unsupervised optimization and machine learning, **expectation-maximization** (EM) approach. The general idea of EM is to randomly initialize the quantities that we want to estimate and then iteratively recalculate each quantity, using the information from the neighbors, to "move" it closer to the value that ensures optimality of the target function. Epochs (an iteration that spans the whole dataset using each node at most once) of such recalculation should continue until either the whole epoch doesn't produce a significant change of the loss function we're optimizing, that is, we have reached the stationary point, or a satisfactory number of iterations was performed. Sometimes a stationary point either can't be reached or will take too long to reach, but, according to Pareto's principle, 20% of effort might have brought us 80% to the goal.

In each epoch, we recalculate the PageRank of all nodes by transferring weights from a node equally to all of its neighbors. The neighbors with more inbound connections will thus receive more weight. However, the PageRank concept adds a condition that an imaginary surfer who is randomly clicking links will eventually stop clicking. The probability that the transfer will continue is called a damping factor d. Various studies have tested different damping factors, but it is generally assumed that the damping factor for the web graph will be set around 0.85. The damping factor is subtracted from 1 (and in some variations of the algorithm, the result is divided by the number of documents in the collection), and this term is then added to the product of the damping factor and the sum of the incoming PageRank scores. The damping factor is subtracted from 1 (and in some variations of the algorithm, the result is divided by the number of documents (N) in the collection), and this term is then added to the product of the damping factor and the sum of the incoming PageRank scores. So the PageRank of a page is mostly derived from the PageRanks of other pages. The damping factor adjusts the derived value downward.

Implementation

Actually, PageRank can be computed both iteratively and algebraically. In algebraic form, each PageRank iteration may be expressed simply as

```
(setf pr (+ (* d (mat* g pr))
            (/ (- 1 d) n)))
```

where g is the graph incidence matrix and `pr` is the vector of PageRank for each node.

However, the definitive property of PageRank is that it is estimated for huge graphs. That is, directly representing them as matrices isn't possible, nor is performing the matrix operations on them. The iterative algorithm gives more control, as well as distribution of the computation, so it is usually preferred in practice not only for PageRank but also for most other optimization techniques. So PageRank should be viewed primarily as a distributed algorithm. The need to implement it on a large cluster triggered the development by Google of the influential MapReduce distributed computation framework.

Here is a simplified PageRank implementation of the iterative method:

```
(defun pagerank (g &key (d 0.85) (repeat 100))
  (rtl:with ((n (length (nodes g)))
             (pr (make-array n :initial-element (/ 1 n))))
    (loop :repeat repeat :do
      (let ((pr2 (map 'vector (lambda (x) (- 1 (/ d n)))
                      pr)))
        (dokv (i node nodes)
          (let ((p (aref pr i))
                (m (length (node-children node))))
            (rtl:dokv (j child (node-children node))
              (incf (aref pr2 j) (* d (/ p m))))))
        (setf pr pr2)))
    pr))
```

We use the same graph representation as previously and perform the update "backward": not by gathering all incoming edges, which will require us to add another layer of data that is both not necessary and hard to maintain, but transferring the PR value over outgoing edges one by one. Such an approach also makes the computation trivial to distribute as we can split the whole graph into arbitrary sets of nodes and the computation for each set can be performed in parallel: we'll just need to maintain a local copy of the pr2 vector and merge it at the end of each iteration by simple summation. This method naturally fits the MapReduce framework that was invented at Google to perform PageRank and other similar calculations distributed over thousands of machines. The inner node loop constitutes the essence of the map step, while the reduce step consists in merging of the vectors obtained from each mapper. To see that, let's refactor the preceding code:

```
;; this function will be executed by mapper workers
(defun pr1 (node n p &key (d 0.85))
  (let ((pr (make-array n :initial-element 0))
        (m (hash-table-count (node-children node))))
    (rtl:dokv (j child (node-children node))
      (setf (aref pr j) (* d (/ p m))))
    pr))

(defun pagerank-mr (g &key (d 0.85) (repeat 100))
  (rtl:with ((n (length (nodes g)))
             (pr (make-array n :initial-element (/ 1 n))))
    (loop :repeat repeat :do
      (setf pr (map 'vector (lambda (x)
                              (- 1 (/ d n)))
                    (reduce 'vec+ (map 'vector (lambda (node p)
                                                 (pr1 node n p :d d))
                                       (nodes g)
                                       pr)))))
    pr))
```

Here, we have used the standard Lisp map and reduce functions, but a MapReduce framework will provide replacement functions which, behind the scenes, will orchestrate parallel execution of the provided code. We will talk a bit more about MapReduce and see such framework in Chapter 15 of this book.

One more thing to note is that the latter approach differs from the original version in that each mapper operates independently on an isolated version of the pr vector and thus the execution of PageRank on the subsequent nodes during a single iteration will see an older input value p. However, since the algorithm is stochastic and the order of calculations is not deterministic, this is acceptable: it may impact only the speed of convergence (and hence the number of iterations needed) but not the final result.

Takeaways

1. The more we progress into advanced topics of this book, the more apparent will be the tendency to reuse the approaches, tools, and technologies we have developed previously. Graph algorithms are good demonstrations of new features and qualities that can be obtained by a smart combination and reuse of existing data structures.

2. Many graph algorithms are greedy, which means that they use the locally optimal solution trying to arrive at a global one. This phenomenon is conditioned by the structure—or rather lack of structure—of graphs that don't have a specific hierarchy to guide the optimal solution. The greediness, however, shouldn't mean suboptimality. In many greedy algorithms, like FFA, there is a way to play back the wrong solution. Others provide a way to trade off execution speed and optimality. A good example of the latter approach is beam search that has a configurable beam size parameter that allows the programmer to choose speed or optimality of the end result.

3. In A*, we had a first glimpse of heuristic algorithms—an area that may be quite appealing to many programmers who are used to solving the problem primarily optimizing for its main scenarios. This approach may lack some mathematical rigor, but it also has its place; and we'll see other heuristic algorithms in the following chapters that are, like A*, the best practical solution in their domains, for instance, the Monte Carlo tree search (MCTS).

4. Another thing that becomes more apparent in the progress of this book is how small the percentage of the domain we can cover in detail in each chapter. This is true for graphs: we have just scratched the surface and outlined the main approaches to handling them. We'll see more of graph-related stuff in the

following chapters, as well. Graph algorithms may be quite useful in a great variety of areas that do not necessarily have a direct formulation as graph problems (like maps or networks do), and so developing an intuition to recognize the hidden graph structure may help the programmer reuse the existing elegant techniques instead of having to deal with their own cumbersome ad hoc solutions.

CHAPTER 11

Strings

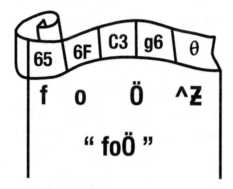

It may not be immediately obvious why the whole chapter is dedicated to strings. Aren't they just glorified arrays? There are several answers to these challenges:

- Indeed, strings are not just arrays or, rather, not only arrays: in different contexts, other representations, such as trees or complex combinations of arrays, may be used. And, besides, there are additional properties that are important for strings even when they are represented as arrays.

- There are a lot of string-specific algorithms that deserve their own chapter.

- Finally, strings play a significant role in almost every program, so they have specific handling: in the OS, the standard library, and even, sometimes, your application framework.

In the base case, a string is, indeed, an array. As we already know, this array may either store its length or be a 0-terminated security catastrophe, like in C (see buffer overflow). So, to iterate, strings should store their length. **Netstrings** are a notable take

© Vsevolod Domkin 2021
V. Domkin, *Programming Algorithms in Lisp*, https://doi.org/10.1007/978-1-4842-6428-7_11

on the idea of the length-aware strings. It's a simple external format that serializes a string as a tuple of length and contents, separated by a colon and ending with a comma: 3:foo, is the netstring for the string foo.

More generally, a string is a sequence of characters. The characters themselves may be single bytes as well as fixed or variable-length byte sequences. The latter character encoding poses a challenging question of what to prefer, correctness or speed. With variable-length Unicode code points, the simplest and fastest string variant, a byte array, breaks, for it will incorrectly report its length (in bytes, not in characters) and fail to retrieve the character by index. Different language ecosystems address this issue differently, and the majority is, unfortunately, broken in one aspect or another. Overall, two approaches are possible:

- The first one is to use a fixed-length representation and pad shorter characters to full length. Generally, such representation will be 32-bit UTF-32 resulting in up to 75% storage space waste for the most common 1-byte ASCII characters.

- The alternative approach lies in utilizing a more advanced data structure. The naive variant is a list, which implies an unacceptable slowdown of character access operation to $O(n)$. A more balanced approach would combine minimal additional space requirements with acceptable speed. One of the solutions may be to utilize the classic **bitmap** trick: use a bit array indicating, for each byte, whether it's the start of a character (only a 12% overhead). Determining the character position with a bitmap may be performed in a small number of steps with the help of an infamous, in close circles, operation—**population count** a.k.a. **Hamming weight**. This hardware instruction calculates the number of 1-bits in an integer and is accessible via logcount Lisp standard library routine. Behind the scenes, it is also called for bit arrays if you invoke count 1 on them. At least this is the case for SBCL:

```
CL-USER> (disassemble (lambda (x)
                        (declare (type (simple-array bit) x))
                        (count 1 x)))
```

```
; disassembly for (LAMBDA (X))
; Size: 267 bytes. Origin: #x100FC9FD1A
...
; DA2:        F3480FB8FA        POPCNT RDI, RDX
```

The indexing function implementation may be quite tricky, but the general idea is to try to jump ahead n characters and calculate the popcount of the substring from the previous position to the current that will tell us the number of characters we have skipped. For the base case of a 1-byte string, we will get exactly where we wanted in just one jump and one popcount. However, if there were multibyte characters in the string, the first jump would have skipped less than n characters. If the difference is sufficiently small (say, below 10), we can just perform a quick linear scan of the remainder and find the position of the desired character. If it's larger than n/2, we can jump ahead n characters again (this will repeat at most three times as the maximum byte length of a character is 4), and if it's below n/2, we can jump n/2 characters. And if we overshoot, we can reverse the direction of the next jump or search. You can see where it's heading: if at each step (or, at least, at each fourth step) we are constantly half dividing our numbers, this means O(log n) complexity. That's the worst performance for this function we can get, and it will very efficiently handle the cases when the character length doesn't vary: be it 1 byte—just two operations—or 4 bytes—eight ops.

Here is the prototype of the char-index operation implemented according to the described algorithm (without the implementation of the mb-linear-char-index that performs the final linear scan):

```
(defstruct (mb-string (:conc-name mbs-))
  bytes
  bitmap)

(defparameter *mb-threshold* 10)

(defun mb-char-index (string i)
  (let ((off 0))
    (loop
      (rtl:with ((cnt (count 1 (mbs-bitmap string)
                            :start off :end (+ off i))))
               (diff (- i cnt)))
        (cond
```

```
((= cnt i)
 (return (+ off i)))
((< diff *mb-threshold*)
 (return (mb-linear-char-index string diff off)))
((< cnt (floor i 2))
 (incf off i)
 (decf i cnt))
(t
 (incf off (floor i 2))
 (decf i cnt)))))))
```

The `length` of such a string may be calculated by performing the popcount on the whole bitmap:

```
(defun mb-length (string)
  (count 1 (mbs-bitmap string)))
```

It's also worth taking into account that there exists a set of rules assembled under the umbrella of the Unicode collation algorithm that specifies how to order strings containing Unicode code points.

Basic String-Related Optimizations

Strings are often subject to subsequencing, so an efficient implementation may use structure sharing. As we remember, in Lisp, this is accessible via the displaced array mechanism (and a convenience RUTILS function `slice` that we have already used in the preceding code). Yet, structure sharing should be utilized with care as it opens a possibility for action-at-a-distance bugs if the derived string is modified, which results in parallel modification of the original. However, strings are rarely modified in-place, so, even in its basic form (without mandatory immutability), the approach works well. Moreover, some programming language environments make strings immutable by default. In such cases, to perform on-the-fly string modification (or, rather, creation), such patterns as the Java `StringBuilder` are used, which create the string from parts by first accumulating them in a list and then, when necessary, concatenating the list's contents into a single final string. An alternative approach is string formatting (the `format` function in Lisp) that is a higher-level interface, which still needs to utilize some underlying mutation/combination mechanism.

Another important string-related technology is **interning**. It is a space-saving measure to avoid duplicating the same strings over and over again, which operates by putting a string in a table and using its index afterward. This approach also enables efficient equality comparison. Interning is performed by the compiler implicitly for all constant strings (in the special segment of the program's memory called "string table"/`strtab`) and also may be used explicitly. In Lisp, there's a standard function `intern` that performs a similar action although in a more dynamic way. Lisp symbols use interned strings as their names. Another variant of interning is string pooling. The difference is that interning uses a global string table, while the pools may be local.

Strings in the Editor

Now, let's consider situations in which representing strings as arrays doesn't work. The primary one is in the editor, that is, when constant random modification is the norm. There's another not so obvious requirement related to editing: handle potentially arbitrary long strings that still need to be dynamically modified. Have you tried opening a hundred-megabyte text document in your favorite editor? You'd better not unless you're a vim user. :) Finally, an additional limitation of handling the strings in the editor is posed when we allow concurrent modification. This we'll discuss in Chapter 15.

So why does an array as a string back end not work well in the editor? Because of content relocation required by all edit operations. $O(n)$ editing is, obviously, not acceptable. What to do? There are several more advanced approaches:

1. The simplest change will be, once again, to use an array of arrays, for example, for each line. This will not change the general complexity of $O(n)$ but, at least, will reduce n significantly. The issue is that, still, it will depend on the length of the line, so, for a not so rare degraded case, when there are few or no linebreaks, the performance will seriously deteriorate. And, moreover, having observable performance differences between editing different paragraphs of the text is not user-friendly at all.

2. A more advanced approach would be to use trees, reducing access time to $O(\log n)$. There are many different kinds of trees, and, in fact, only a few may work as efficient string representations. Among them a popular data structure, for representing strings, is a **rope**. It's a binary tree where each leaf holds a substring and its

length and each intermediate node further holds the sum of the lengths of all the leaves in its left subtree. It's a more-or-less classic application of binary trees to a storage problem, so we won't spend more time on it here. Suffice to say that it has the expected binary tree performance of $O(\log n)$ for all operations, provided that we keep it balanced. It's an OK alternative to a simple array, but, for such a specialized problem, we can do better with a custom solution.

3. And the custom solution is to return to arrays. There's one clever way to use them that works very well for dynamic strings. It is called a **gap buffer**. This structure is an array (buffer) with a gap in the middle. That is, let's imagine that we have a text of n characters. The gap buffer will have a length of n + k where k is the gap size—some value, derived from practice, that may fluctuate in the process of string modification. You can recognize this gap as the position of the cursor in the text. Insertion operation in the editor is performed exactly at this place, so it's $O(1)$. Just afterward, the gap will shrink by one character, so we'll have to resize the array, at some point, if there are too many insertions and the gap shrinks below some minimum size (maybe, below 1). The deletion operation will act exactly the opposite by growing the gap at one of the sides. The gap buffer is an approach that is especially suited for normal editing—a process that has its own pace. It also allows the system to represent multiple cursors by maintaining several gaps. Also, it may be a good idea to represent each paragraph as a gap buffer and use an array of them for the whole text. The gap buffer is a special case of the zipper pattern that we'll discuss in Chapter 15.

Substring Search

One of the most common string operations is substring search. For ordinary sequences, we, usually, search for a single element, but strings, on the contrary, more often need subsequence search, which is more complex. A naive approach will start by looking for the first character and then trying to match the next character and the next, until either something ends or there's a mismatch. Unlike with hash-tables, the Lisp standard library has good support for string processing, including such operations as search and mismatch that compare two strings from a chosen side and return the position at which they start to diverge (both of these operations, actually, operate on any sequence).

If we were to implement our own string-specific search, the most basic version would, probably, look like this:

```
(defun naive-match (pat str)
  (dotimes (i (- (1+ (length str)) (length pat)))
    (when (= (mismatch pat (rtl:slice str i))
             (length pat))
      (return-from naive-match i))))
```

If the strings had been random, the probability that we are correctly matching each subsequent character would have dropped to 0 very fast. Even if we consider just the English alphabet, the probability of the first character being the same in two random strings is 1/26, the first and second 1/676, and so on. And if we assume that the whole charset may be used, we'll have to substitute 26 with 256 or a greater value. So, in theory, such naive approach has almost $O(n)$ complexity, where n is the length of the string. Yet, the worst case has $O(n * m)$, where m is the length of the pattern. Why? If we try to match a pattern a..ab against a string aa.....ab, at each position, we'll have to check the whole pattern until the last character mismatches. This may seem like an artificial example, and, indeed, it rarely occurs. But, still, real-world strings are not so random and are much closer to the uniform corner case than to the random one. So researchers have come up with a number of ways to improve subsequence matching performance. These include the four well-known inventor-glorifying substring search algorithms: Knuth-Morris-Pratt (KMP), Boyer-Moore (BM), Rabin-Karp (RK), and Aho-Corasick (AC). Let's discuss each one of them and try to determine their interesting properties.

Knuth-Morris-Pratt (KMP)

Knuth-Morris-Pratt is the most basic of these algorithms. Prior to performing the search, it examines the pattern to find repeated subsequences in it and creates a table containing, for each character of the pattern, the length of the prefix of the pattern that can be skipped if we have reached this character and failed the search at it. This table is also called the "failure function." The number in the table is calculated as the length of the proper suffix[1] of the pattern substring ending before the current character that matches the start of the pattern.

I'll repeat here the example provided in Wikipedia that explains the details of the table-building algorithm, as it's somewhat tricky.

Let's build the table for the pattern abdcabd. We set the table entry for the first char a to -1. To find the entry for b, we must discover a proper suffix of a which is also a prefix of the pattern. But there are no proper suffixes of a, so we set this entry to 0. To find the entry with index 2, we see that the substring ab has a proper suffix b. However, b is not a prefix of the pattern. Therefore, we also set this entry to 0.

For the next entry, we first check the proper suffix of length 1, and it fails like in the previous case. Should we also check longer suffixes? No. We can formulate a shortcut rule: at each stage, we need to consider checking suffixes of a given size (1+ n) only if a valid suffix of size n was found at the previous stage and should not bother checking longer lengths. So we set the table entry for c to 0 also.

We pass to the subsequent character a. The same logic shows that the longest substring we need to consider has length 1, and as in the previous case, it fails since d is not a prefix. But instead of setting the table entry to 0, we can do better by noting that a is also the first character of the pattern and also that the corresponding character of the string can't be a (as we're calculating for the mismatch case). Thus, there is no point in trying to match the pattern for this character again—we should begin one character ahead. This means that we may shift the pattern by match length plus one character, so we set the table entry to -1.

Considering now the next character b: though by inspection the longest substring would appear to be a, we still set the table entry to 0. The reasoning is similar to the previous case. b itself extends the prefix match begun with a, and we can assume that the corresponding character in the string is not b. So backtracking before it is pointless, but that character may still be a; hence, we set the entry not to -1, but to 0, which means shifting the pattern by one character to the left and trying to match again.

Finally, for the last character d, the rule of the proper suffix matching the prefix applies, so we set the table entry to 2.

---

[1]A proper suffix is a suffix that is at least one character shorter than the string itself. For example, in the string abc, the proper suffices are bc and c.

The resulting table is

a	b	c	d	a	b	d
-1	0	0	0	-1	0	2

Here's the implementation of the table-building routine:

```
(defun kmp-table (pat)
  (let ((rez (make-array (length pat)))
        (i 0))  ; prefix length
    (setf (aref rez 0) -1)
    (loop :for j :from 1 :below (length pat) :do
      (if (char= (char pat i) (char pat j))
          (setf (aref rez j) (aref rez i))
          (progn ;; we have to use parallel version of setf here
                 (psetf (aref rez j) i
                        i (aref rez i))
                 (loop :while (and (>= i 0)
                                   (not (char= (char pat i)
                                               (char pat j))))
                       :do (setf i (aref rez i)))))
      (incf i))
    rez))
```

It can be proven that it runs in O(m). We won't show it here, so coming up with proper calculations is left as an exercise to the reader.

Now, the question is: How shall we use this table? Let's look at the code:

```
(defun kmp-match (pat str)
  (let ((s 0)
        (p 0)
        (ff (kmp-table pat)))
    (loop :while (< s (length str)) :do
      (if (char= (char pat p) (char str s))
          ;; if the current chars match
          (if (= (1+ p) (length pat))
              ;; if we reached the end of the pattern - success
              (return (- s p))
```

```
    ;; otherwise, match the subsequent chars
    (setf p (1+ p)
          s (1+ s)))
  ;; if the characters don't match
  (if (= -1 (aref ff p))
      ;; shift the pattern for the whole length
      (setf p 0
            ;; and skip to the next char in the string
            s (1+ s))
      ;; try matching the current char again,
      ;; shifting the pattern to align the prefix
      ;; with the already matched part
      (setf p (aref ff p)))))))
```

As we see, the index in the string (s) is incremented at each iteration except when the entry in the table is positive. In the latter case, we may examine the same character more than once but not more than we have advanced in the pattern. And the advancement in the pattern meant the same advancement in the string (as the match is required for the advancement). In other words, we can backtrack not more than n times over the whole algorithm runtime, so the worst-case number of operations in kmp-search is 2n, while the best-case is just n. Thus, the total complexity is $O(n + m)$.

And what will happen in our aa..ab example? The failure function for it will look like the following: -1 -1 -1 -1 (- m 2). Once we reach the first mismatch, we'll need to backtrack by one character; perform the comparison, which will mismatch; advance by one character (to b); mismatch again; again backtrack by one character; and so on until the end of the string. So this case will have almost the abovementioned 2n runtime.

To conclude, the optimization of KMP lies in excluding unnecessary repetition of the same operations by memoizing the results of partial computations—both in table-building and matching parts. The next chapter of the book will be almost exclusively dedicated to studying this approach in algorithm design.

Boyer-Moore (BM)

Boyer-Moore algorithm is conceptually similar to KMP, but it matches from the end of the pattern. It also builds a table, or rather three tables, but using a different set of rules, which also involve the characters in the string we search. More precisely, there are two basic rules instead of one for KMP. Besides, there's another rule, called the Galil rule, that is required to ensure the linear complexity of the algorithm. Overall, BM is pretty complex in the implementation details and also requires more preprocessing than KMP, so its utility outweighs these factors only when the search is repeated multiple times for the same pattern.

Overall, BM may be faster with normal text (and the longer the pattern, the faster), while KMP will work the best with strings that have a short alphabet (like DNA). However, I would choose KMP as the default due to its relative simplicity and much better space utilization.

Rabin-Karp (RK)

Now, let's talk about alternative approaches that rely on techniques other than pattern preprocessing. They are usually used to find matches of multiple patterns in one go as, for the base case, their performance will be worse than that of the previous algorithms.

Rabin-Karp algorithm uses an idea of the **rolling hash**. It is a hash-function that can be calculated incrementally. The RK hash is calculated for each substring of the length of the pattern. If we were to calculate a normal hash-function like FNV-1, we'd need to use each character for the calculation—resulting in $O(n * m)$ complexity of the whole procedure. The rolling hash is different as it requires, at each step of the algorithm, to perform just two operations: as the "sliding window" moves over the string, subtract the part of the hash corresponding to the character that is no longer part of the substring and add the new value for the character that has just become the part of the substring.

Here is the skeleton of the RK algorithm:

```
(defun rk-match (pat str)
  (let ((len (length pat))
        (phash (rk-hash pat)))
    (loop :for i :from len :to (length str)
          :for beg := (- i len)
          :for shash := (rk-hash (rtl:slice str 0 len))
            :then (rk-rehash len shash
                             (char str beg) (char str i))
          :when (and (= phash shash)
                     (string= pat (rtl:slice str beg len)))
          :collect beg)))
```

A trivial `rk-hash` function would be just

```
(defun rk-hash (str)
  (loop :for ch :across str :sum (char-code ch)))
```

But it is, obviously, not a good hash-function as it doesn't ensure the equal distribution of hashes. Still, in this case, we need a reversible hash-function. Usually, such hashes add position information into the mix. An original hash-function for the RK algorithm is the Rabin fingerprint that uses random irreducible polynomials over Galois fields of order 2. The mathematical background needed to explain it is somewhat beyond the scope of this book. However, there are simpler alternatives such as the following:

```
(defun rk-hash (str)
  (assert (> (length str) 0))
  (let ((rez (char-code (char str 0))))
    (loop :for ch :across (rtl:slice str 1) :do
      (setf rez (+ (rem (* rez 256) 101)
                   (char-code ch))))
    (rem rez 101)))
```

Its basic idea is to treat the partial values of the hash as the coefficients of some polynomial. The implementation of `rk-rehash` for this function will look like this:

```
(defun rk-rehash (hash len ch1 ch2)
  (rem (+ (* (+ hash 101
               (- (rem (* (char-code ch1)
                          (expt 256 (1- len)))
                       101)))
            256)
          (char-code ch2))
       101))
```

Our `rk-match` could be used to find many matches of a single pattern. To adapt it for operating on multiple patterns at once, we'll just need to pre-calculate the hashes for all patterns and look up the current rk-hash value in this set. Additional optimization of this lookup may be performed with the help of a Bloom filter—a stochastic data structure we'll discuss in more detail later.

Finally, it's worth noting that there are other similar approaches to the rolling hash concept that trade some of the uniqueness properties of the hash-function for the ability to produce hashes incrementally or have similar hashes for similar sequences. For instance, the **perceptual hash** (phash) is used to find near-match images.

Aho-Corasick (AC)

Aho-Corasick is another algorithm that allows matching multiple strings at once. The preprocessing step of the algorithm constructs a **finite-state machine** (FSM) that resembles a trie with additional links between the various internal nodes. The FSM is a graph data structure that encodes possible states of the system and actions needed to transfer it from one state to the other.

The AC FSM is constructed in the following manner:

1. Build a trie of all the words in the set of search patterns (the search dictionary). This trie represents the possible flows of the program when there's a successful character match at the current position. Add a loop edge for the root node.

2. Add backlinks transforming the trie into a graph. The backlinks are used when a failed match occurs. These backlinks are pointing either to the root of the trie or, if there are some prefixes that correspond to the part of the currently matched path, to the end of the longest prefix. The longest prefix is found using BFS of the trie. This approach is, basically, the same idea used in KMP and BM to avoid reexamining the already matched parts. So backlinks to the previous parts of the same word are also possible. Here is the example FSM for the search dictionary `'("the" "this" "that" "it" "his")`:

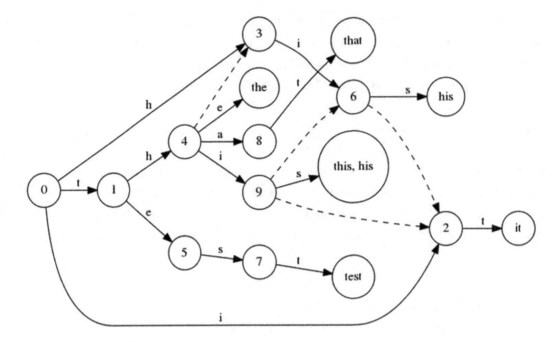

Basically, it's just a trie with some backlinks to account for already processed prefixes. One more detail missing for this graph to be a complete FSM is an implicit backlink from all nodes without an explicit backlink that don't have backlinks to the root node.

The main loop of the algorithm is rather straightforward: examine each character and then

- Either follow one of the transitions (direct edge) if the character of the edge matches.

- Or follow the backlink if it exists.

- Or reset the FSM state—go to root.

- If the transition leads us to a terminal node, record the match(es) and return to root as well.

As we see from the description, the complexity of the main loop is linear in the length of the string: at most, two matches are performed, for each character. The FSM construction is also linear in the total length of all the words in the search dictionary.

The algorithm is often used in antivirus software to perform an efficient search for code signatures against a database of known viruses. It also formed the basis of the original Unix command fgrep. And, from my point of view, it's the simplest to understand yet pretty powerful and versatile substring search algorithm that may be a default choice if you ever have to implement one yourself.

Regular Expressions

Searching is, probably, the most important advanced string operation. Besides, it is not limited to mere substring search—matching of more complex patterns is even in higher demand. These patterns, which are called "regular expressions" or, simply, **regex**es, may include optional characters, repetition, alternatives, backreferences, and so on. Regexes play an important role in the history of the Unix command line, being the principal technology of the infamous grep utility and then the cornerstone of Perl. All modern programming languages support them either in the standard library or, as Lisp, with high-quality third-party add-ons (cl-ppcre).

One of my favorite programming books, *Beautiful Code*, has a chapter on implementing simple regex matching from Brian Kernighan with code written by Rob Pike. It shows how easy it is to perform basic matching of the following patterns:

```
c    matches any literal character c
.    matches any single character
^    matches the beginning of the input string
$    matches the end of the input string
*    matches zero or more occurrences of the previous character
```

In the following, the C code from the book is translated into an equivalent Lisp version:

```lisp
(defun match (regex text)
  "Search for REGEX anywhere in TEXT."
  (if (rtl:starts-with "^" regex)
      (match-here (rtl:slice regex 1) text)
      (dotimes (i (length text))
        (when (match-here regex (rtl:slice text i))
          (return t)))))
```

```
(defun match-here (regex text)
  "Search for REGEX at beginning of TEXT."
  (cond ((= 0 (length regex))
           t)
          ((and (> (length regex) 1)
                (char= #\* (char regex 1)))
           (match-star (char regex 1) (rtl:slice regex 2) text))
          ((string= "$" regex)
           (= 0 (length text)))
          ((and (> (length text) 0)
                (member (char text 0) (list #\. (char text 0)))
           (match-here (rtl:slice regex 1) (rtl:slice text 1))))))

(defun match-star (c regex text)
  "Search for C*REGEX at beginning of TEXT."
  (loop
    (when (match-here regex text) (return t))
    (setf text (rtl:slice text 1))
    (unless (and (> (length text) 0)
                 (member c (list #\. (char text 0))))
      (return))))
```

This is a greedy linear algorithm. However, modern regexes are much more advanced than this naive version. They include such features as register groups (to record the spans of text that match a particular subpattern), backreferences, non-greedy repetition, and so on and so forth. Implementing those will require changing the simple linear algorithm to a backtracking one. And incorporating all of them would quickly transform the preceding code into a horrible unmaintainable mess: not even due to the number of cases that have to be supported but due to the need of accounting for the complex interdependencies between them.

And, what's worse, soon there will arise a need to resort to backtracking. Yet, a backtracking approach has a critical performance flaw: potential exponential runtime for certain input patterns. For instance, the Perl regex engine (PCRE) requires over 60 seconds to match a 30-character string aa..a against the pattern a? {15}a{15} (on standard hardware), while the alternative approach, which we'll discuss next, requires just 20 microseconds—a million times faster. And it handles a 100-character string of a similar kind in under 200 microseconds, while Perl would require over 1015 years.[2]

This issue is quite severe and has even prompted Google to release their own regex library with strict linear performance guarantees—RE2. The goal of the library is not to be faster than all other engines under all circumstances. Although RE2 guarantees linear-time performance, the linear-time constant varies depending on the overhead entailed by its way of handling of the regular expression. In a sense, RE2 behaves pessimistically, whereas backtracking engines behave optimistically, so it can be outperformed in various situations. Also, its goal is not to implement all of the features offered by PCRE and other engines. As a matter of principle, RE2 does not support constructs for which only backtracking solutions are known to exist. Thus, backreferences and look-around assertions are not supported.

The preceding figures are taken from a seminal article by Russ Cox. He goes on to add:

> *Historically, regular expressions are one of computer science's shining examples of how using good theory leads to good programs. They were originally developed by theorists as a simple computational model, but Ken Thompson introduced them to programmers in his implementation of the text editor QED for CTSS. Dennis Ritchie followed suit in his own implementation of QED, for GE-TSS. Thompson and Ritchie would go on to create Unix, and they brought regular expressions with them. By the late 1970s, regular expressions were a key feature of the Unix landscape, in tools such as ed, sed, grep, egrep, awk, and lex. Today, regular expressions have also become a shining example of how ignoring good theory leads to bad programs. The regular expression implementations used by today's popular tools are significantly slower than the ones used in many of those thirty-year-old Unix tools.*

The linear-time approach to regex matching relies on a similar technique to the one in the Aho-Corasick algorithm—the FSM. Actually, if by regular expressions we mean a set of languages that abide by the rules of the regular grammars in the Chomsky hierarchy of languages, the FSM is their exact theoretical computation model. Here is how an FSM for a simple regex a*b$ might look like:

---

[2]Perl is only the most conspicuous example of a large number of popular programs that use the same algorithm; the same applies to Python or PHP or Ruby or many other languages.

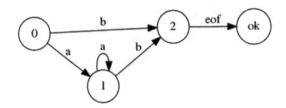

Such FSM is called an **NFA** (Nondeterministic Finite Automaton) as some states have more than one alternative successor. Another type of automata are **DFAs** (Deterministic Finite Automata) that permit transitions to at most one state for each state. The method to transform the regex into an NFA is called Thompson's construction. And an NFA can be made into a DFA by the powerset construction and then be minimized to get an optimal automaton. DFAs are more efficient to execute than NFAs, because DFAs are only ever in one state at a time: they never have a choice of multiple next states. But the construction takes additional time. Anyway, both NFAs and DFAs guarantee linear-time execution.

Thompson's algorithm builds the NFA up from partial NFAs for each subexpression, with a different construction for each operator. The partial NFAs have no matching states: instead, they have one or more dangling arrows, pointing to nothing. The construction process will finish by connecting these arrows to a matching state:

- The NFA for matching a single character e is a single node with a slot for an incoming arrow and a pending outgoing arrow labeled with e.

- The NFA for the concatenation e1e2 connects the outgoing arrow of the e1 machine to the incoming arrow of the e2 machine.

- The NFA for the alternation e1|e2 adds a new start state with a choice of either the e1 machine or the e2 machine.

- The NFA for e? alternates the e machine with an empty path.

- The NFA for e* uses the same alternation but loops a matching e machine back to the start.

- The NFA for e+ also creates a loop, but one that requires passing through e at least once.

Counting the states in the preceding constructions, we can see that this technique creates exactly one state per character or metacharacter in the regular expression. The only exception is the construct c{n} or c{n,m} which requires to duplicate the single character automaton n or m times, respectively, but it is still a constant number. Therefore, the number of states in the final NFA is at most equal to the length of the original regular expression plus some constant.

Implementation of Thompson's Construction

The core of the algorithm could be implemented very transparently with the help of the Lisp generic functions. However, to enable their application, we'd first need to transform the raw expression into a sexp (tree-based) form. Such representation is supported, for example, in the CL-PPCRE library:

```
PPCRE> (parse-string "ab[0-9]+c$")
(:SEQUENCE "ab"
           (:GREEDY-REPETITION 1 NIL (:RANGE #\0 #\9))
           #\c
           :END-ANCHOR)
```

Parsing is a whole separate topic that will be discussed next. But once we have performed it, we gain a possibility to straightforwardly implement Thompson's construction by traversing the parse tree and emitting, for each state, the corresponding part of the automaton. The Lisp generic functions are a great tool for implementing such transformation as they allow to define methods that are selected based on either the type or the identity of the arguments. And those methods can be added independently, so the implementation is clear and extensible. We will define two generic functions: one to emit the automaton fragment (th-part) and another to help in transition selection (th-match).

First, let's define the state node of the FSM. We will use a linked graph representation for the automaton. So a variable for the FSM in the code will point to its start node, and it will, in turn, reference the other nodes. There will also be a special node that will be responsible for recording the matches (*matched-state*):

```
(defstruct th-state
  transitions)

(defparameter *initial-state* nil)
(defparameter *matched-state* (make-th-state))
```

```
(defun th-state (&rest transitions)
  "A small convenience function to construct TH-STATE structs."
  (make-th-state :transitions (loop :for (cond state) :on transitions :by 'cddr
                                    :collect (rtl:pair cond state)))))
```

And now, we can define the generic function that will emit the nodes:

```
(define-condition check-start-anchor () ())

(defgeneric th-part (next-state kind &rest args)
  (:documentation
   "Emit the TH-STATE structure of a certain KIND
    (which may be a keyword or a raw string)
    using the other ARGS and pointing to NEXT-STATE struct.")
  (:method (next-state (kind (eql :sequence)) &rest args)
    (apply 'th-part (if (rest args)
                        (apply 'th-part :sequence (rest args))
                        next-state)
           (first args)))
  (:method (next-state (kind (eql :greedy-repetition)) &rest args)
    ;; this method can handle *, +, {n}, and {n,m} regex modifiers
    ;; in any case, there's a prefix sequence of fixed nonnegative length
    ;; of identical elements that should unconditionally match,
    ;; followed by a bounded or unbounded sequence that,
    ;; in case of a failed match, transitions to the next state
    (apply 'th-part
           (let ((*initial-state* next-state))
             (apply 'th-part next-state :sequence
                    (loop :repeat (or (second args) 1)
                          :collect (rtl:mklist (third args)))))
           :sequence (loop :repeat (first args)
                           :collect (rtl:mklist (third args)))))
  (:method (next-state (kind character) &rest args)
    (th-state kind next-state
              ;; Usually, *initial-state* will be null,
              ;; i.e. further computations along this path will be aborted,
```

```
      ;; but, for some variants (? or *), they will just continue
      ;; normally to the next state.
      ;; The special variable controls this setting,
      ;; as you can see in the method for :greedy-repetition
      t *initial-state*))
  (:method (next-state (kind (eql :end-anchor)) &rest args)
    (th-state nil *matched-state*
              t *initial-state*))
  (:method (next-state (kind (eql :start-anchor)) &rest args)
    ;; This part is unique as all the other parts consume the next
    ;; character (we're not implementing lookahead here),
    ;; but this one shouldn't.
    ;; To implement such behavior without the additional complexity
    ;; of passing the search string to this function (which we'll still
    ;; probably need to do later on, but were able to avoid so far),
    ;; we can resort to a cool Lisp technique of signaling a condition
    ;; that can be handled specially in the top-level code
    (signal 'check-start-anchor)
    next-state))
```

Here, we have defined some of the methods of th-part that are specialized for the following patterns: the basic :sequence of expressions, :greedy-repetition (regexes * and +), a single character, and single symbols :start-anchor and :end-anchor (regexes ^ and $). As you can see, some of them dispatch (are chosen based) on the identity of the first argument (using eql specializers), while the character-related method specializes on the class of the arg. As we develop this facility, we could add more methods with defmethod. Running th-part on the whole parse tree will produce the complete automaton; we don't need to do anything else!

To use the constructed FSM, we run it with the string as input. NFAs are endowed with the ability to guess perfectly when faced with a choice of next state: to run the NFA on a real computer, we must find a way to simulate this guessing. One way to do that is to guess one option, and if that doesn't work, try the other. A more efficient way to simulate perfect guessing is to follow all admissible paths simultaneously. In this approach, the simulation allows the machine to be in multiple states at once. To process each letter, it advances all the states along all the arrows that match the letter. In the worst case, the NFA might be in every state at each step, but this results in at worst a constant amount of work independent of the length of the string, so arbitrarily large input strings can be processed in linear time. The efficiency comes from tracking the set of reachable states but not which paths were used to reach them. In an NFA with n nodes, there can only be n reachable states at any step:

```
(defun run-nfa (nfa str)
  (let ((i 0)
        (start 0)
        (matches (list))
        (states (list nfa)))
    ;; this is the counterpart for the start-anchor signal
    (handler-bind ((check-start-anchor
                      ;; there's no sense to proceed matching
                      ;; a ^... regex if the string is not
                      ;; at its start
                      (lambda (c)
                        (when (> i 0) (return-from run-nfa)))))
      (dovec (char (concatenate 'vector str
                                 #(nil)))  ; end-anchor
        (let ((new-states (list)))
          (dolist (state states)
            (dolist (tr (th-state-transitions state))
              (when (th-match tr char)
                (case (rtl:rt tr)
                  (*matched-state* (push start matches))
                  ((nil) )  ; ignore it
                  (t (pushnew (rtl:rt tr) new-states)))
                (return))))
          (if new-states
              (setf states new-states)
              (setf states (list nfa)
                    start nil)))
        (incf i)
        (unless start (setf start i))))
    matches))
```

The th-match function may have methods to match a single char and a character range, as well as a particular predicate. Its implementation is trivial and left as an exercise to the reader.

Overall, interpreting an automaton is a simple and robust approach, yet if we want to squeeze all the possible performance, we can compile it directly to machine code. This is much easier to do with the DFA as it has at most two possible transitions from each state, so the automaton can be compiled to a multilevel conditional and even a jump-table.

Grammars

Regexes are called "regular" for a reason: there's a corresponding mathematical formalism "regular languages" that originates from the hierarchy of grammars compiled by Noam Chomsky. This hierarchy has four levels, each one allowing strictly more complex languages to be expressed with it. And for each level, there's an equivalent computation model:

- Type 0: Recursively enumerable (or universal) grammars—Turing machine

- Type 1: Context-dependent (or context-sensitive) grammars—a linear bounded automaton

- Type 2: Context-free grammars—pushdown automaton

- Type 3: Regular grammars—FSM

We have already discussed the bottom layer of the hierarchy. Regular languages are the most limited (and thus the simplest to implement): for example, you can write a regex a{15}b{15}, but you won't be able to express a{n}b{n} for an arbitrary n, that is, ensure that b is repeated the same number of times as a. The top layer corresponds to all programs, and so all the programming science and lore, in general, is applicable to it. Now, let's talk about context-free grammars which are another type that is heavily used in practice and even has a dedicated set of algorithms. Such grammars can be used not only for simple matching but also for parsing and generation. **Parsing**, as we have seen in the preceding text, is the process of transforming a text that is assumed to follow the rules of a certain grammar into the structured form that corresponds to the particular rules that can be applied to this text. And generation is the reverse process: apply the rules and obtain the text. This topic is huge, and there's a lot of literature on it including the famous Dragon Book.

Parsing is used for processing both artificial (including programming) and natural languages. And, although different sets of rules may be used, as well as different approaches for selecting a particular rule, the resulting structure will be a tree. In fact, formally, each grammar consists of four items:

- The set of terminals (leaves of the parse tree) or tokens of the text: These could be words or characters for the natural language; keywords, identifiers, and literals for the programming language; and so on.

- The set of nonterminals—symbols used to name different items in the rules and in the resulting parse tree, the non-leaf nodes of the tree. These symbols are abstract and not encountered in the actual text. The examples of nonterminals could be VB (verb) or NP (noun phrase) in natural language parsing and if-section or template-argument in parsing of C++ code.

- The root symbol (which should be one of the nonterminals).

- The set of production rules that have two sides—a left-hand (lhs) and a right-hand (rhs) one: On the left-hand side, there should be at least one nonterminal, which is substituted with a number of other terminals or nonterminals on the right-hand side. During generation, the rule allows the algorithm to select a particular surface form for an abstract nonterminal (e.g., turn a nonterminal VB into a word do). During parsing, which is a reverse process, it allows the program, when it's looking at a particular substring, to replace it with a nonterminal and expand the tree structure. When the parsing process reaches the root symbol by performing such substitution and expansion, it is considered terminated.

Each compiler has to use parsing as a step in transforming the source into executable code. Also, parsing may be applied for any data format (for instance, JSON) to transform it into machine data. In natural language processing, parsing is used to build the various tree representations of the sentence, which encode linguistic rules and structure.

There are many different types of parsers that differ in the additional constraints they impose on the structure of the production rules of the grammar. The generic context-free constraint is that in each production rule, the left-hand side may only be a single nonterminal. The most widespread of context-free grammars are LL(k) (in particular, LL(1)) and LR (LR(1), SLR, LALR, GLR, etc.). For example, LL(1) parser (one of the easiest to build) parses the input from left to right, performing leftmost derivation of the sentence, and it is allowed to look ahead at most one character. Not all combinations of derivation rules allow the algorithm to build a parser that will be able to perform unambiguous rule selection under such constraints. But, as the LL(1) parsing is simple and efficient, some authors of grammars specifically target their language to be LL(1)-parseable. For example, Pascal and other programming languages created by Niklaus Wirth fall into this category.

There are also two principal approaches to implementing the parser: a top-down and a bottom-up one. In a top-down approach, the parser tries to build the tree from the root, while, in a bottom-up one, it tries to find the rules that apply to groups of terminal symbols and then combine those until the root symbol is reached. Obviously, we can't enumerate all parsing algorithms here, so we'll study only a single approach, which is one of the most widespread, efficient, and flexible ones—**shift-reduce parsing**. It's a bottom-up linear algorithm that can be considered one of the instances of the pushdown automaton approach—a theoretical computational model for context-free grammars.

A shift-reduce parser operates on a queue of tokens of the original sentence. It also has access to a stack. At each step, the algorithm can perform

- Either a `shift` operation: Take the token from the queue and push it onto the stack.

- Or a `reduce` operation: Take the top items from the stack, select a matching rule from the grammar, and add the corresponding subtree to the partial parse tree, in the process removing the items from the stack.

Thus, for each token, it will perform exactly two "movement" operations: push it onto the stack and pop from the stack. Plus, it will perform rule lookup, which requires a constant number of operations (maximum length of the rhs of any rule) if an efficient structure is used for storing the rules. A hash-table indexed by the rhs's and a trie are good choices for that.

Here's a small example from the domain of NLP syntactic parsing. Let's consider a toy grammar:

```
S -> NP VP .
NP -> DET ADJ NOUN
NP -> PRP$ NOUN  ; PRP$ is a possessive pronoun
VP -> VERB VP
VP -> VERB NP
```

and the following vocabulary:

```
DET -> a|an|the
NOUN -> elephant|pyjamas
ADJ -> large|small
VERB -> is|wearing
PRP$ -> my
```

No, let's parse the sentence (already tokenized): `A large elephant is wearing my pyjamas`. First, we'll need to perform part-of-speech (POS) tagging, which, in this example, is a matter of looking up the appropriate nonterminals from the vocabulary grammar. This will result in the following:

```
DET ADJ    NOUN   VERB  VERB PRP$  NOUN   .
 |   |      |      |     |    |     |     |
 A large elephant is wearing my pyjamas .
```

This POS tags will serve the role of terminals for our parsing grammar. Now, the shift-reduce process itself begins:

1. Initial queue: (DET ADJ NOUN VERB VERB PRP$ NOUN .)
   Initial stack: ()
   Operation: shift

2. Queue: (ADJ NOUN VERB VERB PRP$ NOUN .)
   Stack: (DET)
   Operation: shift (as there are no rules with the rhs DET)

3. Queue: (NOUN VERB VERB PRP$ NOUN .)
   Stack: (ADJ DET)
   Operation: shift

4. Queue: (VERB VERB PRP$ NOUN .)
   Stack: (NOUN ADJ DET)
   Operation: reduce (rule NP -> DET ADJ NOUN)
   ; we match the rules in reverse to the stack

5. Queue: (VERB VERB PRP$ NOUN .)
   Stack: (NP)
   Operation: shift

6. Queue: (VERB PRP$ NOUN .)
   Stack: (VERB NP)
   Operation: shift

7. Queue: (PRP$ NOUN .)
   Stack: (VERB VERB NP)
   Operation: shift

8. Queue: (NOUN .)
   Stack: (PRP$ VERB VERB NP)
   Operation: shift

9. Queue: (.)
   Stack: (NOUN PRP$ VERB VERB NP)
   Operation: reduce (rule: NP -> PRP$ NOUN)

10. Queue: (.)
    Stack: (NP VERB VERB NP)
    Operation: reduce (rule: VP -> VERB NP)

11. Queue: (.)
    Stack: (VP VERB NP)
    Operation: reduce (rule: VP -> VERB VP)

12. Queue: (.)
    Stack: (VP NP)
    Operation: shift

11. Queue: ()
    Stack: (. VP NP)
    Operation: reduce (rule: S -> NP VP .)

243

12. Reached root symbol - end.

The resulting parse tree is:

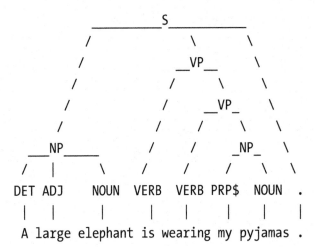

```
                        _____S_____
                    /            \        \
                  /              __VP__       \
                /             /      \      \
              /             /        __VP_     \
            /             /       /      \    \
        ___NP____       /      /     _NP_    \
      /    |      \    /      /     /    \    \
    DET  ADJ     NOUN  VERB  VERB PRP$   NOUN   .
     |    |       |     |     |    |      |     |
     A  large elephant  is wearing my pyjamas  .
```

The implementation of the basic algorithm is very simple:

```lisp
(defstruct grammar
  rules
  max-length)

(defmacro grammar (&rest rules)
  `(make-grammar
    :rules (pairs->ht (mapcar (lambda (rule)
                                (rtl:pair (nthcdr 2 rule) (first rule)))
                       ',rules))
    :max-length
    (let ((max 0))
      (dolist (rule ',rules)
        ;; Here, #1= and #1# are reader-macros for capturing
        ;; a form and re-evaluating it again
        (when (> #1=(length (nthcdr 2 rule)) max)
          (setf max #1#)))
      max)))

(defun parse (grammar queue)
  (let ((stack (list)))
```

```
    (loop :while queue :do
      (print stack)   ; diagnostic output
      (rtl:if-it (find-rule stack grammar)
                 ;; reduce
                 (dotimes (i (length (cdr rtl:it))
                            (push rtl:it stack))
                   (pop stack))
                 ;; shift
                 (push (pop queue) stack))
      :finally (return (find-rule stack grammar)))))

(defun find-rule (stack grammar)
  (let (prefix)
    (loop :for item in stack
          :repeat (grammar-max-length grammar) :do
          (push (first (rtl:mklist item)) prefix)
          (rtl:when-it (rtl:? grammar 'rules prefix)
            ;; otherwise parsing will fail with a stack
            ;; containing a number of partial subtrees
            (return (cons rtl:it (reverse (subseq stack 0
                                  (length prefix)))))))))

CL-USER> (parse (print (grammar (S -> NP VP |.|)
                                (NP -> DET ADJ NOUN)
                                (NP -> PRP$ NOUN)
                                (VP -> VERB VP)
                                (VP -> VERB NP)))
                '(DET ADJ NOUN VERB VERB PRP$ NOUN |.|))
#S(GRAMMAR
    :RULES #{
             '(NP VP |.|) S
             '(DET ADJ NOUN) NP
             '(PRP$ NOUN) NP
             '(VERB VP) VP
             '(VERB NP) VP
            }
    :MAX-LENGTH 3)
```

```
NIL
(DET)
(ADJ DET)
(NOUN ADJ DET)
((NP DET ADJ NOUN))
(VERB (NP DET ADJ NOUN))
(VERB VERB (NP DET ADJ NOUN))
(PRP$ VERB VERB (NP DET ADJ NOUN))
(NOUN PRP$ VERB VERB (NP DET ADJ NOUN))
((NP PRP$ NOUN) VERB VERB (NP DET ADJ NOUN))
((VP VERB (NP PRP$ NOUN)) VERB (NP DET ADJ NOUN))
((VP VERB (VP VERB (NP PRP$ NOUN))) (NP DET ADJ NOUN))
(S (NP DET ADJ NOUN) (VP VERB (VP VERB (NP PRP$ NOUN))) |.|)
```

However, the additional level of complexity of the algorithm arises when the grammar becomes ambiguous, that is, there may be situations when several rules apply. Shift-reduce is a greedy algorithm, so, in its basic form, it will select some rule (for instance, with the shortest rhs or just the first match), and it cannot backtrack. This may result in a parsing failure. If some form of rule weights is added, the greedy selection may produce a suboptimal parse. Anyway, there's no option of backtracking to correct a parsing error. In the NLP domain, the peculiarity of shift-reduce parsing application is that the number of rules is quite significant (it can reach thousands) and, certainly, there's ambiguity. In this setting, shift-reduce parsing is paired with machine learning techniques, which perform a "soft" selection of the action to take at each step, as reduce is applicable almost always, so a naive greedy technique becomes pointless.

Actually, shift-reduce would better be called something like stack-queue parsing, as different parsers may not limit the implementation to just the shift and reduce operations. For example, an NLP parser that allows the construction of non-projective trees (those where the arrows may cross, that is, subsequent words may not always belong to a single or subsequent upper-level categories) adds a swap operation. A more advanced NLP parser that produces a graph structure called an AMR (abstract meaning representation) has nine different operations.

Shift-reduce parsing is implemented in many of the parser generator tools, which generate a parser program from a set of production rules. For instance, the popular Unix tool yacc is a LALR parser generator that uses shift-reduce. Another popular tool ANTLR is a parser generator for LL(k) languages that uses a non-shift-reduce direct pushdown automaton-based implementation.

Besides shift-reduce and similar automaton-based parsers, there are many other parsing techniques used in practice. For example, CYK probabilistic parsing was popular in NLP for some time, but it's a $O(n^3)$ algorithm, so it gradually fell from grace and lost to machine learning–enhanced shift-reduce variants. Another approach is packrat parsing (based on PEG—parsing expression grammars) that has a great Lisp parser generator library esrap. Packrat is a more powerful top-down parsing approach with backtracking and unlimited lookahead that nevertheless guarantees linear parse time. Any language defined by an LL(k) or LR(k) grammar can be recognized by a packrat parser, in addition to many languages that conventional linear-time algorithms do not support. This additional power simplifies the handling of common syntactic idioms such as the widespread but troublesome longest-match rule, enables the use of sophisticated disambiguation strategies such as syntactic and semantic predicates, provides better grammar composition properties, and allows lexical analysis to be integrated seamlessly into parsing. The last feature makes packrat very appealing to the programmers as they don't have to define separate tools for lexical analysis (tokenization and token categorization) and parsing. Moreover, the rules for tokens use the same syntax, which is also quite similar to regular expression syntax. For example, here's a portion of the esrap rules for parsing tables in Markdown documents. The Markdown table may look something like this:

```
| Left-Aligned  | Center Aligned  | Right Aligned |
| :------------ |:---------------:|         -----:|
| col 3 is      | some wordy text |         $1600 |
| col 2 is      | centered        |           $12 |
| zebra stripes | are neat        |            $1 |
```

You can see that the code is quite self-explanatory: each defrule form consists of a rule name (lhs), its rhs, and a transformation of the rhs into a data structure. For instance, in the rule table-row, the rhs is (and (& #\|) (+ table-cell) #\| sp newline). The row should start with a | char followed by one or more table-cells (a separate rule) and ended by | with some space characters and a newline. And the transformation (:destructure (_ cells &rest) ... only cares about the content, that is, the table cells:

```
(defrule sp (* space-char)
  (:text t))

(defrule table-cell (and #\|
                      sp
                      (* (and (! (or (and sp #\|) endline)) inline))
                      sp
                      (& #\|))
  (:destructure (_ __ content &rest ___)
    (mapcar 'second content)))

(defrule table-row (and (& #\|) (+ table-cell) #\| sp newline)
  (:destructure (_ cells &rest __)
    (mapcar (lambda (a) (cons :plain a))
            cells)))

(defrule table-align-cell (and sp (? #\:) (+ #\-) (? #\:) sp #\|)
  (:destructure (_ left __ right &rest ___)
    (if right (if left 'center 'right) (when left 'left))))

(defrule table-align-row (and #\| (+ table-align-cell) sp newline)
  (:destructure (_ aligns &rest __)
    aligns))

(defrule table-head (and table-row table-align-row))
```

To conclude the topic of parsing, I wanted to pose a question: Can it be used to match the regular expressions? And the answer, of course, is that it can, as we are operating in a more powerful paradigm that includes the regexes as a subdomain. However, the critical showstopper of applying parsing to this problem is the need to define the grammar instead of writing a compact and more or less intuitive regex...

String Search in Action: Plagiarism Detection

Plagiarism detection is a very challenging problem that doesn't have an exact solution. The reason is that there's no exact definition of what can be considered plagiarism and what can't; the boundary is rather blurry. Obviously, if the text or its part is just copy-pasted, everything is clear. But, usually (and especially when they know that plagiarism detection is at play), people will apply their creativity to alter the text in some slight or even significant ways. However, over the years, researchers have come up with numerous algorithms of plagiarism detection, with quality good enough to be used in our educational institutions. The problem is very popular, and there are even shared task challenges dedicated to improving plagiarism catchers. It's somewhat an arms race between the plagiarists and the detection systems.

One of the earliest but, still, quite effective ways of implementing plagiarism detection is the Shingle algorithm. It is also based on the idea of using hashes and some basic statistical sampling techniques. The algorithm operates in the following stages:

1. Text normalization (this may include case normalization, reduction of the words to basic forms, error correction, cleanup of punctuation, stopwords, etc.)

2. Selection of the shingles and calculation of their hashes

3. Sampling the shingles from the text at question

4. Comparison of the hashes of the original shingles to the sampled hashes and evaluation

The single shingle is a contiguous sequence of words from the normalized text (another name for this object, in NLP, is `ngram`). The original text will give us (1-n) shingles, where n is the number of words. The hashes of the shingles are normal string hashes (like FNV-1).

The text, which is analyzed for plagiarism, is also split into shingles, but not all of them are used—just a random sample of m. The sampling theorem can give a good estimate of the number that can be trusted with a high degree of confidence. For efficient comparison, all the original hashes can be stored in a hash-set. If the number of overlapping shingles exceeds some threshold, the text can be considered plagiarized. The other take on the result of the algorithm application may be to return the plagiarism degree, which will be the percentage of the overlapping shingles. The complexity of the algorithm is O(n + m).

In a sense, the Shingle algorithm may be viewed as an instance of massive string search, where the outcome we're interested in is not so much the positions of the patterns in the text (although those may also be used to indicate the parts of the text that are plagiarism-suspicious) as the fact that they are present in it.

Takeaways

Strings are peculiar objects: initially, it may seem that they are just arrays. But, beyond this simple understanding, due to the main usage patterns, a much more interesting picture can be seen. Advanced string representations and algorithms are examples of special-purpose optimization applied to general-purpose data structures. This is another reason why strings are presented at the end of the part on derived data structures: string algorithms make heavy use of the material we have covered previously, such as trees and graphs.

We have also discussed the FSM—a powerful data structure that can be used to reliably implement complex workflows. FSMs may be used not only for string matching but also for implementing protocol handling (e.g., in the HTTP server), complex user interactions, and so on. The Erlang programming language even has a standard library behavior gen_fsm (replaced by the newer gen_statem) that is a framework for easy implementation of FSMs—as many Erlang applications are mass service systems that have state machine–like operation.

P.S. Originally, I anticipated this chapter to be one of the shortest in the book, but it turned out to be the longest one. Strings are not so simple as they might seem... ;)

CHAPTER 12

Dynamic Programming

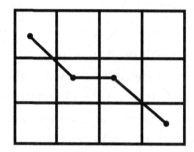

This chapter opens the final part of the book. In it, we're going to apply the knowledge from the previous chapters in analyzing a selection of important problems that are mostly application-independent and find usages in many applied domains: optimization, synchronization, compression, and similar.

We will start with a single approach that is arguably the most powerful algorithmic technique in use. If we managed to reduce the problem to dynamic programming (DP), in most of the cases, we can consider it solved. The fact that we progressed so far in this book without mentioning DP is quite amazing. Actually, we could have already talked about it several times, especially in Chapter 11, but I wanted to contain this topic to its own chapter, so I deliberately didn't start the exposition earlier. Indeed, strings are one of the domains where dynamic programming is used quite heavily, but the technique finds application in almost every area.

Also, DP is one of the first marketing terms in CS. When Bellman had invented it, he wanted to use the then hyped term "programming" to promote his idea. This has, probably, caused more confusion over the years than benefit. In fact, a good although unsexy name for this technique could be simply "filling the table" as the essence of

© Vsevolod Domkin 2021
V. Domkin, *Programming Algorithms in Lisp*, https://doi.org/10.1007/978-1-4842-6428-7_12

the approach is an exhaustive evaluation of all variants with memoization of partial results (in a table) to avoid repetition of redundant computations. Obviously, it will have any benefits only when there are redundant computations, which is not the case, for example, with combinatorial optimization. To determine if a problem may be solved with DP, we need to validate that it has the **optimal substructure property**:

> *A problem has optimal substructure if when we take its subproblem an optimal solution to the whole problem includes an optimal solution to this subproblem.*

An example of the optimal substructure is the shortest path problem. If the shortest path from point A to point B passes through some point C and there are multiple paths from C to B, the one included in the shortest path A–B should be the shortest of them. In fact, the shortest path is an archetypical DP problem which we'll discuss later in this chapter. A counterexample is a Travelling Salesman Problem (TSP): if it had optimal substructure, the subpath between any two nodes in the result path should have been the shortest possible path between these nodes. But it isn't true for all nodes because it can't be guaranteed that the edges of the path will form a cycle with all the other shortest paths.

Fibonacci Numbers

So, as we said, the essence of DP is filling a table. This table, though, may have a different number of dimensions for different problems. Let's start with a 1D case. What book on algorithms can omit discussing the Fibonacci numbers? Usually, they are used to illustrate recursion, yet they are also a great showcase for the power of memoization. Besides, recursion is, conceptually, also an integral part of DP.

A naive approach to calculating the i-th number will be directly coding the Fibonacci formula:

```
(defun naive-fib (i)
  (check-type i (integer 0))
  (if (< i 2) 1
      (+ (naive-fib (- i 1))
         (naive-fib (- i 2)))))
```

However, applying it will result in an exponential growth of the number of computations: each call to `naive-fib` results in two more calls. So the number of calls needed for the n-th number, with this approach, is O(2^n):

```
CL-USER> (time (naive-fib 40))
Evaluation took: 3.390 seconds of real time
165580141
CL-USER> (time (naive-fib 42))
Evaluation took: 7.827 seconds of real time
433494437
```

Yet, we can see here a direct manifestation of an optimal substructure property: the i-th number calculation uses the result of the (1- i)-th one. To utilize this recurrence, we'll need to store the previous results and reuse them. It may be achieved by changing the function call to the table access. Actually, from the point of view of math, tables and functions are, basically, the same thing:

```
(let ((fib (vec 1 1)))  ; our table will be an adjustable vector
  (defun fib (i)
    (when (< (length fib) i)
      (vector-push-extend (fib (- i 1)) fib))
    (+ (aref fib (- i 1))
       (aref fib (- i 2)))))
```

What we've done here is added a layer of memoization to our function that uses an array `fib` that is filled with the consecutive Fibonacci numbers. The array is hidden inside the closure of the `fib` procedure, so it will persist between the calls to it and accumulate the numbers as they are requested. There will also be no way to clear it, apart from redefining the function, as the closed-over variables of this kind are not accessible outside of the function. The consecutive property is ensured by the arrangement of the recursive calls: the table is filled on the recursive ascent starting from the lowest yet unknown number. This approach guarantees that each Fibonacci number is calculated exactly once and reduces our dreaded O(2^n) running time to a mere O(n)!

Such a calculation is the simplest example of top-down DP that is performed using recursion. Despite its natural elegance, it suffers from a minor problem that may turn significant, in some cases: extra space consumption by each recursive call. It's not only

O(n) in time but also in space. The alternative strategy that gets rid of redundant space usage is called bottom-up DP and is based on loops instead of recursion. Switching to it is quite trivial, in this case:

```
(let ((fib (vec 1 1)))
  (defun bottom-up-fib (i)
    (let ((off (length fib)))
      (adjust-array fib (1+ i) :fill-pointer t)
      (dotimes (j (- (1+ i) off))
        (let ((j (+ j off)))
          (setf (aref fib j)
                (+ (aref fib (- j 1))
                   (aref fib (- j 2)))))))))
    (aref fib i)))
```

```
CL-USER> (time (bottom-up-fib 42))
Evaluation took: 0.000 seconds of real time
CL-USER> (time (bottom-up-fib 4200))
Evaluation took: 0.004 seconds of real time
4051274663782640767950407815583314544208670701385703251 7543...
;; the last number is a Lisp bignum (a number that has unbounded size)
```

Funny enough, a real-word-ready implementation of Fibonacci numbers ends up not using recursion at all...

String Segmentation

Let's consider another 1D problem: suppose we have a dictionary of words and a string consisting of those words that somehow lost the spaces between them—the words got glued together. We need to restore the original string with spaces or, to phrase it differently, split the string into words. This is one of the instances of string segmentation problems, and if you're wondering how and where such a situation could occur for real, consider a Chinese text that doesn't have to contain spaces. Every Chinese language processing system needs to solve a similar task.

Here's an example input:[1]

```
String: thisisatest
Dictionary: a, i, s, at, is, hi, ate, his, sat, test, this
Expected output: this is a test
```

It is clear that even with such a small dictionary, there are multiple ways we could segment the string. The straightforward and naive approach is to use a greedy algorithm. For instance, a shortest-first solution will try to find the shortest word from the dictionary starting at the current position and then split it (as a prefix) from the string. It will result in the following split: `this i sat est`. But the last part `est` isn't in the dictionary, so the algorithm has failed to produce some of the possible correct splits (although, by chance, if the initial conditions were different, it could have succeeded). Another version—the longest-first approach—could look for the longest words instead of the shortest. This would result in: `this is ate st`. Once again the final token is not a word. It is pretty obvious that these simple takes are not correct and we need a more nuanced solution.

As a common next step in developing such brute-force approaches, a developer would resort to backtracking: when the computation reaches the position in the string, from which no word in the dictionary may be recovered, it unwinds to the position of the previous successful split and tries a different word. This procedure may have to return multiple steps back—possibly to the very beginning. As a result, in the worst case, to find a correct split, we may need to exhaustively try all possible combinations of words that fit into the string.

Here's an illustration of the recursive shortest-first greedy algorithm operation:

```
(defun shortest-first-restore-spaces (dict str)
  (dotimes (i (length str))
    (let ((word (rtl:slice str 0 (1+ i))))
      (when (rtl:? dict word)
        (return (rtl:cond-it
                  ((= (1+ i) (length str))
                   word)
```

---

[1]If you wonder, s is a word that is usually present in English programmatic dictionaries because when it's and friends are tokenized, they're split into two tokens, and the apostrophe may be missing sometimes. Also, our dictionary is case-insensitive.

```
            ((shortest-first-restore-spaces dict (rtl:slice str (1+ i)))
             (format nil "~A ~A" word rtl:it)))))))))
```

```
CL-USER> (defparameter *dict* (rtl:hash-set 'equal "a" "i" "at" "is" "hi" "ate"
                                            "his" "sat" "test" "this"))
CL-USER> (trace shortest-first-restore-spaces)
CL-USER> (shortest-first-restore-spaces *dict* "thisisatest")
  0: (SHORTEST-FIRST-RESTORE-SPACES #<HASH-TABLE :COUNT 10> "thisisatest")
    1: (SHORTEST-FIRST-RESTORE-SPACES #<HASH-TABLE :COUNT 10> "isatest")
      2: (SHORTEST-FIRST-RESTORE-SPACES #<HASH-TABLE :COUNT 10> "satest")
        3: (SHORTEST-FIRST-RESTORE-SPACES #<HASH-TABLE :COUNT 10> "est")
        3: SHORTEST-FIRST-RESTORE-SPACES returned NIL
      2: SHORTEST-FIRST-RESTORE-SPACES returned NIL
    1: SHORTEST-FIRST-RESTORE-SPACES returned NIL
  0: SHORTEST-FIRST-RESTORE-SPACES returned NIL
NIL
```

To add backtracking into the picture, we need to avoid returning in the case of the failure of the recursive call:

```
(defun bt-shortest-first-restore-spaces (dict str)
  (dotimes (i (length str))
    (let ((word (rtl:slice str 0 (1+ i))))
      (when (rtl:in# word dict)
        (when (= (1+ i) (length str))
          (return word))
        (rtl:when-it (bt-shortest-first-restore-spaces
                      dict (slice str (1+ i)))
          (return (format nil "~A ~A" word rtl:it)))))))
```

```
CL-USER> (trace shortest-first-restore-spaces)
CL-USER> (bt-best-first-restore-spaces *dict* "thisisatest")
  0: (BT-SHORTEST-FIRST-RESTORE-SPACES #<HASH-TABLE :COUNT 10>
     "thisisatest")
    1: (BT-SHORTEST-FIRST-RESTORE-SPACES #<HASH-TABLE :COUNT 10> "isatest")
```

```
2: (BT-SHORTEST-FIRST-RESTORE-SPACES #<HASH-TABLE :COUNT 10>
   "satest")
  3: (BT-SHORTEST-FIRST-RESTORE-SPACES #<HASH-TABLE :COUNT 10> "est")
  3: BT-SHORTEST-FIRST-RESTORE-SPACES returned NIL
2: BT-SHORTEST-FIRST-RESTORE-SPACES returned NIL
;; backtracking kicks in here
2: (BT-SHORTEST-FIRST-RESTORE-SPACES #<HASH-TABLE :COUNT 10> "atest")
  3: (BT-SHORTEST-FIRST-RESTORE-SPACES #<HASH-TABLE :COUNT 10>
     "test")
  3: BT-SHORTEST-FIRST-RESTORE-SPACES returned "test"
2: BT-SHORTEST-FIRST-RESTORE-SPACES returned "a test"
1: BT-SHORTEST-FIRST-RESTORE-SPACES returned "is a test"
0: BT-SHORTEST-FIRST-RESTORE-SPACES returned "this is a test"
"this is a test"
```

Lisp `trace` is an invaluable tool to understand the behavior of recursive functions. Unfortunately, it doesn't work for loops, with which one has to resort to debug printing.

Realizing that this is brute force, we could just as well use another approach: generate all combinations of words from the dictionary of the total number of characters (n) and choose the ones that match the current string. The exact complexity of this scheme is $O(2^n)$.[2] In other words, our solution leads to a **combinatorial explosion** in the number of possible variants—a clear no-go for every algorithmic developer.

So we need to come up with something different, and, as you might have guessed, DP fits in perfectly as the problem has the optimal substructure: a complete word in the substring of the string remains a complete word in the whole string as well. Based on this understanding, let's reframe the task in a way that lends itself to DP better: find each character in the string that ends a complete word so that all the words combined cover the whole string and do not intersect.[3]

Here is an implementation of the DP-based procedure. Apart from calculating the maximum length of a word in the dictionary, which usually may be done offline, it requires single forward and backward passes. The forward pass is a linear scan of the

---

[2]The intuition for it is the following: in the worst case, every character has two choices—either to be the last letter of the previous word or the first one of the next word, hence the branching factor is 2.

[3]Actually, the condition of complete string coverage may be lifted, which will allow to use almost the same algorithm but skip over "undictionary" words like misspellings.

string that at each character tries to find all the words starting at it and matching the string. The complexity of this pass is $O(n * w)$, where w is the constant length of the longest word in the dictionary, that is, it is, actually, $O(n)$. The backward pass (called, in the context of DP, **decoding**) restores the spaces using the so-called backpointers stored in the dp array. In the following is a simplistic implementation that returns a single match. A recursive variant is possible with or without a backward pass that will accumulate all the possible variants:

```
(defun dp-restore-spaces (dict str)
  (let ((dp (make-array (1+ (length str)) :initial-element nil))
        ;; in the production implementation, the following calculation
        ;; should be performed at the pre-processing stage
        (w (reduce 'max (mapcar 'length (keys dict))))
        (begs (list))
        (rez (list)))
    ;; the outer loop tries to find the next word
    ;; only starting from the ends of the words that were found previously
    (do ((i 0 (pop begs)))
        ((or (null i)
             (= i (length str))))
      ;; the inner loop checks all substrings of length 1..w
      (do ((j (1+ i) (1+ j)))
          ((>= j (1+ (min (length str)
                          (+ w i)))))
        (when (rtl:? dict (rtl:slice str i j))
          (setf (aref dp j) i)
          (push j begs)))
      (setf begs (reverse begs)))
    ;; the backward pass
    (do ((i (length str) (aref dp i)))
        ((null (aref dp i)))
      (push (rtl:slice str (aref dp i) i) rez))
    (strjoin #\Space rez)))
```

```
CL-USER> (dp-restore-spaces *dict* "thisisatest")
"this is a test"
```

Similarly to the Fibonacci numbers, the solution to this problem doesn't use any additional information to choose between several variants of a split; it just takes the first one. However, if we wanted to find the variant that is most plausible to the human reader, we'd need to add some measure of plausibility. One idea might be to use a frequency dictionary, that is, prefer the words that have a higher frequency of occurrence in the language. Such an approach, unfortunately, also has drawbacks: it overemphasizes short and frequent words, such as determiners, and also doesn't account for how words are combined in context. A more advanced option would be to use a frequency dictionary not just of words but of separate phrases (ngrams). The longer the phrases used, the better from the standpoint of linguistics, but also the worse from the engineering point of view: more storage space needed and more data to process if we want to collect reliable statistics for all the possible variants. And, once again, with the rise of the number of words in an ngram, we will be facing the issue of combinatorial explosion pretty soon. The optimal point for this particular task might be bigrams or trigrams, that is, phrases of two or three words. Using them, we'd have to supply another dictionary to our procedure and track the measure of plausibility of the current split as a product of the frequencies of the selected ngrams. Formulated this way, our exercise becomes not merely an algorithmic task but an optimization problem. And DP is also suited to solving such problems. In fact, that was the primary purpose it was intended for, in the Operations Research community.[4] We'll see it in action with our next problem—text justification. Then you'll be able to apply the same approach to create a smarter procedure (let's call it `restore-spaces-plausibly`).

Text Justification

The task of text justification is relevant to both editing and reading software: given a text, consisting of paragraphs, split each paragraph into lines that contain whole words only with a given line length limit so that the variance of line lengths is the smallest. Its solution may be used, for example, to display text in HTML blocks with an `align=justify` property.

---

[4]See, for example, Stuart Dreyfus' "Richard Bellman on the Birth of Dynamic Programming."

A more formal task description would be the following:

- The algorithm is given a text string and a line length limit (say, 80 characters).

- There's a plausibility formula that specifies the penalty for each line being shorter than the length limit. A usual formula is this:

```
(defun penalty (limit length)
  (if (<= length limit)
      (expt (- limit length) 3)
      most-positive-fixnum))
```

- The result should be a list of strings.

As we are discussing this problem in the context of DP, first, we need to determine what is its optimal substructure. Superficially, we could claim that lines in the optimal solution should contain only the lines that have the smallest penalty, according to the formula. However, this doesn't work as some of the potential lines that have the best plausibility (length closest to 80 characters) may overlap, that is, the optimal split may not be able to include all of them. What we can reliably claim is that, if the text is already justified from position 0 to i, we can still justify the remainder optimally regardless of how the prefix is split into lines. This is, basically, the same as with string segmentation where we didn't care how the string was segmented before position i. And it's a common theme in DP problems: the key feature that allows us to save on redundant computation is that we only remember the optimal result of the computation that led to a particular partial solution, but we don't care about what particular path was taken to obtain it (except we care to restore the path, but that's what the backpointers are for—it doesn't impact the forward pass of the algorithm). So the optimal substructure property of text justification is that if the best split of the whole string includes the consecutive indices x and y, then the best split from 0 to y should include x.

Let's justify the following text with a line limit of 50 chars:

```
Common Lisp is the modern, multi-paradigm, high-performance, compiled,
ANSI-standardized, most prominent descendant of the long-running family
of Lisp programming languages.
```

Suppose we've already justified the first 104 characters. This leaves us with a suffix that has a length of 69: `descendant of the long-running family of Lisp programming languages.` As its length is above 50 chars, but below 100, we can conclude that it requires exactly one split. This split may be performed after the first token, second, third, and so on. Let's calculate the total plausibility of each candidate:

```
after "the": 5832 + 0 = 5832
after "long-running": 6859 + 2197 = 9056
after "family": 1728 + 8000 = 9728
after "of": 729 + 12167 = 12896
after "Lisp": 64 + 21952 = 22016
```

So the optimal split starting at index 105[5] is into strings: `"descendant of the"` and `"long-running family of Lisp programming languages."` Now, we haven't guaranteed that index 105 will be, in fact, the point in the optimal split of the whole string, but, if it were, we would have already known how to continue. This is the key idea of the DP-based justification algorithm: starting from the end, calculate the cost of justifying the remaining suffix after each token using the results of previous calculations. At first, while suffix length is below line limit, it is trivially computed by a single call to the plausibility function. After exceeding the line limit, the calculation will consist of two parts: the plausibility penalty and the previously calculated value.

```
(defun justify (limit str)
  (rtl:with ((toks (reverse (split #\Space str)))
             (n (length toks))
             (penalties (make-array n))
             (backptrs (make-array n))
             (lengths (make-array n)))
    ;; forward pass (from the end of the string)
    (rtl:doindex (i tok toks)
      (let ((len (+ (length tok) (max 0 (aref lengths (1- i))))))
        (setf (aref lengths i) (1+ len))
        (if (<= len limit)
            (setf (aref penalties i) (penalty len limit)
                  (aref backptrs i) -1)
```

---

[5]A space at the end of the line is discarded.

```
          ;; minimization loop
          (let ((min most-positive-fixnum)
                arg)
            (dotimes (j i)
              (rtl:with ((j (- i j 1))
                         (len (- (aref lengths i)
                                 (aref lengths j)))
                         (penalty (+ (penalty len limit)
                                     (aref penalties j))))
                (cond ((> len limit) (return))
                      ((< penalty min) (setf min penalty
                                             arg j)))))
            (setf (aref penalties i) min
                  (aref backptrs  i) arg)))))
  ;; backward pass (decoding)
  (loop :for end := (1- n) :then beg
        :for beg := (aref backptrs end)
        :do (fmt "~A~%"
                 (rtl:strjoin #\Space (reverse (subseq toks
                                                       (1+ beg)
                                                       (1+ end)))))
        :until (= -1 beg))))
CL-USER> (justify 50 "Common Lisp is the modern, multi-paradigm, high-
performance, compiled, ANSI-standardized, most prominent descendant of the
long-running family of Lisp programming languages.")

Common Lisp is the modern, multi-paradigm,
high-performance, compiled, ANSI-standardized,
most prominent descendant of the long-running
family of Lisp programming languages.
```

This function is somewhat longer, but, conceptually, it is pretty simple. The only insight I needed to implement it efficiently was the additional array for storing the lengths of all the string suffixes we have examined so far. This way, we apply memoization twice—to prevent recalculation of both the penalties and the suffix lengths—and all of the ones we have examined so far are used at each iteration. If we were to store the suffixes themselves, we would have had to perform an additional $O(n)$-length calculation at each iteration.

The algorithm performs two passes. In the forward pass (which is, in fact, performed from the end), it fills the slots of the DP arrays using the minimum joint penalty for the potential current line and the remaining suffix, the penalty for which was calculated during one of the previous iterations of the algorithm. In the backward pass, the resulting lines are extracted by traversing the backpointers starting from the last index.

The key difference from the previous DP example are these lines:

```
(setf (aref penalties i) min
      (aref backptrs  i) arg)
```

Adding them (alongside the whole minimization loop) turns DP into an optimization framework that, in this case, is used to minimize the penalty. The backptrs array, as we said, is used to restore the steps which have led to the optimal solution. As, eventually (and this is true for the majority of the DP optimization problems), we care about this sequence and not the optimization result itself.

As we can see, for the optimization problems, the optimal substructure property is manifested as a mathematical formula called the **recurrence relation**. It is the basis for the selection of a particular substructure among several variants that may be available for the current step of the algorithm. The relation involves an already memoized partial solution and the cost of the next part we consider adding to it. For text justification, the formula is the sum of the current penalty and the penalty of the newly split suffix. Each DP optimization task is based on a recurrence relation of a similar kind.

Now, let's look at this problem from a different perspective. We can represent our decision space as a directed acyclic graph. Its leftmost node (the "source") will be index 0, and it will have several direct descendants: nodes with those indices in the string, at which we can potentially split it not exceeding the 50-character line limit or, alternatively, each substring that spans from index 0 to the end of some token and is not longer than 50 characters. Next, we'll connect each descendant node in a similar manner with all nodes that are "reachable" from it, that is, they have a higher value of associated string position and the difference between their index and this node is below 50. The final node of the graph ("sink") will have the value of the length of the string. The cost of each edge is the value of the penalty function. Now, the task is to find the shortest path from source to sink.

Here is the DAG for the example string with the nodes labeled with the indices of the potential string splits. As you can see, even for such a simple string, it's already quite big. What to speak of real texts. But it can provide some sense of the number of variants that an algorithm has to evaluate.

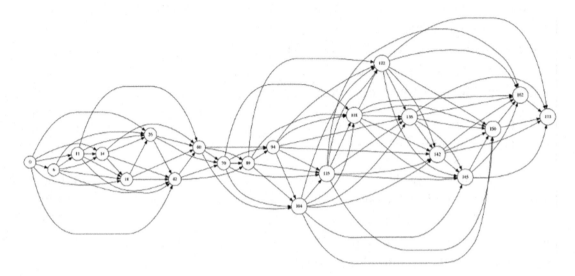

What is the complexity of this algorithm? On the surface, it may seem to be O(m^2) where m is the token count, as there are two loops: over all tokens and over the tail. However, the line (when (> len limit) (return)) limits the inner loop to only the part of the string that can fit into limit chars, effectively reducing it to a constant number of operations (not more than limit , but, in practice, an order of magnitude less). Thus, the actual complexity is O(m).[6]

Pathfinding Revisited

In fact, any DP problem may be reduced to pathfinding in the graph: the shortest path, if optimization is involved, or just any path otherwise. The nodes in this graph are the intermediate states (for instance, a split at index x or an i-th Fibonacci number) and the edges are possible transitions that may bear an associated cost (as in text justification)

---

[6]Provided all the length calculations are implemented efficiently. For simplicity, I have used plain lists here with a linear length complexity, but a separate variable may be added to avoid the extra cost.

or not (as in string segmentation). And the classic DP algorithm to solve the problem is called the Bellman-Ford (BF) algorithm. Not incidentally, one of its authors, Bellman, is the "official" inventor of DP:

```
(defun bf-shortest-path (g)
  (rtl:with ((n (array-dimension g 0))
             (edges (edges-table g))
             (dists (make-array n :initial-element most-positive-fixnum))
             (backptrs (make-array n))
             (path (list)))
    (setf (aref dists (1- n)) 0)
    (dotimes (v (vertices g))
      (dotimes (e (? edges v))
        (rtl:with ((u (src e))
                   (dist (+ (dist e)
                            (aref dists u))))
          (when (< dist (aref dists u))
            (setf (aref dists u) dist
                  (aref backptrs u) v)))))
    (loop :for v := (1- n) :then (aref backptrs v) :do
      (push v path))
    (values path
            (aref dists (1- n)))))
```

The code for the algorithm is very straightforward, provided that our graph representation already has the vertices and edges as a data structure in convenient format or implements such operations (in the worst case, the overall complexity should be not greater than $O(V * E)$). For the edges, we need a kv indexed by the edge destination—an opposite to the usual representation that groups them by their sources.[7]

Compared to text justification, this function looks simpler as we don't have to perform task-specific processing that accounts for character limit and spaces between words. However, if we were to use bf-shortest-path, we'd have to first create the graph data structure from the original text. So all that complexity would go into the graph creation routine. However, from the architectural points of view, such split may be beneficial as the pathfinding procedure could be reused for other problems.

---

[7] However, if we think of it, we could reuse the already proven linked representation just putting the incoming edges into the node structure instead of the outgoing ones.

One might ask a reasonable question: How does Bellman-Ford fare against Dijkstra's algorithm (DA)? As we have already learned, Dijkstra's is a greedy and optimal solution to pathfinding, so why consider yet another approach? Both algorithms operate by relaxation, in which approximations to the correct distance are replaced by better ones until the final result is reached. And in both of them, the approximate distance to each vertex is always an overestimate of the true distance, and it is replaced by the minimum of its old value and the length of a newly found path. Turns out that DA is also a DP-based approach, but with additional optimizations! It uses the same optimal substructure property and recurrence relations. The advantage of DA is the utilization of the priority queue to effectively select the closest vertex that has not yet been processed. Then it performs the relaxation process on all of its outgoing edges, while the Bellman-Ford algorithm relaxes all the edges. This method allows BF to calculate the shortest paths not to a single node but to all of them (which is also possible for DA but will make its runtime, basically, the same as for BF). So Bellman-Ford complexity is $O(V * E)$ compared to $O(E + V \log V)$ for the optimal implementation of DA. Besides, BF can account for negative edge weights, which will break DA.

So DA remains the algorithm of choice for the standard shortest path problem, and it's worth keeping in mind that it can also be applied as a solver for some DP problems if they are decomposed into graph construction + pathfinding. However, some DP problems have additional constraints that make using DA for them pointless. For example, in text justification, the number of edges to consider at each step is limited by a constant factor, so the complexity of the exhaustive search is, in fact, $O(V)$. Proving that for our implementation of justify is left as an exercise to the reader...

LCS and Diff

Let's return to strings and the application of DP to them. The ultimate DP-related string problem is string alignment. It manifests in many formulations. The basic one is the Longest Common Subsequence (LCS) task: determine the length of the common part among two input strings. Solving it, however, provides enough data to go beyond that—it enables determining the best alignment of the strings, as well as enumerating the edit operations needed to transform one string into another. The edit operations, which are usually considered in the context of LCS, are

- Insertion of a character

- Deletion of a character

- Substitution of a character

Based on the number of those operations, we can calculate a metric of commonality between two strings that is called the **Levenshtein distance**. It is one of the examples of the so-called **edit distances**. The identical strings have a Levenshtein distance of 0 and strings foobar and baz of 4 (three deletion operations for the prefix foo and a substitution operation of r into z). There are also other variants of edit distances. For instance, the Damerau-Levenshtein distance that is better suited to compare texts with misspellings produced by humans adds another modification operation: swap, which reduces the edit distance in the case of two adjacent characters being swapped to 1 instead of 2 for the Levenshtein (one deletion and one insertion).

The Levenshtein distance, basically, gives us for free the DP recurrence relations: when we consider the i-th character of the first string and the j-th one of the second, the edit distance between the prefixes 0,i and 0,j is either the same as for the pair of chars (1- i) and (1- j), respectively, if the current characters are the same, or 1+, the minimum of the edit distances of the pairs i (1- j), (1- i) (1- j), and (1-i) j.

We can encode this calculation as a function that uses a matrix for memoization. Basically, this is the DP solution to the LCS problem: now, you just have to subtract the length of the string and the bottom-right element of the matrix, which will give you the measure of the difference between the strings:

```
(defun lev-dist (s1 s2 &optional
                    (i1 (1- (length s1)))
                    (i2 (1- (length s2)))
                    (ld (make-array (list (1+ (length s1))
                                          (1+ (length s2)))
                               :initial-element nil)
                        ldp))  ; a flag indicating that the argument
                               ; was supplied
  ;; initialization of the 0-th column and row
  (unless ldp
    (dotimes (k (1+ (length s1))) (setf (aref ld k 0) K))
    (dotimes (k (1+ (length s2))) (setf (aref ld 0 k) K)))
```

```
(values (or (aref ld (1+ i1) (1+ i2))
            (setf (aref ld (1+ i1) (1+ i2))
                  (if (eql (aref s1 i1) (aref s2 i2))
                      (lev-dist s1 s2 (1- i1) (1- i2) ld)
                      (1+ (min (lev-dist s1 s2 (1- i1) (1- i2) ld)
                               (lev-dist s1 s2 i1 (1- i2) ld)
                               (lev-dist s1 s2 (1- i1) i2 ld))))))
        ld))
```

However, if we want to also use this information to align the sequences, we'll have to make a reverse pass:[8]

```
(defun align (s1 s2)
  (rtl:with ((i1 (length s1))
             (i2 (length s2))
             ;; our Levenshtein distance procedure returns
             ;; the whole DP matrix as a second value
             (ld (nth-value 1 (lev-dist s1 s2)))
             (rez (list)))
    (loop
      (let ((min (min (aref ld (1- i1) (1- i2))
                      (aref ld      i1  (1- i2))
                      (aref ld (1- i1)      i2))))
        (cond ((= min (aref ld (1- i1) (1- i2)))
               (push (rtl:pair (char s1 (1- i1))
                               (char s2 (1- i2)))
                     rez)
               (decf i1)
               (decf i2))
              ((= min (aref ld (1- i1) i2))
               (push (rtl:pair (char s1 (1- i1)) nil)
                     rez)
               (decf i1))
```

---

[8]Here, a separate backpointers array isn't necessary as we can infer the direction by reversing the distance formula.

```
              ((= min (aref ld i1 (1- i2)))
                (push (rtl:pair nil (char s2 (1- i2)))
                      rez)
                (decf i2))))
      (when (= 0 i1)
        (loop :for j :from (1- i2) :downto 0 :do
          (push (rtl:pair #\* (char s2 j)) rez))
        (return))
      (when (= 0 i2)
        (loop :for j :from (1- i1) :downto 0 :do
          (push (rtl:pair (char s1 j) nil) rez))
        (return)))
    ;; pretty output formatting
    (with-output-to-string (s1)
      (with-output-to-string (s2)
        (with-output-to-string (s3)
          (loop :for (c1 c2) :in rez :do
            (format s1 "~C " (or c1 #\.))
            (format s2 "~C " (cond ((null c1) #\↓)
                                   ((null c2) #\↑)
                                   ((char= c1 c2) #\|)
                                   (t #\x)))
            (format s3 "~C " (or c2 #\.)))
          (format t "~A~%~A~%~A~%"
                  (get-output-stream-string s1)
                  (get-output-stream-string s2)
                  (get-output-stream-string s3)))))
  rez))

CL-USER> (align "democracy" "remorse")
d e m o c r a c y
x | | | ↑ | ↑ x x
r e m o . r . s e

CL-USER> (lev-dist "democracy" "remorse")
5
```

```
#2A((0 1 2 3 4 5 6 7)
    (1 1 2 3 4 5 6 7)
    (2 2 1 2 3 4 5 6)
    (3 3 2 1 2 3 4 5)
    (4 4 3 2 1 2 3 4)
    (5 5 4 3 2 2 2 3 4)
    (6 5 5 4 3 2 3 4)
    (7 6 6 5 4 3 3 4)
    (8 7 7 6 5 4 4 4)
    (9 8 8 7 6 5 5 5)))
```

It should be pretty clear how we can also extract the edit operations during the backward pass: depending on the direction of the movement, horizontal, vertical, or diagonal, it's an insertion, deletion, or substitution. The same operations may be also grouped to reduce noise. The alignment task is an example of a 2D DP problem. Hence, the diff computation has a complexity of $O(n^2)$. There are other notable algorithms, such as CYK parsing or the Viterbi algorithm, that also use a 2D array, although they may have higher complexity than just $O(n^2)$. For instance, the CYK parsing is $O(n^3)$, which is very slow compared to the greedy $O(n)$ shift-reduce algorithm.

However, the diff we will obtain from the basic LCS computation will still be pretty basic. There are many small improvements that are made by production diff implementation both on the UX and performance sides. Besides, the complexity of the algorithm is $O(n^2)$, which is quite high, so many practical variants perform many additional optimizations to reduce the actual number of operations, at least, for the common cases.

The simplest improvement is a **preprocessing** step that is warranted by the fact that, in many applications, the diff is performed on texts that are usually mostly identical and have a small number of differences between them localized in an even smaller number of places. For instance, consider source code management, where diff plays an essential role: the programmers don't tend to rewrite whole files too often; on the contrary, such practice is discouraged due to programmer collaboration considerations.

So some heuristics may be used in the library diff implementations to speed up such common cases:

- Check that the texts are identical.

- Identify common prefix/suffix and perform the diff only on the remaining part.

- Detect situations when there's just a single or two edits.

A perfect diff algorithm will report the minimum number of edits required to convert one text into the other. However, sometimes the result is too perfect and not very good for human consumption. People will expect operations parts to be separated at token boundaries when possible; also larger contiguous parts are preferred to an alteration of small changes. All these and other diff ergonomic issues may be addressed by various **postprocessing** tweaks.

But, besides these simple tricks, are global optimizations to the algorithm possible? After all, $O(n^2)$ space and time requirements are still pretty significant. Originally, diff was developed for Unix by Hunt and McIlroy. Their approach computes matches in the whole file and indexes them into the so-called k-candidates, k being the LCS length. The LCS is augmented progressively by finding matches that fall within proper ordinates (following a rule explained in their paper). While doing this, each path is memoized. The problem with the approach is that it performs more computation than necessary: it memoizes all the paths, which requires $O(n^2)$ memory in the worst case and $O(n^2 \log n)$ for the time complexity!

The current standard approach is the divide-and-conquer Myers algorithm. It works by finding recursively the central match of two sequences with the smallest edit script. Once this is done, only the match is memoized, and the two subsequences preceding and following it are compared again recursively by the same procedure until there is nothing more to compare. Finding the central match is done by matching the ends of subsequences as far as possible and, any time it is not possible, augmenting the edit script by one operation, scanning each furthest position attained up to there for each diagonal, and checking how far the match can expand. If two matches merge, the algorithm has just found the central match. This approach has the advantage of using only $O(n)$ memory and executes in $O(n * d)$, where d is the edit script complexity (d is less than n, usually much less). The Myers algorithm wins because it does not memoize the paths while working and does not need to "foresee" where to go. So it can concentrate only on the furthest positions it could reach with an edit script of the smallest complexity. The smallest complexity constraint ensures that what is found in the LCS. Unlike the Hunt-McIlroy algorithm, the Myers one doesn't have to memoize the paths. In a sense, the Myers algorithm compared to the vanilla DP diff, like Dijkstra's one vs. Bellman-Ford, cuts down on the calculation of the edit distances between the substrings that don't contribute to the optimal alignment, while solving LCS and building the whole edit distance matrix performs the computation for all substrings.

The diff tool is a prominent example of a transition from quite an abstract algorithm to a practical utility that is an essential part of many ubiquitous software products and the additional work needed to ensure that the final result is not only theoretically sane but also usable.

P.S. Ever wondered how GitHub, when displaying the diff, not only shows the changed line but also highlights the exact changes? It runs diff twice: first, at the line level (using each line as a single unit/token) and then at the character level, as you would normally expect. Then the results are just combined.

DP in Action: Backprop

As we said in the beginning, DP has applications in many areas: from machine learning to graphics to source code management. Literally, you can find an algorithm that uses DP in every specialized domain, and if you don't, this means you, probably, can still advance this domain and create something useful by applying DP to it. Deep learning is the fastest developing area of the machine learning domain, in recent years. At its core, the discipline is about training huge multilayer optimization functions called "neural networks." And the principal approach to doing that, which, practically speaking, has enabled the rapid development of machine learning techniques that we see today, is the backpropagation (backprop) optimization algorithm.

As pointed out by Christopher Olah, for modern neural networks, it can make training with gradient descent as much as ten million times faster, relative to a naive implementation. That's the difference between a model taking a week to train and taking 200,000 years. Beyond its use in deep learning, backprop is a computational tool that may be applied in many other areas, ranging from weather forecasting to analyzing numerical stability—it just goes by different names there. In fact, the algorithm has been reinvented at least dozens of times in different fields. The general, application-independent name for it is reverse-mode differentiation. Essentially, it's a technique for calculating partial derivatives quickly using DP on computational graphs.

Computational graphs are a nice way to think about mathematical expressions. For example, consider the expression (setf e (* (+ a b) (1+ b))). There are four operations: two additions, one multiplication, and an assignment. Let's arrange those computations in the same way they would be performed on the computer:

```
(let ((c (+ a b))
      (d (1+ b)))
  (setf e (* c d)))
```

To create a computational graph, we make each of these operations, along with the input variables, into nodes. When the outcome of one expression is an input to another one, a link points from one node to another:

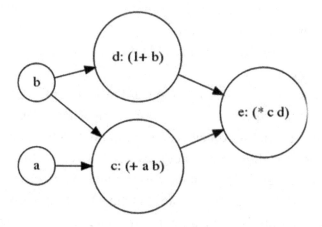

We can evaluate the expression by setting the values in the input nodes (a and b) to certain values and computing nodes in the graph along the dependency paths. For example, let's set a to 2 and b to 1: the result in node e will be, obviously, 6.

The derivatives in a computational graph can be thought of as edge labels. If a directly affects c, then we can write a partial derivative $\partial c/\partial a$ along the edge from a to c.

Here is the computational graph with all the derivatives for the evaluation with the values of a and b set to 2 and 1:

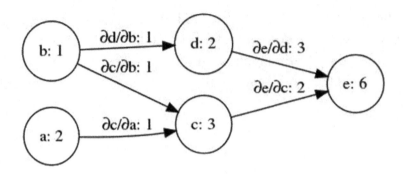

But what if we want to understand how nodes that aren't directly connected affect each other? Let's consider how e is affected by a. If we change a at a speed of 1, c also changes at a speed of 1. In turn, c changing at a speed of 1 causes e to change at a speed of 2. So e changes at a rate of (* 1 2) with respect to a. The general rule is to sum over all possible paths from one node to the other, multiplying the derivatives on each edge of the path together. We can see that this graph is, basically, the same as the graph we used to calculate the shortest path.

This is where forward-mode differentiation and reverse-mode differentiation come in. They're algorithms for efficiently computing the sum by factoring the paths. Instead of summing over all of the paths explicitly, they compute the same sum more efficiently by merging paths back together at every node. In fact, both algorithms touch each edge exactly once. Forward-mode differentiation starts at the input to the graph and moves toward the output node. At every node, it sums all the paths feeding in. Each of those paths represents one way in which the input affects that node. By adding them up, we get the total derivative. Reverse-mode differentiation, on the other hand, starts at the output of the graph and moves toward the input nodes. At each node, it merges all paths which originated at that node. Forward-mode differentiation tracks how one input affects every node. Reverse-mode differentiation tracks how every node affects one output.

So what if we do reverse-mode differentiation from e down? This gives us the derivative of e with respect to every node. Forward-mode differentiation gave us the derivative of our output with respect to a single input, but reverse-mode differentiation gives us all of the derivatives we need for gradient descent in one go. When training neural networks, the cost is a function of the weights of each edge. And using reverse-mode differentiation (a.k.a. backprop), we can calculate the derivatives of the cost with respect to all the weights in a single pass through the graph. As there are millions and tens of millions of weights, in a neural network, reverse-mode differentiation results in a speedup of the same factor!

Backprop is an example of simple memoization DP. No selection of the optimal variant is needed; it's just a proper arrangement of the operations to avoid redundant computations.

Takeaways

DP-based algorithms may operate on one of these three levels:

- Just systematic memoization, when every intermediate result is cached and used to compute subsequent results for larger problems (Fibonacci numbers, backprop)

- Memoization + backpointers that allow for the reconstruction of the sequence of actions that lead to the final solution (text segmentation)

- Memoization + backpointers + a target function that selects the best intermediate solution (text justification, diff, shortest path)

If we want to apply DP to some task, we need to find its optimal substructure, that is, verify that an optimal solution to a subproblem will remain a part of the optimal solution to the whole problem. Next, if we deal with an optimization task, we may have to formulate the recurrence relations. After that, it's just a matter of technique: those relations may be programmed either directly as a recursive or iterative procedure (like in LCS) or indirectly using the method of consecutive approximations (like in Bellman-Ford).

Ultimately, all DP problems may be reduced to pathfinding in the graph, but it doesn't always make sense to have this graph explicitly as a data structure in the program. If it does, however, remember that Dijkstra's algorithm is the optimal algorithm to find a single shortest path in it.

DP, usually, is a reasonable next thing to think about after the naive greedy approach (which, let's be frank, everyone tends to take initially) stumbles over backtracking. However, we saw that DP and greedy approaches do not contradict each other: in fact, they can be combined as demonstrated by Dijkstra's algorithm. Yet, an optimal greedy algorithm is more of an exception than a rule. However, there are a number of problems for which a top-n greedy solution (the so-called **beam search**) can be a near-optimal solution that is good enough.

Also, DP doesn't necessarily mean optimal. A vanilla dynamic programming algorithm exhaustively explores the decision space, which may be excessive in many cases. It is demonstrated by the examples of Dijkstra's and Myers algorithms that improve on the DP solution by cutting down some of the corners.

P.S. We have also discussed, the first time in this book, the value of heuristic pre- and postprocessing. From the theoretical standpoint, it is not something you have to pay attention to, but, in practice, that's a very important aspect of the production implementation of many algorithms and, thus, shouldn't be frowned upon or neglected. In an ideal world, an algorithmic procedure should have both optimal worst-case complexity and the fastest operation in the common cases.

CHAPTER 13

Approximation

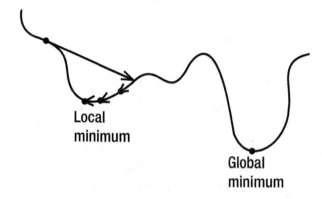

This chapter will be a collection of stuff from somewhat related but still distinct domains. What unites it is that all the algorithms we will discuss are, after all, targeted at calculating approximations to some mathematical functions. There are no advanced data structures involved, neither is the aim to find a clever way to improve the runtime of some common operations. No, these algorithms are about calculations and computing an acceptable result within the allocated time budget.

Combinatorial Optimization

Dynamic programming is a framework that can be used for finding the optimal value of some loss function when there are multiple configurations of the problem space that result in different values. Such search is an example of discrete optimization for there is a countable number of states of the system and a distinct value of the cost function we're optimizing corresponding to each state. There are also similar problems that have an unlimited and uncountable number of states, but there is still a way to find a global or local optimum of the cost function for them. They comprise the continuous optimization domain. Why is optimization not just a specialized area relevant to a few practitioners

© Vsevolod Domkin 2021
V. Domkin, *Programming Algorithms in Lisp*, https://doi.org/10.1007/978-1-4842-6428-7_13

but a toolbox that every senior programmer should know how to utilize? The primary reason is that it is applicable in almost any domain: the problem just needs to be large enough to rule out simple brute force. You can optimize how the data is stored or how the packets are routed, how the blueprint is laid out or how the servers are loaded. Many people are just not used to looking at their problems this way. Also, understanding optimization is an important prerequisite for having a good grasp of machine learning, which is revolutionizing the programming world.

DP is an efficient and, overall, great optimization approach, but it can't succeed if the problem doesn't have an optimal substructure. Combinatorial optimization approaches deal with finding a near optimum for the problems where an exhaustive search requires $O(2^n)$ computations. Such problems are called NP-hard, and a classic example of these is the Travelling Salesman Problem (**TSP**). The task is to find an optimal order of edges in a cycle spanning all vertices of a fully connected weighted graph. As we saw previously, this problem doesn't have an optimal substructure, that is, an optimal partial solution isn't necessarily a part of the best overall one and so taking the shortest edge doesn't allow the search procedure to narrow down the search space when looking at the next vertex. A direct naive approach to TSP will enumerate all the possible variants and select the one with a minimal cost. However, the number of variants is $n!$, so this approach becomes intractable very fast. A toy example of visiting all the capitals of the 50 US states has 10^{64} variants. This is where quantum computers promise to overturn the situation, but while we're waiting for them to mature, the only feasible approach is developing approximation methods that will get us a good enough solution in polynomial (ideally, linear) time. TSP may look like a purely theoretical problem, but it has some real-world applications. Besides vehicle routing, automated drilling and soldering in electronics is another example. Yet, even more important is that there are many other combinatorial optimization problems, but, in essence, the approaches to solving one of them apply to all the other NP-hard problems. That is, like with shortest path, coming up with an efficient solution to TSP allows one to unlock the option to efficiently solve a very broad range of problems over a variety of domains.

So let's write down the code for the basic TSP solution. As usual, we have to select the appropriate graph representation. From one point of view, we're dealing with a fully connected graph, so every representation will work and a matrix one will be the most convenient. However, storing an n^2-sized array is not the best option, especially for a large n. A better "distributed" representation might be useful here. Yet, for the TSP graph, an even better approach would be to do the opposite of our usual optimization trick:

trade computation for storage space. When the graph is fully connected, usually, there exists some kind of an underlying metric space that contains all the vertices. A common example is a Euclidian space, in which each vertex has a coordinate (e.g., the latitude and longitude). Anyway, whichever way to represent the vertex position is used, the critical requirement is the existence of the metric that may be calculated at any time (and fast). Under such conditions, we don't have to store the edges at all. So our graph will be just a list of vertices.

Let's use the example with the US state capitals. Each vertex will be represented as a pair of floats (lat and lon). We can retrieve the raw data from the Wikipedia article about the US capitols (with an "o") and extract the values we need with the following code snippet,[1] which cuts a few corners:

```
(defstruct city
  name lat lon)
```

```
(defparameter *wp-link* "https://en.wikipedia.org/w/index.
php?title=List_of_state_and_territorial_capitols_in_the_United_
States&action=edit&section=1")
```

```
(defparameter *cs*
  (rtl:with ((raw (drakma:http-request *wp-link*))
             (coords-regex (ppcre:create-scanner
                              "\\{\\{coord\\|(\\d+)\\|(\\
d+)\\|([.\\d]+)\\|.\\|(\\d+)\\|(\\d+)\\|([.\\d]+)\\|.\\|type"))
             (capitals (list)))
    (flet ((dms->rad (vec off)
             (* (/ pi 180)
                (+    (aref vec (+ off 0))
                   (/ (aref vec (+ off 1)) 60)
                   (/ (aref vec (+ off 2)) 3600)))))
      (dolist (line (rtl:split
                      #\Newline
                      (rtl:slice raw
                                 (search "{| class=\"wikitable sortable\""
                                         raw)
```

---

[1] It uses the popular drakma HTTP client and cl-ppcre regex library.

```
                              (search "</textarea><div
                              class='editOptions'>"
                                        raw))))
        (when (and (rtl:starts-with "|" line)
                 (search "{{coord" line))
          (rtl:with ((_ coords (ppcre:scan-to-strings coords-regex line))
                     (coords (rtl:map* 'read-from-string coords)))
            (push (make-city
                   :name (slice line (position-if 'alpha-char-p line)
                                (position-if (lambda (ch)
                                               (member ch '(#\] #\|)))
                                             line :start 1))
                   :lat (dms->rad coords 0)
                   :lon (dms->rad coords 3))
                  capitals)))))
    (coerce capitals 'vector)))

CL-USER> (length *cs*)
50
```

We also need to define the metric. The calculation of distances on Earth, though, is not so straightforward as on a plain. Usually, as a first approximation, the haversine formula is used that provides the estimate of the shortest distance over the surface "as the crow flies" (ignoring the relief):

```
(defun earth-dist (c1 c2)
  (rtl:with ((lat1 (city-lat c1))
             (lat2 (ciyte-lat c2))
             (a (+ (expt (sin (/ (- lat2 lat1) 2))
                          2)
                   (* (cos lat1)
                      (cos lat2)
                      (expt (sin (/ (- (city-lon c2) (city-lon c1)) 2))
                            2)))))
    (* 1.2742e7   ; Earth diameter
       (atan (sqrt a) (sqrt (- 1 a))))))
```

With the metric at our disposal, let's define the function that will calculate the length of the whole path and use it for a number of random paths (we'll use the RUTILS function shuffle to produce a random path):

```
(defun path-length (path)
  (let ((rez (earth-dist (aref path 0) (aref path -1))))
    (dotimes (i (1- (length path)))
      (incf rez (earth-dist (aref path i) (aref path (1+ i)))))
    rez))

CL-USER> (path-length *cs*)
9.451802301259182d7
CL-USER> (path-length (rtl:shuffle *cs*))
9.964776273250546d7
CL-USER> (path-length (rtl:shuffle *cs*))
1.009761841183094d8
```

We can see that an average path may have a length of around 10000 kilometers. However, we don't know anything about the shortest or the longest one, and to find out reliably, we'll have to evaluate 50! Paths... Yet, as we accept the sad fact that it is not possible to do with our current technology, it's not time to give up yet. Yes, we may not be able to find the absolute best path, but at least we can try to improve on the random one. Already, the three previous calculations had a variance of 5%. So, if we're lucky, maybe we could hit a better path purely by chance. Let's try a thousand paths using our usual argmin pattern:

```
(defun random-search (path n)
  (let ((min (path-length path))
        (arg path))
    (loop :repeat n :do
      (rtl:with ((path (rtl:shuffle path))
                 (len (path-length path)))
        (when (< len min)
          (setf min len
                arg path))))
    (values arg
            min)))
```

```
CL-USER> (setf *print-length* 2)
2
CL-USER> (random-search *cs* 1000)
(#S(CITY :NAME "Atlanta" :LAT 0.5890359059538811d0 ...)
 #S(CITY :NAME "Montpelier, Vermont" :LAT 0.772521512027179d0 ...) ...)
7.756170773802838d7
```

OK, we've got a sizable 20% improvement. What about 1,000,000 combinations?

```
CL-USER> (time (random-search *cs* 1000000))
Evaluation took:
  31.338 seconds of real time
...
(#S(CITY :NAME "Boise, Idaho" :LAT 0.7612723873453388d0 ...)
 #S(CITY :NAME "Helena, Montana" :LAT 0.813073800024579d0 ...) ...)
6.746660953705506d7
```

Cool, another 15%. Should we continue increasing the size of the sample? Maybe, after a day of computations, we could get the path length down by another 20–30%. And that's already a good gain. Surely, we could also parallelize the algorithm or use a supercomputer in order to analyze many more variants. But there should be something smarter than simple brute force, right?

Local Search

Local search is the "dumbest" of these smart approaches, built upon the following idea: if we had a way to systematically improve our solution, instead of performing purely random sampling, we could arrive at better variants much faster. The local search procedure starts from a random path and continues improving it until the optimum is reached. This optimum will be a local one (hence the name), but it will still be better than what we have started with. Besides, we could run the optimization procedure many times from a different initial point, basically, getting the benefits of the brute-force approach. We can think of the repeated local search as sampling + optimization:

```
(defun local-search (path improve-fn)
  (let ((min (path-length path))
        (cc 0))  ; iteration count
```

```
(loop
  (incf cc)
  (rtl:if-it (funcall improve-fn path)
             (setf min (path-length rtl:it)
                   path rtl:it)
             (return (values path
                             min
                             cc))))))))
```

For this code to work, we also need to supply the improve-fn. Coming up with it is where the creativity of the algorithmic researcher needs to be channeled into. Different problems (and even a single problem) may allow for different approaches. For TSP, there are several improvement possibilities discovered so far. And all of them use the planar (2D) nature of the graph we're processing. It is an additional constraint that has a useful consequence: if the paths between two pairs of nodes intersect, definitely, there are also shorter paths between them that are nonintersecting. So swapping the edges will improve the whole path. If we were to draw a picture of this swap, it would look like this (the edges A-D and C-B intersect, while A-B and C-D don't, and hence their total length is shorter):

```
- A   B -       - A - B -
     X      ==>
- C   D -       - C - D -
```

This rule allows us to specify the so-called 2-opt improvement procedure:

```
(defun 2-opt (path)
  (loop :repeat (* 2 (length path)) :do
    (rtl:with ((len (length path))
               (v1 (random len))
               (v1* (if (= (1+ v1) len) 0 (1+ v1)))
               (v2 (loop :for v := (random len)
                         :when (and (/= v v1) (/= v (1- v1)))
                         :do (return v)))
               (v2* (if (= #2=(1+ v2) len) 0 #2#)))
      (when (< (+ (path-length (vec (aref path v1) (aref path v2)))
               (path-length (vec (aref path v1*) (aref path v2*))))
```

```
              (+ (path-length (vec (aref path v1) (aref path v1*)))
                 (path-length (vec (aref path v2) (aref path v2*)))))
      (let ((beg (min v1* v2*))
            (end (max v1* v2*)))
        (return (concatenate 'vector
                              (subseq path 0 beg)
                              (reverse (subseq path beg end))
                              (subseq path end)))))))))
```

Note that we do not need to perform a complicated check for path intersection (which requires an algorithm of its own, and there are a number of papers dedicated to this task). In fact, we don't care if there is an intersection: we just need to know that the new path, which consists of the newly replaced edges and a reversed part of the path between the two inner nodes of the old edges, is shorter. One more thing to notice is that this implementation doesn't perform an exhaustive analysis of all possible edge swaps, which is suggested by the original 2-opt algorithm (a O(n^2) operation). Here, we select just a random pair. Both variants are acceptable, and ours is simpler to implement:

```
CL-USER> (local-search *cs* '2-opt)
#(#S(CITY :NAME "Jackson, Mississippi" :LAT 0.5638092223095238d0 ...)
  #S(CITY :NAME "Baton Rouge, Louisiana" :LAT 0.5315762080646039d0 ...) ...)
3.242702077795514d7
111
```

So, outright, we've got a 100% improvement on the random-search path obtained after a much larger number of iterations. Iteration counting was added to the code in order to estimate the work we had to do. To make a fair comparison, let's run random-search with the same n (111):

```
CL-USER> (random-search *cs* 111)
#(#S(CITY :NAME "Boise, Idaho" :LAT 0.7612723873453388d0 ...)
  #S(CITY :NAME "Springfield, Illinois" :LAT 0.69461512973363367d0 ...) ...)
7.522044767585556d7
```

But this is still not 100% fair as we haven't yet factored in the time needed for the 2-opt call which is much heavier than the way random search operates. In my estimates, 111 iterations of local-search took four times as long, so...

```
CL-USER> (random-search *cs* 444)
#(#S(CITY :NAME "Lansing, Michigan" :LAT 0.745844229097319d0 ...)
  #S(CITY :NAME "Springfield, Illinois" :LAT 0.69461512973633670d0 ...) ...)
7.537249874357127d7
```

Now, the runtimes are the same, but there's not really much improvement in the random search outcome. That's expected for, as we have already observed, achieving a significant improvement in random-search results requires performing orders of magnitude more operations.

Finally, let's define multi-local-search to leverage the power of random sampling:

```
(defun multi-local-search (path n)
  (let ((min (path-length path))
        (arg path))
    (loop :repeat n :do
      (rtl:with ((cur (local-search (rtl:shuffle path) '2-opt)))
        (when (< #1=(path-length cur) min)
          (setf min #1#
                arg cur))))
    (values arg
            min)))
CL-USER> (time (multi-local-search *cs* 1000))
Evaluation took:
  22.394 seconds of real time
...
#(#S(CITY :NAME "Atlanta" :LAT 0.5890359059538811d0 ...)
  #S(CITY :NAME "Montgomery, Alabama" :LAT 0.5650930224896327d0 ...) ...)
2.8086843039667137d7
```

Quite a good improvement that took only 20 seconds to achieve!

As a final touch, let's draw the paths on the map. It's always good to double-check the result using some visual approach when it's available. Here is our original random path (Anchorage and Honolulu are a bit off due to the issues with the map projection):

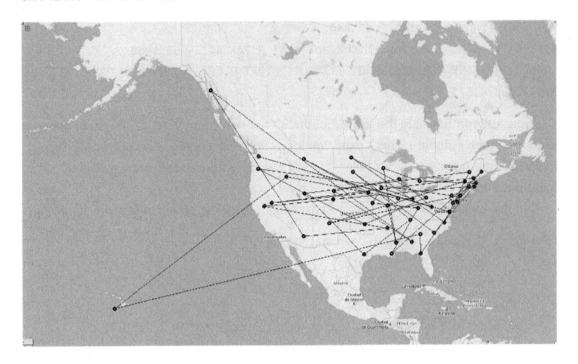

This is the result of random search with a million iterations:

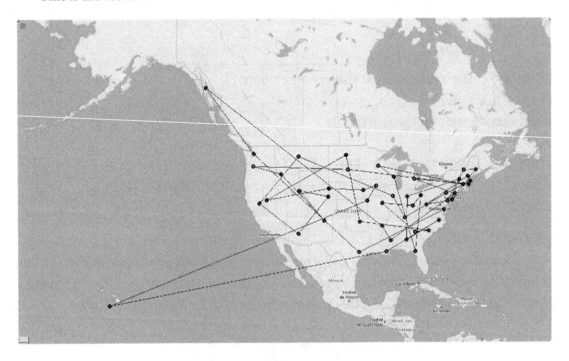

And this is our multistart local search outcome. Looks nice, doesn't it?

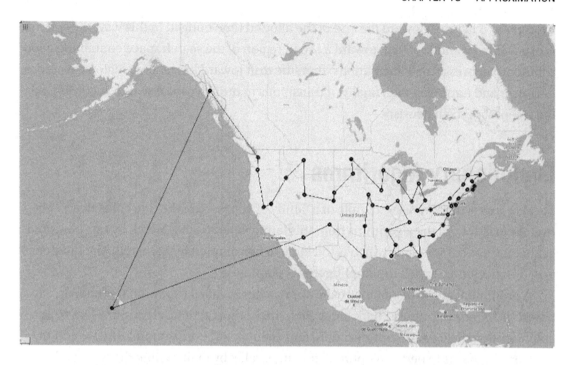

2-opt is the simplest path-improving technique. There are more advanced ones like 3-opt and Lin-Kernighan heuristic. Yet, the principle remains the same: for local search to work, we have to find a way to locally improve our current best solution.

Another direction of the development of the basic algorithm, besides better local improvement procedures and trying multiple times, is devising a way to avoid being stuck in local optima. **Simulated annealing** is the most well-known technique for that. The idea is to replace unconditional selection of a better variant (if it exists) with a probabilistic one. The name and inspiration for the technique come from the physical process of cooling molten materials down to the solid state. When molten steel is cooled too quickly, cracks and bubbles form, marring its surface and structural integrity. Annealing is a metallurgical technique that uses a disciplined cooling schedule to efficiently bring the steel to a low-energy, optimal state. The application of this idea to the optimization procedure introduces the temperature parameter T. At each step, a new state is produced from the current one. For instance, it can be achieved using 2-opt, although the algorithm doesn't impose the limitation on the state to necessarily be better than the current one, so even such a simple thing as a random swap of vertices in the path is admissible. Next, unlike with local search, the transition to the candidate step doesn't happen unconditionally, but with a probability proportional to (/ 1 T). Initially, we start with a high value of T and then decrease it following some annealing schedule.

Eventually, T falls to 0 toward the end of the allotted time budget. In this way, the system is expected to wander, at first, toward a broad region of the search space containing good solutions, ignoring small fluctuations; then the drift toward low-energy regions becomes narrower and narrower; and, finally, it transitions to ordinary local search according to the steepest descent heuristic.

Evolutionary Algorithms

Local search is the simplest example of a family of approaches that are collectively called **metaheuristics**. All the algorithms from this family operate, in general, by sampling and evaluating a set of solutions which is too large to be completely evaluated. The difference is in the specific approach to sampling that is employed.

A prominent group of metaheuristic approaches is called evolutionary (and/or nature-inspired) algorithms. It includes such methods as genetic algorithms (GAs), ant colony and particle swarm optimization, and cellular and even grammatical evolution. The general idea is to perform optimization in parallel by maintaining the so-called population of states and alter this population using a set of rules that improve the aggregate quality of the whole set while permitting some outliers in hopes that they may lead to better solutions unexplored by the currently fittest part of the population.

We'll take a brief glance at evolutionary approaches using the example of **genetic algorithms**, which are, probably, the most well-known technique among them. The genetic algorithm (GA) views each possible state of the system as an individual "genome" (encoded as a vector). GA is best viewed as a framework that requires specification of several procedures that operate on the genomes of the current population:

- The initialization procedure which creates the initial population. After it, the size of the population remains constant, but each individual may be replaced with another one obtained by applying the evolution procedures.

- The fitness function that evaluates the quality of the genome and assigns some weight to it. For TSP, the length of the path is the fitness function. For this problem, the smaller the value of the function, the better.

- The selection procedure specifies which items from the population to use for generating new variants. In the simplest case, this procedure can use the whole population.

- The evolution operations which may be applied. The usual GA operations are mutation and crossover, although others can be devised also.

Mutation operates on a single genome and alters some of its slots according to a specified rule. 2-opt may be a valid mutation strategy, although even the generation of a random permutation of the TSP nodes may work if it is applied to a part of the genome and not to the whole. By controlling the magnitude of mutation (what portion of the genome is allowed to be involved in it), it is possible to choose the level of stochasticity in this process. But the key idea is that each change should retain at least some resemblance with the previous version, or we'll just end up with stochastic search.

The crossbreeding operation isn't, strictly speaking, necessary in the GA, but some of the implementations use it. This process transforms two partial solutions into two others by swapping some of the parts. Of course, it's not possible to apply directly to TSP, as it would result in the violation of the main problem constraint of producing a loop that spans all the nodes. Instead, another procedure called the ordered crossover should be used. Without crossbreeding, GA may be considered a parallel version of local search.

Here is the basic GA skeleton. It requires definition of the procedures init-population, select-candidates, mutate, crossbread, and score-fitness:

```
(defun ga (population-size &key (n 100))
  (let ((genomes (init-population population-size)))
    (loop :repeat n :do
      (let ((candidates (select-candidates genomes)))
        (dolist (ex (mapcar 'mutate candidates))
          (push ex genomes))
        (dolist (ex (crossbread candidates))
          (push ex genomes)))
      (setf genomes (rtl:take population-size (sort genomes
      'score-fitness))))))
```

This template is not a gold standard; it can also be tweaked and altered, but you've got a general idea. The other evolutionary optimization methods also follow the same principles but define different ways to evolve the population. For example, particle swarm optimization operates by moving candidate solutions (particles) around in the search space according to simple mathematical formulas over their position and velocity. The movement of each particle is influenced by its local best-known position, as well as guided toward the global best-known positions in the search space. And those are, in turn, updated as better positions are found by other particles. By the way, the same idea underlies the particle filter algorithm used in signal processing and statistical inference.

Branch and Bound

Metaheuristics can be, in general, classified as local search optimization methods for they operate in a bottom-up manner by selecting a random solution and trying to improve it by gradual change. The opposite approach is global search that tries to systematically find the optimum by narrowing the whole problem space. We have already seen the same pattern of two alternative ways to approach the task—top-down and bottom-up—in parsing, and it also manifests in other domains that permit problem formulation as a search task.

How is a top-down systematic evaluation of the combinatorial search space even possible? Obviously, not in its entirety. However, there are methods that allow the algorithm to rule out significant chunks that certainly contain suboptimal solutions and narrow the search to only the relevant portions of the domain that may be much smaller in cardinality. If we manage to discard, this way, a large number of variants, we have more time to evaluate the other parts, thus achieving better results (e.g., with local search).

The classic global search is represented by the branch and bound (B&B) method. It views the set of all candidate solutions as a rooted tree with the full set being at the root. The algorithm explores branches of this tree, which represent subsets of the solution set. Before enumerating the candidate solutions of a branch, the branch is checked against upper and lower estimated bounds on the optimal solution and is discarded if it cannot produce a better solution than the best one found so far by the algorithm. The key feature of the algorithm is efficient bounds estimation. When it is not possible, the algorithm degenerates to an exhaustive search.

Here is a skeleton B&B implementation. Similar to the one for genetic algorithms, it relies on providing implementations of the key procedures separately for each search problem. For the case of TSP, the function will accept a graph, and all the permutations of its vertices comprise the search space. We'll use the branch struct to represent the subspace we're dealing with. We can narrow down the search by pinning a particular subset of edges—this way, the subspace will contain only the variants originating from the possible permutations of the vertices that are not attached to those edges:

```
(defstruct branch
  (upper most-positive-fixnum)
  (lower 0)
  (edges (list)))
```

The b&b procedure will operate on the graph g and will have an option to either work until the shortest path is found or terminate after n steps:

```
(defun b&b (g &key n)
  (rtl:with ((cur (vertices g))
             (min (cost cur)))
             (arg cur)
             (q (make-branch :upper min :lower (lower-bound g (list))))
    (loop :for i :from 0
          :for branch := (pop q) :while branch :do
      (when (eql i n) (return))
      (if (branchp branch)
          (dolist (item (branch-out branch))
            ;; we leave only the subbranches that can,
            ;; at least in theory, improve on the current solution
            (when (< (branch-lower item) upper)
              (push item q)))
          (let ((cost (branch-upper branch)))
            (when (< cost lower)
              (setf lower cost
                    arg branch)))))
    (values cur
            cost)))
```

Implementing the function branch-out is trivial: it needs to generate all the possible variants by expanding the current edge set with a single new edge, and it should also calculate the bounds for each variant by calling lower-bound on them.

The most challenging part is figuring out the way to compute the `lower-bound`. The key insight here is the observation that each path in the graph is not shorter than half the sum of the shortest edges attached to each vertex. So the lower bound for a branch with pinned edges e1, e2, and e3 will be the sum of the lengths of these edges plus half the sum of the shortest edges attached to all the other vertices that the pinned edges don't cover. It is the most straightforward and raw approximation that will allow the algorithm to operate:

```
(defun lower-bound (graph pinned-edges)
  (let ((cost 0)
        (forbidden-edges (apply 'rtl:hash-set 'eql pinned-edges)))
    (dolist (v (vertices graph))
      (let ((min1 most-positive-fixnum)
            (min2 most-positive-fixnum))
        (dolist (e (edges v))
          (unless (rtl:in# e forbidden-edges))
            (let ((len (edge-length e)))
              (cond ((< len min1) (setf min1 len))
                    ((< len min2) (setf min2 len))))))
        (incf cost (/ (+ min1 min2) 2)))
    (reduce '+ (mapcar 'edge-length pinned-edges)
            :initial-value cost)))
```

This implementation can be further improved both in terms of efficiency and finding smarter ways to estimate the lower bound. Devising ways to make it more precise and estimating if they are worth applying in terms of computational complexity is left as an exercise for the reader.

B&B may also use additional heuristics to further optimize its performance at the expense of producing a slightly more suboptimal solution. For example, one may wish to stop branching when the gap between the upper and lower bounds becomes smaller than a certain threshold. Another improvement may be to use a priority queue instead of a stack, in the example, in order to process the most promising branches first.

One more thing I wanted to mention in the context of global heuristic search is **Monte Carlo tree search** (MCTS), which, in my view, uses a very similar strategy to B&B. It is the currently dominant method for finding near-optimal paths in the decision tree for turn-based and other similar games (like go or chess). The difference between

B&B and MCTS is that, typically, B&B will use a conservative exact lower bound for determining which branches to skip. MCTS, instead, calculates the estimate of the potential of the branch to yield the optimal solution by performing the sampling of a number of random items from the branch and averaging their scores. So it can be considered a "softer" variant of B&B. The two approaches can be also combined, for example, to prioritize the branch in the B&B queue. The term "Monte Carlo," by the way, is applied to many algorithms that use uniform random sampling as the basis of their operation.

Gradient Descent

The key idea behind local search was to find a way to somehow improve the current best solution and change it in that direction. It can be similarly utilized when switching from discrete problems to continuous ones. And in this realm, the direction of improvement (actually, the best possible one) is called the **gradient** (or, rather, the opposite of the gradient). Gradient descent (GD) is the principal optimization approach, in the continuous space, that works in the same manner as local search: find the direction of improvement and progress alongside it. There's also a vulgar name for this approach: hill climbing. It has a lot of variations and improvements that we'll discuss in this chapter. But we'll start with the code for the basic algorithm. Once again, it will be a template that can be filled in with specific implementation details for the particular problem. We see this "framework" pattern recurring over and over in optimization methods as most of them provide a general solution that can be applied in various domains and be appropriately adjusted for each one:

```
(defun gd (fn data &key n (learning-rate 0.1) (precision 1e-6))
  (let ((ws (init-weights fn))
        (cost (cost fn ws))
        (i 0))
    (loop
      (update-weights ws learning-rate
                      (grad fn ws data))
      (let ((prev cost))
        (setf cost (cost fn ws))
```

```
      (when (or (< (abs (- cost prev)) precision)
                (eql n (incf i)))
        (return))))
  (values ws
          cost))
```

This procedure optimizes the weights (ws) of some function fn. Moreover, whether we know or not the mathematical formula for fn doesn't really matter: the key is to be able to compute grad, which may be done analytically (using a formula that is just coded) or in a purely data-driven fashion (what backprop, which we have seen in the previous chapter, does). ws will usually be a vector or a matrix, and grad will be an array of the same dimensions. In the simplest and not interesting toy case, both are just scalar numbers.

Besides, in this framework, we need to define the following procedures:

- init-weights sets the starting values in the ws vector according to fn. There are several popular ways to do that: the obvious one to set it to all zeroes, which doesn't work in conjunction with backprop; sample from a uniform distribution with a small amplitude; and more advanced heuristics like Xavier initialization.

- update-weights has a simple mathematical formulation: (decf ws (* learning-rate gradient)). But as ws is usually a multidimensional structure, in Lisp, we can't just use - and * on it as these operations are reserved for dealing with numbers.

- It is also important to be able to calculate the cost function (also often called "loss"). As you can see from the code, the GD procedure may terminate in two cases: either it has used the whole iteration budget assigned to it, or it has approached the optimum very closely, so that, at each new iteration, the change in the value of the cost function is negligible. Apart from this usage, tracking the cost function is also important to monitor the "learning" process (another name for the optimization procedure, popular in this domain). If GD is operating correctly, the cost should monotonically decrease at each step.

This template is the most basic one, and you can see a lot of ways of its further improvement and tuning. One important direction is controlling the learning rate: similar to simulated annealing, it may change over time according to some schedule or heuristics.

Another set of issues that we won't elaborate upon now are related to dealing with numeric precision, and they also include such problems as vanishing/exploding gradients.

Improving GD

In the majority of interesting real-world optimization problems, the gradient can't be computed analytically using a formula. Instead, it has to be recovered from the data, and this is a computationally intensive process: for each item in the dataset, we have to run the "forward" computation and then compute the gradient in the "backward" step. A diametrically opposite approach in terms of both computation speed and quality of the gradient would be to take just a single item and use the gradient for it as an approximation of the actual gradient. From the statistics point of view, after a long sequence of such samples, we have to converge to some optimum anyway. This technique, called **stochastic gradient descent** (SGD), can be considered a form of combining sampling with gradient descent. Yet, sampling could be also applied to the dataset directly. The latter approach is called **batch gradient descent**, and it combines the best of both worlds: decent performance and a much more predictable and close to the actual value of the gradient, which is more suitable for supporting the more advanced approaches, such as momentum.

In essence, momentum makes the gradient that is calculated on a batch of samples more straightforward and less prone to oscillation due to the random fluctuations of the batch samples. It is, basically, achieved by using the moving average of the gradient. Different momentum-based algorithms operate by combining the currently computed value of the update with the previous value. For example, the simple SGD with momentum will have the following update code:

```
(let ((dws 0))
  (loop
    (rtl:with ((batch (sample data batch-size))
               (g (calculate-gradient batch)))
      (setf dws (- (* decay-rate dws)
                   (* learning-rate g)))
      (incf ws dws))))
```

An alternative variant is called the Nesterov accelerated gradient which uses the following update procedure:

```
(let ((dws 0))
  (loop
    (incf ws dws)
    (rtl:with ((batch (sample data batch-size))
               (g (- (* learning-rate (calculate-gradient batch)))))
      (setf dws (+ (* decay-rate dws) g))
      (incf ws g))))
```

That is, we first perform the update using the previous momentum and only then calculate the gradient and perform the gradient-based update. The motivation for it is the following: while the gradient term always points in the right direction, the momentum term may not. If the momentum term points in the wrong direction or overshoots, the gradient can still "go back" and correct it in the same update step.

Another direction of GD improvement is using the adaptive learning-rate. For instance, the famous **Adam** algorithm tracks per-cell learning rate for the ws matrix.

These are not all the ways in which plain gradient descent may be made more sophisticated—in order to converge faster. I won't mention here second-order methods or conjugate gradients. Numerous papers exploring this space continue being published.

Sampling

Speaking about sampling that we have mentioned several times throughout this book, I think this is a good place to mention a couple of simple sampling tricks that may prove useful in many different problems.

The sampling that is used in SGD is the simplest form of random selection that is executed by picking a random element from the set and repeating it the specified number of times. This sampling is called "with replacement." The reason for this is that after picking an element, it is not removed from the set (i.e., it can be considered "replaced" by an equal element), and so it can be picked again. Such an approach is the simplest one to implement and reason about. There's also the "without replacement" version that removes the element from the set after selecting it. It ensures that each element may be picked only once, but also causes the change in probabilities of picking elements on subsequent iterations.

Here is an abstract (as we don't specify the representation of the set and the related size, remove-item, and empty? procedures) implementation of these sampling methods:

```
(defun sample (n set &key (with-replacement t))
  (loop :repeat n
        :for i := (random (size set))
        :collect (rtl:? set i)
        :unless with-replacement :do
          (remove-item set i)
          (when (empty? set) (loop-finish)))
```

This simplest approach samples from a uniform probability distribution, that is, it assumes that the elements of the set have an equal chance of being selected. In many tasks, these probabilities have to be different. For such cases, a more general sampling implementation is needed:

```
(defun sample-from-dist (n dist)
  ;; here, DIST is a hash-table with keys being items
  ;; and values — their probabilities
  (let ((scale (reduce '+ (rtl:vals dist))))
    (loop :repeat n :collect
      (let ((r (* scale (random 1.0)))
            (acc 0))
        (rtl:dotable (k v dist)
          (incf acc v)
          (when (>= acc r)
            (return k)))))))
```

```
CL-USER> (sample-from-dist 10 #h(:foo 2 :quux 1 :baz 10))
(:BAZ :BAZ :BAZ :QUUX :BAZ :BAZ :BAZ :BAZ :BAZ :FOO)
```

I'm surprised how often I have to retell this simple sampling technique. In it, all the items are placed on a [0, 1) interval occupying the parts proportionate to their weight in the probability distribution (:baz will have 80% of the weight in the preceding distribution). Then we put a random point in this interval and determine in which part it falls.

The final sampling approach I'd like to show here—quite a popular one for programming interviews—is **reservoir sampling**. It deals with uniform sampling from an infinite set. Well, how do you represent an infinite set? For practical purposes, it can be thought of as a stream. So the items are read sequentially from this stream, and we need to decide which ones to collect and which to skip. This is achieved by the following procedure:

```
(defun reservoir-sample (n stream)
  (let ((rez (make-array n :initial-element nil)))  ; reservoir
    (handler-case
        (loop :for item := (read stream)
              :for i :from 0
              :for r := (random (1+ i))
              :do (cond
                    ;; fill the reservoir with the first N items
                    ((< i n) (setf (aref rez i) item))
                    ;; replace the R-th item with probability
                    ;; proportionate to (- 1 (/ R N))
                    ((< r n) (setf (aref rez r) item))))
      ;; sampling stops when the stream is exhausted
      ;; we'll use an input stream and read items from it
      (end-of-file () rez))))
```

```
CL-USER> (with-input-from-string (in "foo foo foo foo bar bar baz")
           (reservoir-sample 3 in))
#(BAR BAZ FOO)
CL-USER> (with-input-from-string (in "foo foo foo foo bar bar baz")
           (reservoir-sample 3 in))
#(FOO FOO FOO)
CL-USER> (with-input-from-string (in "foo foo foo foo bar bar baz")
           (reservoir-sample 3 in))
#(BAZ FOO FOO)
CL-USER> (with-input-from-string (in (format nil "~{~A ~}"
                                             (loop :for i :from 0 :to 100
                                                   :collect i)))
           (reservoir-sample 10 in))
#(30 42 66 68 76 5 22 39 51 24)   ; note that 5 stayed at the same position
                                  ; where it was placed initially
```

Matrix Factorization

Matrix factorization is a decomposition of a matrix into a product of matrices. It has many different variants that find applications for particular classes of problems. Matrix factorization is a computationally intensive task that has many applications: from machine learning to information retrieval to data compression. Its use cases include background removal in images, topic modeling, collaborative filtering, CT scan reconstruction, and so on.

Among many factorization methods, the following two stand out as the most prominent: singular value decomposition (SVD) and non-negative matrix factorization/ non-negative sparse coding (NNSC). NNSC is interesting as it produces much sharper vectors that still remain sparse, that is, all the information is concentrated in the non-null slots.

Singular Value Decomposition

SVD is the generalization of the eigendecomposition (which is defined only for square matrices) to any matrix. It is extremely important as the eigenvectors define the basis of the matrix, and the eigenvalues, the relative importance of the eigenvectors. Once SVD is performed, using the obtained vectors, we can immediately figure out a lot of useful properties of the dataset. Thus, SVD is behind such methods as PCA in statistical analysis, LSI topic modeling in NLP, and so on.

Formally, the singular value decomposition of an m x n matrix M is a factorization of the form (* U S V), where U is an m x m unitary matrix, V is an n x n unitary matrix, and S (usually, Greek sigma) is an m x n rectangular diagonal matrix with non-negative real numbers on the diagonal. The columns of U are left-singular vectors of M, the rows of V are right-singular vectors, and the diagonal elements of S are known as the singular values of M.

The singular value decomposition can be computed either analytically or via approximation methods. The analytic approach is not tractable for large matrices—the ones that occur in practice. Thus, approximation methods are used. One of the well-known algorithms is QuasiSVD that was developed as a result of the famous Netflix challenge in the 2000s. The idea behind QuasiSVD is, basically, gradient descent. The algorithm approximates the decomposition with random matrices and then iteratively improves it using the following formula:

```
(defun svd-1 (u v rank training-data &key (learning-rate 0.001))
  (dotimes (f rank)
    (loop :for (i j val) :in training-data :do
      (let ((err (- val (predict rank u i v j))))
        (incf (aref u f i) (* learning-rate err (aref v f j)))
        (incf (aref v f j) (* learning-rate err (aref u f i)))))))))
```

The described method is called QuasiSVD because the singular values are not explicit: the decomposition is into just two matrices of non-unit vectors. Another constraint of the algorithm is that the rank of the decomposition (the number of features) should be specified by the user. Yet, for practical purposes, this is often what is actually needed. Here is a brief description of the usage of the method for predicting movie reviews for the Netflix challenge:

> *For visualizing the problem, it makes sense to think of the data as a big sparsely filled matrix, with users across the top and movies down the side, and each cell in the matrix either contains an observed rating (1-5) for that movie (row) by that user (column) or is blank meaning you don't know. This matrix would have about 8.5 billion entries (number of users times number of movies). Note also that this means you are only given values for one in 85 of the cells. The rest are all blank.*

> *The assumption is that a user's rating of a movie is composed of a sum of preferences about the various aspects of that movie. For example, imagine that we limit it to forty aspects, such that each movie is described only by forty values saying how much that movie exemplifies each aspect, and correspondingly each user is described by forty values saying how much they prefer each aspect. To combine these all together into a rating, we just multiply each user preference by the corresponding movie aspect, and then add those forty leanings up into a final opinion of how much that user likes that movie. [...] Such a model requires (* 40 (+ 17k 500k)) or about 20M values—400 times less than the original 8.5B .*

Here is the function that approximates the rating. The QuasiSVD matrix u is user-features and v movie-features. As you see, we don't need to further factor u and v into the matrix of singular values and the unit vectors' matrices:

```
(defun predict-rating (rank user-features user movie-features movie)
  (loop :for f :from 0 :below rank
        :sum (* (aref user-features f user)
                (aref movie-features f movie))))
```

Fourier Transform

The last item we'll discuss in this chapter is not exactly an optimization problem, but it's also a numeric algorithm that bears a lot of significance to the previous one and has broad practical applications. The discrete Fourier transform (DFT) is the most important discrete transform, used to perform Fourier analysis in many practical applications: in digital signal processing, the function is any quantity or signal that varies over time, such as the pressure of a sound wave, a radio signal, or daily temperature readings, sampled over a finite time interval; in image processing, the samples can be the values of pixels along a row or column of a raster image.

It is said that the Fourier transform transforms a "signal" from the time/space domain (represented by observed samples) into the frequency domain. Put simply, a time-domain graph shows how a signal changes over time, whereas a frequency-domain graph shows how much of the signal lies within each given frequency band over a range of frequencies. The inverse Fourier transform performs the reverse operation and converts the frequency-domain signal back into the time domain. Explaining the deep meaning of the transform is beyond the scope of this book; the only thing worth mentioning here is that operating on the frequency domain allows us to perform many useful operations on the signal, such as determining the most important features, compression (that we'll discuss in the following), and so on.

The complexity of computing DFT naively just by applying its definition on n samples is $O(n^2)$:

```
(defun dft (vec)
  (rtl:with ((n (length vec))
             (rez (make-array n))
             (scale (/ (- (* 2 pi #c(0 1))) n)))
    ;; #c(0 1) is imaginary unit (i) - Lisp allows us
    ;; to operate on complex numbers directly
    (dotimes (i n)
      (setf (aref rez i)
            (loop :for j :from 0 :below n
                  :sum (* (aref vec j)
                          (exp (* scale i j))))))))
```

However, the well-known fast Fourier transform (FFT) achieves a much better performance of $O(n \log n)$. Actually, a group of algorithms shares the name FFT, but their main principle is the same. You might have already guessed, from our previous chapters, that such reduction in complexity is achieved with the help of the divide-and-conquer approach. A radix-2 decimation-in-time (DIT) FFT is the simplest and most common form of the Cooley-Tukey algorithm, which is the standard FFT implementation. It first computes the DFTs of the even-indexed inputs (indices `0, 2, ..., (- n 2)`) and of the odd-indexed inputs (indices `1, 3, ..., (-n 1)`) and then combines those two results to produce the DFT of the whole sequence. This idea is utilized recursively. What enables such decomposition is the observation that, thanks to the periodicity of the complex exponential, the elements `(? rez i)` and `(? rez (+ i n/2))` may be calculated from the FFTs of the same subsequences. The formulas are the following:

```
(let ((e (fft-of-even-indexed-part))
      (o (fft-of-odd-indexed-part))
      (scale (exp (/ (- (* 2 pi #c(0 1) i))
                     n)))
      (n/2 (floor n 2)))
  (setf (aref rez i) (+ (aref e i) (* scale (aref o i)))
        (aref rez (+ i n/2)) (- (aref e i) (* scale (aref o i)))))
```

Fourier Transform in Action: JPEG

Fourier transform—or rather its variant that uses only cosine functions[2] and operates on real numbers, the discrete cosine transform (DCT)—is the enabling factor of the main lossy media compression formats, such as JPEG, MPEG, and MP3. All of them achieve the drastic reduction in the size of the compressed file by first transforming it into the frequency domain and then identifying the long tail of low-amplitude frequencies and removing all the data that is associated with these frequencies (which is, basically, noise). Such an approach allows specifying a threshold of the percentage of data that should be discarded and retained. The use of cosine rather than sine functions is critical for compression since it turns out that fewer cosine functions are needed to approximate

---

[2]The standard Fourier transform uses both the sine and cosine functions that are the components of the complex exponent.

a typical signal. Also, this allows sticking to only real numbers. DCTs are equivalent to DFTs of roughly twice the length, operating on real data with even symmetry. There are, actually, eight different DCT variants, and we won't go into detail about their differences.

The general JPEG compression procedure operates in the following steps:

- An RGB to YCbCr color space conversion (a special color space with luminescence and chrominance components more suited for further processing).

- Division of the image into 8 × 8–pixel blocks.

- Shifting the pixel values from $[0,256)$ to $[-128,128)$.

- Applying DCT to each block from left to right, top to bottom.

- Compressing each block through quantization.

- Entropy encoding the quantized matrix (we'll discuss this in the next chapter).

- Compressed image is reconstructed through the reverse process using the inverse discrete cosine transform (IDCT).

The quantization step is where the lossy part of compression takes place. It aims at reducing most of the less important high-frequency DCT coefficients to zero; the more zeroes there are, the better the image will compress. Lower frequencies are used to reconstruct the image because the human eye is more sensitive to them, and higher frequencies are discarded.

P.S. Also, further development of the Fourier-related transforms for lossy compression lies in using the wavelet family of transforms.

Takeaways

It was not easy to select the name for this chapter. Originally, I planned to dedicate it to optimization approaches. Then I thought that a number of other numerical algorithms needed to be presented, but they were not substantial enough to justify a separate chapter. After all, I saw that what all these different approaches are about is, first of all, approximation. And, after gathering all the descriptions in one place and combining them, I came to the conclusion that approximation is, in a way, a more general and correct term than optimization. However, they go hand in hand, and it's somewhat hard to say which one enables the other...

A conclusion that we can draw from this chapter is that the main optimization methods currently in use boil down to greedy local probabilistic search. In both the discrete and continuous domains, the key idea is to quickly find the direction, in which we can somewhat improve the current state of the system, and advance alongside that direction. All the rest is, basically, fine-tuning of this concept. There are alternatives, but local search a.k.a. gradient descent a.k.a. hill climbing dominates the optimization landscape.

Another interesting observation can be made that many approaches we have seen here are more of templates or frameworks than algorithms. Branch and bound, genetic programming, and local search define a certain skeleton that should be filled with domain-specific code which will perform the main computations. Such a "big picture" approach is somewhat uncommon to the algorithm world that tends to concentrate on the low-level details and optimize them down to the last bit. So the skills needed to design such generic frameworks are no less important to the algorithmic developers than knowledge of the low-level optimization techniques.

SGD, SVD, MCTS, NNSC, FFT—this sphere has plenty of algorithms with abbreviated names for solving particular numerical problems. We have discussed only the most well-known and principal ones with broad practical significance in the context of software development. But, besides them, there are many other famous numerical algorithms like the sieve of Eratosthenes, the finite element method, the simplex method, and so on and so forth. Yet, many of the ways to tackle them and the issues you will encounter in the process are, essentially, similar.

CHAPTER 14

Compression

$$\text{foo} \longrightarrow \left\{ \begin{array}{l} a : 10 \\ \dots \\ f : 111 \\ \dots \\ 0 : 101 \end{array} \right\} \longrightarrow 111101101$$

Compression is one of the tools that every programmer should understand and wield confidently. Such situations when the size of the dataset is larger than the program can handle directly and it becomes a bottleneck are quite frequent and can be encountered in any domain. There are many forms of compression, yet the most general subdivision is between lossless one which preserves the original information intact and lossy compression which discards some information (assumed to be the most useless part or just noise). Lossless compression is applied to numeric or text data, whole files, or directories—the data that will become partially or utterly useless if even a slight modification is made. Lossy compression, as a rule, is applied to data that originates in the "analog world": sound or video recordings, images, and so on. We have touched the subject of lossy compression slightly in the previous chapter when talking about such formats as JPEG. In this chapter, we will discuss the lossless variants in more detail. Besides, we'll talk a bit about other, non-compressing forms of encoding.

Encoding

Let's start with encoding. Lossless compression is, in fact, a form of encoding, but there are other, simpler forms. And it makes sense to understand them before moving to compression. Besides, encoding itself is a fairly common task. It is the mechanism that transforms the data from an internal representation of a particular program into some

© Vsevolod Domkin 2021

V. Domkin, *Programming Algorithms in Lisp*, https://doi.org/10.1007/978-1-4842-6428-7_14

305

specific format that can be recognized and processed (decoded) by other programs. What we gain is that the encoded data may be serialized and transferred to other computers and decoded by other programs, possibly, independent of the program that performed the encoding.

Encoding may be applied to different semantic levels of the data. Character encoding operates on the level of individual characters or even bytes, while various serialization formats deal with structured data. There are two principal approaches to serialization: text-based and binary. The pros and cons are the opposite: text-based formats are easier to handle by humans but are usually more expensive to process, while binary variants are not transparent (and so much harder to deal with) but much faster to process. From the point of view of algorithms, binary formats are, obviously, better. But my programming experience is that they constitute a severe form of premature optimization. The rule of thumb should always be to start with text-based serialization and move to binary formats only as a last resort when it was proven that the impact on the program performance from that is significant and critical.

Base64

Encoding may have both a reduction and a magnification effect on the size of the data. For instance, there's a popular encoding scheme—Base64. It is a byte-level (lowest-level) encoding that doesn't discriminate between different input data representations and formats. No, the encoder just takes a stream of bytes and produces another stream of bytes—or, more precisely, bytes in the specific range of English ASCII letters, numbers, and three more characters (usually, +, /, and =). This encoding is often used for transferring data in the Web, in conjunction with SMTP (MIME), HTTP, and other popular protocols. The idea behind it is simple: split the data stream into sextets (6-bit parts—there are 64 different variants of those), and map each sextet to an ASCII character according to a fixed dictionary. As the last byte of the original data may not align with the last sextet, an additional padding character (=) is used to indicate 2 (=) or 4 (==) misaligned bits. As we see, Base64 encoding increases the size of the input data by a factor of 1.33.

Here is one of the ways to implement a Base64 serialization routine:

```lisp
(defparameter *b64-dict*
  (coerce (append (loop :for ch :from (char-code #\A) :to (char-code #\Z)
                        :collect (code-char ch))
                  (loop :for ch :from (char-code #\a) :to (char-code #\z)
                        :collect (code-char ch))
                  (loop :for ch :from (char-code #\0) :to (char-code #\9)
                        :collect (code-char ch))
                  '(#\+ #\/ #\=))
          'simple-vector))

(defun b64-encode (in out)
  (let ((key 0)
        (limit 6))
    (flet ((fill-key (byte off beg limit)
             (setf (ldb (byte limit off) key)
                   (ldb (byte limit beg) byte))
             (setf off (- 6 beg)))
           (emit1 (k)
             (write-byte (char-code (svref *b64-dict* k)) out)))
      (loop :for byte := (read-byte in nil) :while byte :do
        (let ((beg (- 8 limit)))
          (fill-key byte 0 beg limit)
          (emit1 key)
          (fill-key byte (setf limit (- 6 beg)) 0 beg)
          (when (= 6 beg)
            (emit1 key)
            (setf limit 6))))
      (when (< limit 6)
        (setf (ldb (byte limit 0) key)
              (ldb (byte limit 0) 0))
        (emit1 key)
        (loop :repeat (ceiling limit 2) :do
          (emit1 64))))))
```

This is one of the most low-level pieces of Lisp code in this book. It could be written in a much more high-level manner: utilizing the generic sequence access operations, say, on bit-vectors, instead of the bit-manipulating ones on numbers. However, it would be also orders of magnitude slower due to the need to constantly "repackage" the bits, converting the data from integers to vectors and back. I also wanted to show a bit of bit fiddling, in Lisp. The standard, in fact, defines a comprehensive vocabulary of bit manipulation functions; and there's nothing stopping the programmer from writing performant code operating at a single bit level.

One important choice made for Base64 encoding is the usage of streams as the input and output. This is a common approach to such problems based on the following considerations:

- It is quite easy to wrap the code so that we could feed/extract strings as inputs and outputs. Doing the opposite and wrapping a string-based code for stream operation is also possible, but it defeats the whole purpose of streams, which is...

- Streams allow to efficiently handle data of any size and not waste memory, as well as CPU, for storing intermediary copies of the strings we're processing. Encoding a huge file is a good illustration of why this matters. With streams, we do it in an obvious manner: (with-open-file (in ...) (rtl:with-out-file (out) (base64-encode in out))). With strings, however, it will mean, first, reading the file contents into memory—and we may not even have enough memory for that—and, after that, filling another big chunk of memory with the encoded data, which we'll still, probably, need to either dump to a file or send over the network.

So what happens in the preceding code? First, the bytes are read from the binary input stream in; then each one is slashed into two parts. The higher bits are set into the current base64 key, which is translated, using *b64-dict*, into an appropriate byte and emitted to the binary output stream out. The lower bits are deposited in the higher bits of the next key in order to use this leftover during the processing of the next byte. However, if the leftover from the previous byte was 4 bits, at the current iteration, we will have 2 base64 bytes available as the first will use 2 bits from the incoming byte and the second will consume the remaining 6 bits. This is addressed in the code block (when (= 6 beg) ...). The function relies on the standard Lisp `ldb` operation which provides access to the individual bits of an integer. It uses the byte-spec (byte limit offset) to control the bits it wants to obtain.

Implementing a decoder procedure is left as an exercise to the reader...

Taking the example from the Wikipedia article, we can see our encoding routine in action (here, we also rely on the FLEXI-STREAMS library to work with binary in-memory streams):

```
CL-USER> (let ((in (flex:make-in-memory-input-stream
                       (map 'vector 'char-code "Man i")))
               (out (flex:make-in-memory-output-stream)))
           (b64-encode in out)
           (map 'string 'code-char (rtl:? out 'vector))))
"TWFuIGk="
```

This function, although it's not big, is quite hard to debug due to the need for careful tracking and updating of the offsets into both the current base64 chunk (key) and the byte being processed. What really helps me tackle such situations is a piece of paper that serves for recording several iterations with all the relevant state changes. Something along these lines:

```
        M (77)      |     a (97)      |     n (110)
   0 1 0 0 1 1 0 1|0 1 1 0 0 0 0 1|0 1 1 0 1 1 1 0
0: 0 1 0 0 1 1     |               |               19 = T
             0 1|               |
1:           0 1|0 1 1 0         |               22 = W
             |         0 0 0 1|
2:           |         0 0 0 1|0 1              5 = F
```

Iteration 0:

beg: 2
off: 0
limit: 6

beg: 0
off: (- 6 2) = 4
limit: 2

Iteration 1:

beg: 4
off: 0
limit: 4

beg: 0
off: (- 6 4) = 2
limit: 4

Another thing that is indispensable, when coding such procedures, is the availability of the reference examples of the expected result, like the ones in Wikipedia. Lisp REPL makes iterating on a solution and constantly rechecking the results, using such available data, very easy. However, sometimes, it makes sense to reject the transient nature of code in the REPL and record some of the test cases as unit tests. As the motto of my test library should-test declares, you should test even Lisp code sometimes. :) The tests also help the programmer to remember and systematically address the various corner cases. In this example, one of the special cases is the padding at the end, which is handled in the code block (when (< limit 6) ...). Due to the availability of a clear spec and reference examples, this algorithm lends itself very well to automated testing. As a general rule, all code paths should be covered by the tests. If I were to write those tests, I'd start with the following simple version. They address all three variants of padding and also the corner case of an empty string:

```
(deftest b64-encode ()
  ;; B64STR would be the function wrapped over the REPL code presented
    above
  (should be rtl:blankp (b64str ""))
  (should be string= "TWFu" (b64str "Man"))
  (should be string= "TWFuIA==" (b64str "Man "))
  (should be string= "TWFuIGk=" (b64str "Man i")))
```

Surely, many more tests should be added to a production-level implementation: to validate operation on non-ASCII characters, handling of huge data, and so on.

Lossless Compression

The idea behind lossless compression is straightforward: find an encoding that is tailored to our particular dataset and allows the encoding procedure to produce a shorter version than using a standard encoding. Not being general-purpose, the vocabulary for this encoding may use a more compact representation for those things that occur often and a longer one for those that appear rarely, skipping altogether those that don't appear at all. Such an encoding scheme will be, probably, structure-agnostic and just convert sequences of bytes into other sequences of a smaller size, although custom structure-aware compression is also possible.

This approach can be explained with a simple example. The phrase "this is a test" uses 8-bit ASCII characters to represent each letter. There are 256 different ASCII characters in total. However, for this particular message, only seven characters are used: t, h, i, s, Space, a, and e. Seven characters, according to the entropy definition, need only 2.81 bits to be distinguished. Encoding them in just 3 ((ceiling 2.81)) bits instead of 8 will reduce the size of the message almost thrice. In other words, we could create the following vocabulary (where #*000 is a Lisp literal representation of a zero bit-vector of 3 bits):

```
#h(#\t  #*000
   #\h  #*001
   #\i  #*010
   #\s  #*011
   #\a  #*100
   #\e  #*101
   #\Space  #*110)
```

Using this vocabulary, our message could be encoded as the following bit-vector: #*000001010011110010011110100110000101011000. The downside, compared to using some standard encoding, is that we now need to package the vocabulary alongside the message, which will make its total size larger than the original that used an 8-bit standard encoding with a known vocabulary. It's clear, though, that, as the message becomes longer, the fixed overhead of the vocabulary will quickly be exceeded by the gain from message size reduction. However, we have to account for the fact that the vocabulary may also continue to grow and require more and more bits to represent each entry (for instance, if we use all Latin letters and numbers, it will soon reach 6 or 7 bits, and our gains will diminish as well). Still, the difference may be pre-calculated and the decision made for each message or a batch of messages. For instance, in this case, the vocabulary size may be, say, 30 bytes, and the message size reduction is 62.5%, so a message of 50 or more characters will be already more compact if encoded with this vocabulary even when the vocabulary itself will be sent with it. The case of only seven characters is pretty artificial, but consider that DNA strings have only four characters.

However, this simplistic approach is just the beginning. Once again, if we use an example of the Latin alphabet, some letters, like q or x, may end up used much less frequently, than, say, p or a. Our encoding scheme uses equal-length vectors to represent them all. Yet, if we were to use shorter representations for more frequently used chars at the expense of longer ones for the characters occurring less often, additional compression could be gained. That's exactly the idea behind Huffman coding.

Huffman Coding

Huffman coding tailors an optimal "alphabet" for each message, sorting all letters based on their frequency and putting them in a binary tree, in which the most frequent ones are closer to the top and the less frequent ones to the bottom. This tree allows calculating a unique encoding for each letter based on a sequence of left or right branches that need to be taken to reach it, from the top. The key trick of the algorithm is the usage of a heap to maintain the characters (both individual and groups of already processed ones) in sorted order. It builds the tree bottom-up by first extracting two least frequent letters and combining them: the least frequent on the left, the more frequent on the right. Let's consider our test message. In it, the letters are sorted by frequency in the following order:

```
((#\a 1) (#\e 1) (#\h 1) (#\i 2) (#\s 3) (#\t 3) (#\Space 3))
```

Extracting the first two letters results in the following treelet:

```
 ((#\a #\e) 2)
  /        \
(#\a 1)  (#\e 1)
```

Uniting the two letters creates a tree node with a total frequency of 2. To use this information further, we add it back to the queue in place of the original letters, and it continues to represent them during the next steps of the algorithm:

```
((#\h 1) ((#\a #\e) 2) (#\i 2) (#\s 3) (#\t 3) (#\Space 3))
```

By continuing this process, we'll come to the following end result:

```
((#\s #\t #\Space #\i #\h #\a #\e) 14)
     /                              \
((#\s #\t) 6)        ((#\Space #\i #\h #\a #\e) 8)
   /     \         /                           \
(#\s 3)  (#\t 3) (#\Space 3)  ((#\i #\h #\a #\e) 5)
                              /                  \
                       (#\i 2)  ((#\h #\a #\e) 3)
                               /               \
                          (#\h 1)  ((#\a #\e) 2)
                                   /          \
                            (#\a 1)   (#\e 1)
```

From this tree, we can construct the optimal encoding:

```
#h(#\s #*00
   #\t #*01
   #\Space #*10
   #\i #*110
   #\h #*1110
   #\a #*11110
   #\e #*11111)
```

Compared to the simple approach that used constantly 3 bits per character, it takes 1 bit less for the three most frequent letters and 2 bits more for two least frequent ones. The encoded message becomes #*01111011000101100010111101001111110001, and it has a length of 38 compared to 43 for our previous attempt.

To be clear, here are the encoding and decoding methods that use the pre-built vocabulary (for simplicity's sake, they operate on vectors and strings instead of streams):

```
(defun huffman-encode (envocab str)
  (let ((rez (make-array 0 :element-type 'bit
                           :adjustable t :fill-pointer t)))
    (rtl:dovec (char str)
      (rtl:dovec (bit (rtl:? envocab char))
        (vector-push-extend bit rez)))
    rez))
```

```
(defun huffman-decode (devocab vec)
  (let (rez)
    (dotimes (i (length vec))
      (dotimes (j (- (length vec) i))
        (rtl:when-it (rtl:? devocab (rtl:slice vec i (+ i j 1)))
          (push rtl:it rez)
          (incf i j)
          (return))))
    (coerce (reverse rez) 'string)))
```

It is worth recalling that vector-push-extend is implemented in a way which will not adjust the array by only 1 bit each time it is called. The efficient implementation "does the right thing," for whatever the right thing means in this particular case (maybe adjusting by one machine word). You can examine the situation in more detail by trying to extend the array by hand (using adjust-array or providing a third optional argument to vector-push-extend) and comparing the time taken by the different variants, to verify my words.

Finally, here is the most involved part of the Huffman algorithm, which builds the encoding and decoding vocabularies (with the help of a heap implementation we developed in Chapter 9):

```
(defun huffman-vocabs (str)
  ;; here we assume more than a single unique character in STR
  (let ((counts #h())
        (q (make-heap :op '< :key 'rt))
        (envocab #h())
        (devocab #h(equal)))   ; bit-vectors as keys require
                               ; equal comparison
    ;; count character frequencies
    (rtl:dovec (char str)
      (incf (gethash char counts 0)))   ; here, we use the default third argument
                                        ; of get# with the value of 0
    ;; heapsort the characters based on their frequency
    (rtl:dotable (char count counts)
      (heap-push (pair char count) q))
```

```
;; build the tree
(dotimes (i (1- (heap-size q)))
  (rtl:with (((lt cl) (heap-pop q))
             ((rt cr) (heap-pop q)))
    (heap-push (pair (list lt rt) (+ cl cr))
               q)))
;; traverse the tree in DFS manner
;; encoding the path to each leaf node as a bit-vector
(labels ((dfs (node &optional (level 0) path)
           (if (listp node)
               (progn
                 (dfs (rtl:lt node) (1+ level) (cons 0 path))
                 (dfs (rtl:rt node) (1+ level) (cons 1 path)))
               (let ((vec (make-array level :element-type 'bit
                                            :initial-contents
                                            (reverse path))))
                 (setf (rtl:? envocab node) vec
                       (rtl:? devocab vec) node)))))
  (dfs (lt (heap-pop q))))
(list envocab devocab)))
```

Huffman Coding in Action: Dictionary Optimization

Compression is one of the areas for which it is especially interesting to directly compare the measured gain in space usage to the one expected theoretically. Yet, as we discussed in one of the previous chapters, such measurements are not so straightforward as execution speed measurements. Yes, if we compress a single sequence of bytes into another one, there's nothing more trivial than to compare their lengths, but, in many tasks, we want to see a cumulative effect of applying compression on a complex data structure. This is what we're going to do next.

Consider the problem that I had in my work on the tool for text language identification wiki-lang-detect. This software relies on a number of big dictionaries that map strings (character trigrams and individual words) to floats. The obvious approach to storing these maps is with a hash-table. However, due to the huge number of keys, such table will, generally, have a sizeable overhead, which we would like to avoid. Besides, the keys are strings, so they have a good potential for reduction in occupied size when compressed. The data is also serialized into per-language files in the tab-separated format. This is the sample of a word-level file for the Danish language:

```
afrika    -8.866735
i     -2.9428265
the     -6.3879676
ngo     -11.449115
of     -6.971129
kanye     -12.925021
e    -8.365895
natal     -12.171249
```

Our task is to load the data in memory so that access to the keys has constant runtime and minimal occupied space.

Let's begin with a simple hash-table-based approach. The following function will load two files from the default directory (*default-pathname-defaults*) and return a list of two hash-tables—for the word and trigram probabilities:

```
(defun load-data-into-hts (lang)
  (declare (optimize sb-c::instrument-consing))
  (mapcar (lambda (kind)
            (let ((rez (make-hash-table :test 'equal)))
              (dolines (line (fmt "~A-~A.csv" lang kind))
                (let ((space (position #\Space line)))
                  (rtl:sethash (slice line 0 space) rez
                               (read-from-string (slice line (1+
                               space))))))
              rez))
          '("words" "3gs")))
```

To measure the space it will take, we'll use a new SBCL extension called allocation profiling from the `sb-aprof` package.[1] To enable the measurement, we have put a special declaration immediately after the defun header: (`optimize sb-c::instrument-consing`).

Now, prior to running the code, let's look at the output of `room`:

```
CL-USER> (room)
Dynamic space usage is:    60,365,216 bytes.
...
```

This is a freshly loaded image, so space usage is minimal. Usually, before proceeding with the experiment, I invoke garbage collection to ensure that we don't have some leftover data from the previous runs that may overlap with the current one. In SBCL, you run it with (`sb-ext:gc:full t`).

Now, let's load the files for the German language (the biggest ones) under `aprof`. The data can be obtained from the GitHub repository of the project. The total size of two German-language files on disk (words and trigram dictionaries) is around 4 MB:

```
CL-USER> (sb-aprof:aprof-run
          (lambda () (defparameter *de* (load-data-into-hts "DE"))))
227 (of 50000 max) profile entries consumed
```

%	Bytes	Count	Function
24.2	34773600	434670	SB-KERNEL:%MAKE-ARRAY - #:|unknown|
19.4	27818880	217335	SB-IMPL::%MAKE-STRING-INPUT-STREAM - SB-IMPL::STRING-INPUT-STREAM
19.4	27818880	434670	SLICE - LIST
17.3	24775088		SB-IMPL::HASH-TABLE-NEW-VECTORS
54.0	13369744	52	SIMPLE-VECTOR
46.0	11405344	156	(SIMPLE-ARRAY (UNSIGNED-BYTE 32) (*))

---

[1]To make full use of this feature and be able to profile SBCL internal functions, you'll need to compile SBCL with the `--with-cons-profiling` flag. Many thanks to Douglas Katzman for developing this feature and guiding me through its usage.

14.9	21406176		SB-IMPL::ANSI-STREAM-READ-LINE-FROM- FRC-BUFFER
99.4	21280192	225209	(SIMPLE-ARRAY CHARACTER (*))
0.6	125984	7874	LIST
4.8	6957184	217412	SB-KERNEL::INTEGER-/-INTEGER - RATIO
00.0	14160		SB-IMPL::%MAKE-PATHNAME
91.8	12992	812	LIST
8.2	1168	1	SIMPLE-VECTOR
00.0	4160	2	SB-IMPL::SET-FD-STREAM-ROUTINES - (SIMPLE-ARRAY CHARACTER (*))
00.0	3712		SB-IMPL::%MAKE-DEFAULT-STRING-OSTREAM
62.1	2304	8	(SIMPLE-ARRAY CHARACTER (*))
37.9	1408	8	SB-IMPL::CHARACTER-STRING-OSTREAM
00.0	1024		MAKE-HASH-TABLE
53.1	544	2	SIMPLE-VECTOR
46.9	480	6	(SIMPLE-ARRAY (UNSIGNED-BYTE 32) (*))
00.0	832		SB-IMPL::%MAKE-FD-STREAM
73.1	608	2	SB-SYS:FD-STREAM
19.2	160	2	SB-VM::ARRAY-HEADER
7.7	64	2	(SIMPLE-ARRAY CHARACTER (*))
00.0	576		GET-OUTPUT-STREAM-STRING
55.6	320	8	SIMPLE-BASE-STRING
44.4	256	8	SB-KERNEL:CLOSURE
00.0	400		SB-KERNEL:VECTOR-SUBSEQ*
60.0	240	6	(SIMPLE-ARRAY CHARACTER (*))
40.0	160	5	SIMPLE-BASE-STRING
00.0	400	5	SB-IMPL::%%MAKE-PATHNAME - PATHNAME
00.0	384	2	SB-IMPL::%MAKE-HASH-TABLE - HASH-TABLE
00.0	288	4	SB-KERNEL:%CONCATENATE-TO-STRING - (SIMPLE-ARRAY CHARACTER (*))

00.0	1w92	12	SB-IMPL::UNPARSE-NATIVE-PHYSICAL- FILE - LIST
00.0	176	2	SB-IMPL::READ-FROM-C-STRING/UTF-8 - (SIMPLE-ARRAY CHARACTER (*))
00.0	128	4	SB-ALIEN-INTERNALS:%SAP-ALIEN - SB-ALIEN-INTERNALS:ALIEN-VALUE
00.0	96		SB-IMPL::QUERY-FILE-SYSTEM
66.7	64	2	SB-KERNEL:CLOSURE
33.3	32	2	SB-VM::VALUE-CELL

```
=======  ===========
 100.0    143576336
```

The profiling report is pretty cryptic, at first sight, and requires some knowledge of SBCL internals to understand. It contains all the allocations performed during the test run, so we should mind that some of the used memory is garbage and will be collected at the next gc. We can confirm that by looking at the room output:

```
CL-USER> (room)
Dynamic space usage is:    209,222,464 bytes.
CL-USER> (sb-ext:gc :full t)
NIL
CL-USER> (room)
Dynamic space usage is:    107,199,296 bytes.
```

Let's study the report in detail. Around 47 MB was, in fact, used for the newly created data structures—more than ten times what was needed to store the data on disk. Well, efficient access requires sacrificing a lot of space. From the report, we can make an educated guess where this 47 MB originates: 24.7 MB was used for the hash-table structures themselves (SB-IMPL::HASH-TABLE-NEW-VECTORS) and 21.4 MB for the keys (SB-IMPL::ANSI-STREAM-READ-LINE-FROM-FRC-BUFFER), plus some small amount of bookkeeping information. We can also infer that the floating-point values required around 7 MB (SB-KERNEL::INTEGER-/-INTEGER - RATIO), but it seems like they were put inside the hash-table arrays without any indirection. To verify that this assumption is correct, we can calculate the total number of keys in the hash-tables, which amounts to

216993, and multiply it by 32 (the number of bits in a short-float used here). Also, the first three lines, which, in total, accrued around 90 MB or almost two-thirds of the memory used, are all related to reading the data and its processing; and this space was freed during gc.

So this report, although it is not straightforward to understand, gives a lot of insight into how space is used during the run of the algorithm. And the ability to specify what to track on a per-code block basis makes it even more useful.

From the obtained breakdown, we can see the optimization potential of the current solution:

- The use of a more space-efficient data structure instead of a hash-table might save us up to 17 MB of space (7 MB of float values will remain intact).

- And another 20 MB may be saved if we compress the keys.

Let's try the second option as it is exactly the focus of this chapter. We'll use the created hash-tables to make new ones with Huffman-encoded keys. Here are the contents of the word probabilities table:

```
;; the following output was obtained with *print-length* set to 10
CL-USER> (rtl:print-ht (first *de*))
#{EQUAL
  "afrika" -9.825206
  "i" -7.89809
  "the" -7.0929685
  "ngo" -12.696277
  "noma" -14.284437
  "of" -6.82038
  "kanye" -14.233144
  "e" -7.7334323
  "natal" -11.476304
  "c" -8.715089
  ...
}
```

And here is the function that will transform the tables:

```
(defun huffman-tables (hts envocab)
  (declare (optimize sb-c::instrument-consing))
  (mapcar (lambda (ht)
            (let ((rez (make-hash-table :test 'equal)))
              (rtl:dotable (str logprob ht)
                (setf (rtl:? rez (huffman-encode envocab str)) logprob))
              rez))
          hts))
;; the Huffman encoding vocabulary *DE-VOCAB* should be built
;; from all the keys of *DE* tables separately

CL-USER> (sb-aprof:aprof-run
          (lambda () (defparameter *de2* (huffman-tables *de* *de-vocab*))))
1294 (of 50000 max) profile entries consumed
```

%	Bytes	Count	Function
42.5	44047104	1376461	SB-VM::ALLOCATE-VECTOR-WITH-WIDETAG - ARRAY
23.9	24775088		SB-IMPL::HASH-TABLE-NEW-VECTORS
54.0	13369744	52	SIMPLE-VECTOR
46.0	11405344	156	(SIMPLE-ARRAY (UNSIGNED-BYTE 32) (*))
20.1	20864160		HUFFMAN-ENCODE
83.3	17386800	217335	SB-VM::ARRAY-HEADER
16.7	3477360	217335	SIMPLE-BIT-VECTOR
6.7	6955072	217335	SB-KERNEL:VECTOR-SUBSEQ* - SIMPLE-BIT-VECTOR
3.4	3477360	217335	(SB-PCL::FAST-METHOD RUTILS.GENERIC::GENERIC-SETF :AROUND (T T)) - LIST
3.4	3477360	217335	(SB-PCL::FAST-METHOD RUTILS.GENERIC::GENERIC-SETF (HASH-TABLE T)) - LIST
00.0	2464	77	SB-KERNEL::INTEGER-/-INTEGER - RATIO

00.0	1024		MAKE-HASH-TABLE
53.1	544	2	SIMPLE-VECTOR
46.9	480	6	(SIMPLE-ARRAY (UNSIGNED-BYTE 32) (*))
00.0	384	2	SB-IMPL::%MAKE-HASH-TABLE - HASH-TABLE
00.0	96		SB-C::%PROCLAIM
66.7	64	2	LIST
33.3	32	1	SB-KERNEL:CLOSURE
00.0	96	2	SB-INT:SET-INFO-VALUE - SIMPLE-VECTOR
00.0	64	2	SB-THREAD:MAKE-MUTEX - SB-HREAD:MUTEX
00.0	32	1	SB-IMPL::%COMPILER-DEFVAR - LIST
00.0	32	2	HUFFMAN-TABLES - LIST
00.0	16	1	SB-KERNEL:ASSERT-SYMBOL-HOME-PACKAGE-UNLOCKED - LIST

```
=======  ===========
 100.0     103600352
CL-USER> (sb-ext:gc :full t)
NIL
CL-USER> (room)
Dynamic space usage is:    139,922,208 bytes.
```

So we have claimed 32 MB of additional space (instead of 47), and some of it seems to be used by other unrelated data (some functions I have redefined in the REPL during the experiment and others), as the compressed keys amount for only 3.5 MB:

```
3477360     217335     SIMPLE-BIT-VECTOR
```

That is more than five times reduction or almost 40% compression of the whole data structure!

And what about performance? Huffman compression will be needed at every data access, so let's measure the time it will take for vanilla string keys and the bit-vector ones. We will use another file from the wiki-lang-detect repository for the smoke test—a snippet from Faust:

```
CL-USER> (defparameter *de-words*
           (let ((words (list))
                 (dict (first *de*)))
             (rtl:dolines (line "data/smoke/de.txt")
               (dolist (word (split #\Space line))
                 (push word words)))
             words))
CL-USER> (length *de-words*)
562

CL-USER> (let ((vocab (first *de*)))
           (time (loop :repeat 1000 :do
                   (dolist (word *de-words*)
                     (gethash word vocab)))))
Evaluation took:
  0.045 seconds of real time

CL-USER> (let ((vocab (first *de2*)))
           (time (loop :repeat 1000 :do
                   (dolist (word *de-words*)
                     (gethash (huffman-encode *de-vocab* word) vocab)))))
Evaluation took:
  0.341 seconds of real time
```

Hmm, with Huffman coding, it's almost 10× slower. :(Is there a way to speed it up somewhat? To answer it, we can utilize another profiler—this time a more conventional one, which measures the time spent in each operation. SBCL provides access to two versions of such profilers: a precise and a statistical one. The statistical doesn't seriously interfere with the flow of the program as it uses sampling to capture the profiling data, and it's the preferred one among the developers. To use it, we need to perform (require 'sb-sprof) and then run the computation with profiling enabled (the lengthy output is redacted to show only the most important parts):

```
CL-USER> (let ((dict (first *de2*)))
          (sb-sprof:with-profiling (:report :graph)
            (loop :repeat 100 :do
              (dolist (word *de-words*)
                (gethash (huffman-encode *de-vocab* word) dict)))))
```

Number of samples: 34
Sample interval: 0.01 seconds
Total sampling time: 0.34 seconds
Number of cycles: 0
Sampled threads:
 #<SB-THREAD:THREAD "repl-thread" RUNNING {100FB19BC3}>

Count	%	Count	%	Callees
24	70.6			"Unknown component: #x52CD6390" [41]
5	14.7	24	70.6	HUFFMAN-ENCODE [1]
1	2.9			SB-IMPL::GETHASH/EQL [17]
1	2.9			SB-IMPL::GETHASH3 [6]
1	2.9			LENGTH [14]
1	2.9			SB-KERNEL:HAIRY-DATA-VECTOR-REF/CHECK-BOUNDS [13]
2	5.9			(SB-VM::OPTIMIZED-DATA-VECTOR-REF BIT) [5]
13	38.2			VECTOR-PUSH-EXTEND [11]
4	11.8			SB-VM::EXTEND-VECTOR [4]
4	11.8	4	11.8	SB-VM::ALLOCATE-VECTOR-WITH-WIDETAG [2]
6	17.6			"Unknown component: #x52CD6390" [41]
3	8.8	6	17.6	SB-IMPL::GETHASH/EQUAL [3]
1	2.9			SXHASH [42]
2	5.9			SB-INT:BIT-VECTOR-= [10]
8	23.5			VECTOR-PUSH-EXTEND [11]
2	5.9	8	23.5	SB-VM::EXTEND-VECTOR [4]
2	5.9			SB-VM::COPY-VECTOR-DATA [9]
4	11.8			SB-VM::ALLOCATE-VECTOR-WITH-WIDETAG [2]

```
-----------------------------------------------------------------
   2   5.9                   HUFFMAN-ENCODE [1]
   2   5.9       2   5.9     (SB-VM::OPTIMIZED-DATA-VECTOR-REF BIT) [5]
-----------------------------------------------------------------
```

...

	Self		Total		Cumul			
Nr	Count	%	Count	%	Count	%	Calls	Function
1	5	14.7	24	70.6	5	14.7	-	HUFFMAN-ENCODE
2	4	11.8	4	11.8	9	26.5	-	SB-VM::ALLOCATE-VECTOR-WITH-WIDETAG
3	3	8.8	6	17.6	12	35.3	-	SB-IMPL::GETHASH/EQUAL
4	2	5.9	8	23.5	14	41.2	-	SB-VM::EXTEND-VECTOR
5	2	5.9	2	5.9	16	47.1	-	(SB-VM::OPTIMIZED-DATA-VECTOR-REF BIT)
6	2	5.9	2	5.9	18	52.9	-	SB-IMPL::GETHASH3
7	2	5.9	2	5.9	20	58.8	-	GETHASH
8	2	5.9	2	5.9	22	64.7	-	(SB-VM::OPTIMIZED-DATA-VECTOR-SET BIT)
9	2	5.9	2	5.9	24	70.6	-	SB-VM::COPY-VECTOR-DATA
10	2	5.9	2	5.9	26	76.5	-	SB-INT:BIT-VECTOR-=
11	1	2.9	13	38.2	27	79.4	-	VECTOR-PUSH-EXTEND
12	1	2.9	1	2.9	28	82.4	-	SB-VM::SLOW-HAIRY-DATA-VECTOR-SET
13	1	2.9	1	2.9	29	85.3	-	SB-KERNEL:HAIRY-DATA-VECTOR-REF/CHECK-BOUNDS
14	1	2.9	1	2.9	30	88.2	-	LENGTH
15	1	2.9	1	2.9	31	91.2	-	SB-KERNEL:HAIRY-DATA-VECTOR-SET
16	1	2.9	1	2.9	32	94.1	-	SB-KERNEL:VECTOR-SUBSEQ*
17	1	2.9	1	2.9	33	97.1	-	SB-IMPL::GETHASH/EQL

...

Unsurprisingly, most of the time is spent in huffman-encode, and of it the biggest chunks are vector-push-extend and hash-table access (to get the Huffman code of a letter). Surely, instead of extending the vector at each iteration, it would be much nicer to just perform a bulk copy of the bits for each character directly into the vector. Let's try that and see the difference:

```
(defun huffman-encode2 (envocab str)
  (let ((vecs (map 'vector (lambda (ch) (get# ch envocab))
                   str))
        (total-size 0))
    (rtl:dovec (vec vecs)
      (incf total-size (length vec)))
    (let ((rez (make-array total-size :element-type 'bit))
          (i 0))
      (rtl:dovec (vec vecs)
        (let ((size (length vec)))
          (setf (subseq rez i) vec)
          (incf i size)))
      rez)))
```

```
CL-USER> (let ((vocab (first *de2*)))
           (time (loop :repeat 1000 :do
                   (dolist (word *de-words*)
                     (gethash (huffman-encode2 *de-vocab* word) vocab)))))
Evaluation took:
  0.327 seconds of real time
```

Almost no difference. Well, it's a usual case with these micro-optimizations: you have a brilliant idea, try it under the profiler, and, bah, no difference... This doesn't have to stop us, though. Another idea could be to use a jump-table instead of a hash-table to store character-vector mappings. There are only around 500 characters that have a mapping in my data, although they span the whole Unicode range:

```
CL-USER> (reduce 'max (mapcar 'char-code (rtl:keys *de-vocab*)))
65533
CL-USER> (defparameter *jvocab* (make-array (1+ 65533)
                                            :element-type 'bit-vector
                                            :initial-element #*))
CL-USER> (rtl:dokv (k v *de-vocab*)
            (setf (aref *jvocab* (char-code k)) v))

(defun huffman-encode3 (envocab str)
  (let ((rez (make-array 0 :element-type 'bit :adjustable t :fill-pointer t)))
    (rtl:dovec (char str)
      ;; here, we have changed the hash-table to a jump-table
      (rtl:dovec (bit (svref envocab (char-code char)))
        (vector-push-extend bit rez)))
    rez))

CL-USER> (let ((vocab (first *de2*)))
            (time (loop :repeat 1000 :do
                    (dolist (word *de-words*)
                      (gethash (huffman-encode3 *jvocab* word) vocab)))))
Evaluation took:
  0.308 seconds of real time
```

OK, we get an improvement of around 10%.[2] That's a start. But many more ideas and experiments are needed if we want to significantly optimize this implementation. Yet, for the sake of space conservation on the pages of this book, we won't continue with it.

Another tool we could use to analyze the performance and think about further improvement is flamegraphs—a way to visualize profiler output. cl-flamegraph is a wrapper around sb-sprof that generates the output in the common format which can be further processed by the Perl tool, in order to generate the image itself. Here is the basic output I got. It's rather rough and, probably, requires some fiddling with the Perl tool to obtain a prettier image:

---

[2]It was verified by taking the average of multiple test runs.

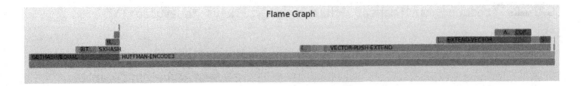
Flame Graph

To conclude, key compression alone gives a sizeable reduction in used space at the cost of deteriorated performance.

Another possible angle of attack is to move from a hash-table to a more space-efficient structure. We have explored this direction somewhat in Chapter 8 already.

Arithmetic Coding

Why does Huffman coding work? The answer lies in Shannon's source coding theorem and has to do with a notion of entropy. Entropy is one of the ways to represent expectation and surprise, in a message. The most random message has the maximal surprise, that is, it's very hard to predict what symbol will appear at a certain position in it, while the least random (for instance, containing only repetitions of a single char) is the least surprising. Obviously, any kind of useful data is not uniformly distributed, or, otherwise, it's indistinguishable from white noise. Most of the data representations use an "alphabet" (encoding) that is redundant, for a particular message. Why? Because it is general-purpose and should allow expressing arbitrary messages. Yet, in practice, some passages appear much more often than the others, some words and some letters are more frequent, and even some patterns in the images may be too.

The idea of character-level compression algorithms is to tailor a custom vocabulary that uses fewer bits for low-entropy (frequent) characters and more bits for high-entropy ones. In general, the probability distribution of characters may be thought of as a $[0,1]$ interval, in which each char occupies a slice proportionate to its frequency. If we rely on standard encoding, the interval for our test example will look like this:

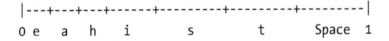

```
|---+---+---+------+---------+---------+---------|
  0 e    a   h    i         s         t       Space 1
```

Here, each subinterval for a character is its probability times the number of bits per character (8 for each). Huffman coding tries to equalize this distribution by assigning fewer bits to characters that occupy larger space. For the Huffman vocabulary we have constructed, the distribution will look like this:

```
|-----+-----+----+------+------+-------+------|
 0   e    a     h    i     s      t      Space 1
```

As you can see, it has become more even, but still not totally. This is due to the discrete nature of the encoding that results in rounding the number of bits to the closest integer value. There's another approach to solving the same problem that aims at reducing the rounding error even further—arithmetic coding. It acts directly on our interval and encodes the whole message in a single number that represents the point in this interval. How is this point found and used? Let's consider a message with a single character i. In our example, the subinterval for it is [0.214285714, 0.357142857). So, if we use any number from this interval and know that the message contains a single character, we can unambiguously decode it back. Ideally, we'd use the number from the interval that has the least count of digits. Here is a simple example of how such a number can be found:

```
(defun find-shortest-bitvec (lo hi)
  (let ((rez (make-array 0 :element-type 'bit :adjustable t :fill-pointer t)))
    (loop
      (rtl:with ((lod lof (floor (* lo 2)))
                 (hid hif (floor (* hi 2))))
        (when (or (zerop lof)
                  (zerop hif)
                  (/= lod hid))
          (vector-push-extend hid rez)
          (return))
        (vector-push-extend lod rez)
        (setf lo lof
              hi hif)))
    rez))
```

```
RTL-USER> (find-shortest-bitvec 0.214285714 0.357142857)
#*01
```

The result is a bit-vector that represents the fractional part of some floating-point number lying within the interval, which may be also used as an encoding of our one-character message. Obviously, we could use just a single bit to encode it with a custom vocabulary of one entry, but, here, for the purpose of illustration, I wanted to use an existing pre-calculated vocabulary that includes other characters as well. Also, if we compare this version with the Huffman coding, the message length is decreased by 1 bit.

Now, how can we process longer messages? In the same manner: by recursively dividing the currently selected part using the same original distribution. For the message is

- On step 1 (for character i), the interval [0.214285714, 0.357142857) will be selected.

- On step 2 (for character s), we'll narrow it down to [0.26530612, 0.29591838) (using the subinterval [0.357142857, 0.5714286) for s).

For this interval, the shortest encoding will be 01001. In this case, it has the same size as the Huffman one.

So the naive arithmetic encoding implementation is quite simple:

```
(defun arithm-encode (envocab message)
  (let ((lo 0.0)
        (hi 1.0))
    (rtl:dovec (char message)
      (let ((coef (- hi lo)))
        (rtl:dotable (ch prob envocab)
          (let ((off (* prob coef)))
            (when (eql char ch)
              (setf hi (+ lo off))
              (return))
            (incf lo off)))))
    (find-shortest-bitvec lo hi)))

CL-USER> (arithm-encode #h(#\e 1/14
                           #\a 1/14
                           #\h 1/14
                           #\i 2/14
```

```
        #\s 3/14
        #\t 3/14
        #\Space 3/14)
    "this is a test")
```
#*10011011010100001110000001

However, this function has a hidden bug. The problem lies in the dreaded floating-point overflow that happens quite soon in the process of narrowing the interval, which results in using more and more digits of the floating-point number until all the bits are utilized and we can't distinguish the intervals any further. If we try to faithfully decode even the short message encoded in the preceding text, we'll already see this effect by getting the output this ist sssst.

The implementation of this approach, which works around the bug, relies on the same idea but uses a clever bit arithmetic trick. Due to that, it becomes less clean and obvious, because it has to work not with the whole number, but with a bounded window in that number (in this case, a 32-bit one), and, also, still take care of potential overflow that may happen when the range collapses around 0.5. Here it is shown, for illustration purposes, without a detailed explanation.[3] This function is another showcase of the Lisp standard support for handling bit-level values. Besides, read-eval (#.) is used here to provide literal values of bitmasks:[4]

```
(defun arithm-encode-correct (envocab message)
  (let ((lo 0)
        (hi (1- (expt 2 32)))
        (pending-bits 0)
        (rez (make-array 0 :element-type 'bit :adjustable t :fill-pointer t)))
    (flet ((emit-bit (bit)
             (vector-push-extend bit rez)
             (let ((pbit (if (zerop bit) 1 0)))
               (loop :repeat pending-bits :do (vector-push-extend pbit rez))
               (setf pending-bits 0))))
```

---

[3]You can study the details in the relevant article.

[4]Some implementations (for instance, SBCL) have "smart enough" compilers to perform constant folding of such expressions. However, read-eval may be used to help the compiler if it is not smart enough.

```
      (rtl:dovec (char message)
        (rtl:with ((range (- hi lo -1))
                   ((plo phi) (rtl:? envocab char)))
          (psetf lo (round (+ lo (* plo range)))
                 hi (round (+ lo (* phi range) -1)))
          (loop
            (cond ((< hi #.(expt 2 31))
                   (emit-bit 0))
                  ((>= lo #.(expt 2 31))
                   (emit-bit 1)
                   (decf lo #.(expt 2 31))
                   (decf hi #.(expt 2 31)))
                  ((and (>= lo #.(expt 2 30))
                        (< hi (+ #.(expt 2 30) #.(expt 2 31))))
                   (decf lo #.(expt 2 30))
                   (decf hi #.(expt 2 30))
                   (incf pending-bits))
                  (t (return)))
            (psetf lo (mask32 (ash lo 1))
                   hi (mask32 (1+ (ash hi 1)))))))
      (incf pending-bits)
      (emit-bit (if (< lo #.(expt 2 30)) 0 1)))
    rez))

(defun mask32 (num)
  ;; this utility is used to confine the number in 32 bits
  (logand num #.(1- (expt 2 32))))

CL-USER> (arithm-encode-correct #h(#\e '(0 1/14)
                                   #\a '(1/14 1/7)
                                   #\h '(1/7 3/14)
                                   #\i '(3/14 5/14)
                                   #\s '(5/14 4/7)
                                   #\t '(4/7 11/14)
                                   #\Space '(11/14 1))
                                "this is a test")
#*10011011010000111000001101010110010101
```

Note that the length of the compressed message is 38 bits—the same as the Huffman version!

And here, for the sake of completeness and verification, is the decoding routine. It works in a similar fashion but backward: we determine the interval into which our current number falls, emit the corresponding character, and narrow the search interval to the currently found one. We'll need to have access to the same vocabulary and know the length of the message:

```
(defun bitvec->int (bits)
  (reduce (lambda (bit1 bit2) (+ (ash bit1 1) bit2)
          bits))

(defun arithm-decode (dedict vec size)
  (rtl:with ((len (length vec))
             (lo 0)
             (hi (1- (expt 2 32)))
             (val (bitvec->int (subseq vec 0 (min 32 len))))
             (off 32)
             (rez (make-string size)))
    (dotimes (i size)
      (rtl:with ((range (- hi lo -1))
                 (prob (/ (- val lo) range)))
        (rtl:dotable (char r dedict)
          (rtl:with (((plo phi) r))
            (when (>= phi prob)
              (psetf (char rez i) char
                     lo (round (+ lo (* plo range)))
                     hi (round (+ lo (* phi range) -1)))
              (return))))
        (print (list val lo hi))
        (loop
          (cond ((< hi #.(expt 2 31))
                 ;; do nothing
                 )
                ((>= lo #.(expt 2 31))
                 (decf lo #.(expt 2 31))
```

```
            (decf hi #.(expt 2 31))
            (decf val #.(expt 2 31)))
           ((and (>= lo #.(expt 2 30))
                 (< hi #.(* 3 (expt 2 30))))
            (decf lo #.(expt 2 30))
            (decf hi #.(expt 2 30))
            (decf val #.(expt 2 30)))
           (t
            (return)))
         (psetf lo (mask32 (ash lo 1))
                hi (mask32 (1+ (ash hi 1)))
                val (mask32 (+ (ash val 1)
                              (if (< off len)
                                  (aref vec off)
                                  0)))
                off (1+ off)))))
    rez)))

CL-USER> (let ((vocab #h(#\e '(0 1/14)
                         #\a '(1/14 1/7)
                         #\h '(1/7 3/14)
                         #\i '(3/14 5/14)
                         #\s '(5/14 4/7)
                         #\t '(4/7 11/14)
                         #\Space '(11/14 1))))
           (arithm-decode vocab
                          (arithm-encode-correct vocab "this is a test")
                          14))
"this is a test"
```

DEFLATE

Entropy-based compression—or, as I would call it, character-level one—can do only so much: it can't account for repetitions of the larger-scale message parts. For instance, a message with a single word repeated twice, when compressed with Huffman or arithmetic encoding, will have twice the length of the message with a single occurrence of that word, the reason being that the probability distribution will not change, and thus the encodings of each character. Yet, there's an obvious possibility to reduce the compressed size here. This and other similar cases are much better treated by dictionary-based or block-level encoding approaches. The most well-known and widespread of them is the DEFLATE algorithm that is a variant of LZ77. Surely, there are other approaches like LZW, LZ78, or the Burrows-Wheeler algorithm (used in bzip2), but they are based on the same principal approach, so studying DEFLATE will allow you to grasp other algorithms if necessary.

But, before considering DEFLATE, let's first look at the simplest block-level scheme—**run-length encoding** (RLE). This is not even a block-level algorithm, in full, as it operates on single characters, once again. The idea is to encode sequences of repeating characters as a single character followed by the number of repetitions. Of course, such an approach will hardly help with natural language texts that have almost no long character repetitions; instead, it was used in images with limited palettes (like those encoded in the GIF format). It is common for such images to have large areas filled with the same color, so the GIF format, for instance, used RLE for each line of pixels. That was one of the reasons that an image with a horizontal pattern like this

xxxxx

xxxxx

xxxxx

lent itself to stellar compression, while the same one rotated by 90 degrees didn't. :)

```
X   X   X
X   X   X
X   X   X
X   X   X
X   X   X
```

LZ77 is a generalization of the RLE approach that considers runs not just of single characters but of variable-length character sequences. Under such conditions, it becomes much better suited for text compression, especially when the text has some redundancies. For example, program code files tend to have some identifiers constantly repeated (like if, `loop`, or `nil`, in Lisp), each code file may have a lengthy identical copyright notice at the top, and so on and so forth. The algorithm operates by replacing repeated occurrences of data with references to a single copy of that data seen earlier in the uncompressed stream. The encoding is by a pair of numbers: the length of the sequence and the offset back into the stream where the same sequence was originally encountered.

The most popular LZ77-based compression method is DEFLATE. In the algorithm, literals, lengths, and a symbol to indicate the end of the current block of data are all placed together into one alphabet. Distances are placed into a separate alphabet as they occur just after lengths, so they cannot be mistaken for another kind of symbol or vice versa. A DEFLATE stream consists of a series of blocks. Each block is preceded by a 3-bit header indicating the position of the block (last or intermediate) and the type of character-level compression used: no compression, Huffman with a predefined tree, and Huffman with a custom tree. Most compressible data will end up being encoded using the dynamic Huffman encoding. The static Huffman option is used for short messages, where the fixed saving gained by omitting the tree outweighs the loss in compression due to using a nonoptimal code.

The algorithm performs the following steps:

1. Matching and replacement of duplicate strings with pointers: Within a single block, if a duplicate series of bytes is spotted (a repeated string), then a backreference is inserted, linking to the previous location of that identical string instead. An encoded match to an earlier string consists of an 8-bit length (the repeated block size is between 3 and 258 bytes) and a 15-bit distance (which specifies an offset of 1–32768 bytes inside the so-called "sliding window") to the beginning of the duplicate. If the distance is less than the length, the duplicate overlaps itself, indicating repetition. For example, a run of any number of identical bytes can be encoded as a single byte followed by a length of (`1-n`).

2. Huffman coding of the obtained block: Instructions to generate the necessary Huffman trees immediately follow the block header. There are, actually, two trees: the 288-symbol length/literal tree and the 32-symbol distance tree, themselves encoded as canonical Huffman codes by giving the bit length of the code for each symbol. The bit lengths are then run-length encoded to produce as compact a representation as possible.

An interesting fact is that DEFLATE compression is so efficient in terms of speed that it is faster to read a compressed file from an ATA hard drive and decompress it in memory than to read an original longer version: disk access is much longer than CPU processing, for this rather simple algorithm! Even more, it applies to network traffic. That's why compression is used (and enabled by default) in many popular network protocols, for instance, HTTP.

Takeaways

This chapter, unlike the previous one, instead of exploring many different approaches, dealt with, basically, just a single one in order to dig deeper and to demonstrate the use of all the tools that can be applied in algorithmic programming: from a piece of paper to sophisticated profilers. Moreover, the case we have analyzed provides a great showcase not just of the tools but of the whole development process with all its setbacks, trial and error, and discoveries.

Bit fiddling was another topic that naturally emerged in this chapter. It may look cryptic to those who have never ventured into this territory, but mastering the technique is necessary to gain access to a number of important areas of the algorithm landscape.

CHAPTER 15

Synchronization

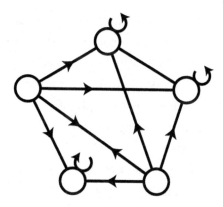

This is the final chapter of the book, in which we will discuss optimization of parallel computations: whether concurrently on a single machine in a shared-memory setting or in a distributed shared-nothing environment. This is a huge topic that spans synchronization itself, parallelization, concurrency, distributed computations, and the functional approach. And every senior software developer should be well versed in it.

Usually, synchronization is studied in the context of system or distributed programming, but it has a significant algorithmic footprint and is also one of the hottest topics for new algorithm research. In fact, there are whole books that concentrate on it, but, usually, they attack the problem from other angles, not focusing on the algorithmic part. This chapter will be more algorithm-centered, although it will also present an overview of the problem space. So, in the end, you'll have a good foundation to explore the topic further if a desire or need for that arises.

Let's start from the basics. In the previous chapters of the book, we, mainly, viewed algorithms as single computations running without external interruptions. This approach, obviously, removes the unnecessary complexity, but it also isn't totally faithful to reality. Most of the programs we deal with, now, run in multiprocessing environments (sometimes, even distributed ones), and even when they don't utilize these capabilities, these are still available, and they sometimes have their impact and, besides, might

V. Domkin, *Programming Algorithms in Lisp*, https://doi.org/10.1007/978-1-4842-6428-7_15

have improved the performance of the programs if they would have been utilized. The majority of the back-end stuff, which, currently, is comprised of services running in the datacenters, is multithreaded. There's a notorious "Zawinski's Law" that states that every program attempts to expand until it can read mail. Those programs which cannot so expand are replaced by ones which can. Being a good joke, it also reflects an important truth about the tendency of all programs over time to become network-aware and thus distributed to at least some extent.

There are two principally different types of environments in which the programs that need synchronization run: shared-memory and shared-nothing ones.

In a shared-memory setting, there exists some shared storage (not necessarily RAM) that can be directly accessed by all the threads[1] of the application. Concurrent access to data in this shared memory is the principal source of the synchronization challenges, although not the only one. The example of a shared-memory program is a normal application that uses multithreading provided either directly by the OS or, more frequently, by the language runtime.[2]

The opposite of shared-memory is a shared-nothing environment, in which all threads[3] don't have any common data storage and can coordinate only by sending messages directly to other processes. The contents of the messages have to be copied from the memory of the sender to the receiver. In this setting, some of the synchronization problems disappear, but others still remain. At the fundamental level, some synchronization or coordination still needs to happen. From a performance standpoint, however, the shared-nothing mode is, usually, inferior due to the need for additional data copying. So both paradigms have their place, and the choice, which one to utilize, depends on the context of a particular task.

The main goal of synchronization is ensuring program correctness when multiple computations are running in parallel. Another side of the coin is achieving optimal performance, which is also addressed by parallelization that we have somewhat discussed in a couple of prior chapters. Prioritizing performance before correctness, although tempting, is one of the primary sources of bugs in the concurrent systems. A trivial example would be building a shared-memory program without explicit use of

---

[1]We will further use the term "thread" to denote a separate computation running as part of our application, as it is less ambiguous than "process" and also much more widespread than all the other terms.

[2]This internal "threading," usually, also relies on the OS threading API behind the scenes.

[3]In this context, they tend to be called "processes," but we'll still stick to the term "thread."

any synchronization mechanisms. It is, definitely, the most performant approach, but non-coordinated access to the shared data will inevitably result in failures like data corruption.

Synchronization Troubles

So let's talk in more detail about the most common synchronization problems that the methods we will discuss next are trying to handle. Such situations are called **race conditions** for there's a situation when multiple threads compete for the same resource—be it data storage or processor—and, in the absence of special coordination, the order of execution will be unspecified, which may result in unpredictable and unintended outcomes. There are two main results of this unpredictability (often, both occur simultaneously):

- Data corruption or loss

- Incorrect order of execution up to total failure of the program

Here is the simplest code segment that is amenable to data corruption in multithreaded programs:

```
(incf i)
```

It seems like there's just one operation involved—how can there be a race condition? From the point of view of a programmer in a high-level language, indeed, we deal with a single operation, but if we go deeper to the level of machine code, we'll see that it is not the case. The relevant assembly snippet will, probably, contain three instructions:

```
mov i, register
inc register
mov register, i
```

You've just seen one more convincing evidence why every programmer should understand how the lower levels of their platform operate. :)

The issue is that modern processors can't directly modify data in the RAM (our variable i). First, the data needs to be moved into a register, only then some operation on it may be performed by the CPU, and, finally, it needs to be put back where the high-level program can find it. If an interrupt occurs (we're talking about multithreaded execution in a single address space, in this context) after mov i, register, the current thread will remember the old value of i (let it be 42) and be put into a waitqueue. If another thread that wants to change i is given processor time next, it may set it to whatever value it wants and continue execution (suppose it will be 0). However, when the turn is returned to the first thread, it will increment the value it remembered (42), so i will change the value in the following sequence: $42 \rightarrow 0 \rightarrow 43$. Hardly, it's an expected behavior.

Such data corruption will only impact the mentioned variable and may not cause catastrophic failures in the program. Its behavior will be incorrect, but in some situations that can be tolerated (for instance, if we gather some statistics and occasional off-by-one errors will not be noticed). Yet, if i was some counter that impacts the core behavior of the program, it might easily lead to a catastrophe.

Ultimately, incorrect execution order should be considered the root cause of all synchronization problems. And here it is also manifest: we expected increment to be a single (**atomic**) operation and thus finish execution before anything else would happen to i.

What are some other common cases of execution order errors? The most well-known and dreaded race condition is a **deadlock**. It is a situation of mutual blocking among two or more threads. Here is the simplest illustration of how it can occur:

```
thread 1 ---> acquire resource1 --> try to acquire resource2
thread 2 --> acquire resource2 ------> try to acquire resource1
```

In other words, two threads need exclusive access to two resources, but the order of access is opposite and the timing of the operations is such that the first thread manages to acquire access to the first resource, while the second to the second. After that, the deadlock is inevitable, and both threads will be blocked as soon as they will try to access the other resource. The period between each thread acquiring the first resource for exclusive access and the release of this resource is called a **critical section** of the program. Only in the critical sections a synchronization issue may manifest.

The only way to untangle "from within" such deadlock situation is for one of the threads to release the resource it already holds. Another approach, which requires external intervention, is often employed in database management systems—deadlock monitoring. A separate thread is periodically examining blocked threads to check for some conditions that signify a deadlock situation, and it resets the threads that were spotted in such a condition. Yet, instead of trying to fix the deadlock situations, it may be better to prevent them from occurring altogether. The prevention techniques may utilize time-limited exclusive leases on resources or mandating the threads to acquire resources in a specific order. However, such approaches are limited and don't cover all the use cases. It would be nice to find some way to totally exclude deadlocks, but we should remember that the original reason why they may occur, at all, is the need to prevent data corruption in the case of uncontrolled access to the data. Exclusive access to the resource ensures that this problem will not occur, but results in the possibility of a deadlock, which is a comparatively lesser evil.

A **livelock** is a dynamic counterpart to deadlock which occurs much rarely. It is a situation when threads don't constantly hold the resources exclusively (for instance, they might release them after a timeout), but the timing of the operations is such that at the time when the resource is needed by one thread, it happens to be occupied by the other, and, ultimately, mutual blocking still occurs.

One more obnoxious race condition is **priority inversion**, a phenomenon one can frequently observe in real life: when a secondary lane of cars merges into the main road, but, for some extraneous reason (traffic light malfunctioning, an accident that is blocking part of the road, etc.), the cars from it have more time to merge than the ones of the main road to progress. Priority inversion may be the reason for a more severe problem, which is **starvation**—a situation when the execution of a thread is stalled as it can't access the resource it needs. Deadlocks result in starvation of all the involved threads, but the issue may occur in other conditions, as well. I would say that starvation or, more generally, underutilization is the most common performance issue of multithreaded applications.

Low-Level Synchronization

I hope, in the previous section, the importance of ensuring proper execution order in the critical sections of the program was demonstrated well enough. How to approach this task? There are many angles of attack. Partially, the problem may be solved by the introduction of atomic operations. Atomic increment and decrement are a common example of those, which may be found in the ecosystem of the majority of the programming languages. For instance, SBCL provides an `sb-ext:atomic-incf` macro that operates on the fixnum slots of structures, array cells, contents of cons pairs, or global variables. Some other languages, like Java, provide `AtomicInteger` and similar structures that guarantee atomic operations on their main slots. In fact, the de facto standard Lisp cross-implementation multithreading library Bordeaux Threads also defines an API for manipulating atomic integers, which means that most of Common Lisp implementations support these operations.

What enables atomic operations are special hardware instructions:

- TSL: Test and set lock

- CAS: Compare and swap

- LL/CS: Load link/store conditional

The most widespread of them is `CAS` that has the same effect as if the following code would work as a single atomic operation:

```
(defmacro cas (place old new)
  `(when (eql ,place ,old)
     (setf ,place ,new))
```

Based on this spec, we could define `atomic-incf` using `cas`:

```
(defmacro atomic-incf (place &optional i)
  (let ((cur (gensym "CUR"))
        (rez (gensym "REZ")))
    `(loop :for ,rez := (let ((,cur ,place))
                          (cas ,place ,cur (+ ,cur ,i)))
           :when ,rez :do (return ,rez))))
```

Here, we read the current value of `place` and then try to set it with `cas`. These two operations happen non-atomically, so there's a chance that `cas` will return nil. In that case, we redo the whole sequence again. It is clear that execution time of such operation is nondeterministic, but, in a reasonably configured multithreaded system, there should be, generally, just a single chance for `cas` to fail: when the thread is preempted between the assignment and `cas`. It shouldn't repeat the second time this thread gets its time slice for it should have enough time to complete both operations considering that it will start from them.

Another important low-level instruction is a **memory barrier**. It causes the CPU to enforce an ordering constraint on memory operations issued before and after the barrier instruction. That is, the operations issued prior to the barrier are guaranteed to be performed before operations issued after the barrier. Memory barriers are necessary because most modern CPUs employ performance optimizations that can result in out-of-order execution. The reordering of memory loads and stores goes unnoticed within a single thread of execution but can cause unpredictable behavior in concurrent programs. One more leak from the low level adding to the list of synchronization worries...

On top of CAS and atomic operations, some higher-level synchronization primitives are provided by the OS and the execution runtimes of most of the programming languages. The most popular of them is the **semaphore**. It is a counter that is initially set to the number of threads that can proceed past querying its value. If the counter is above zero, the thread may continue execution, but it also atomically decrements the counter. This operation is usually called `wait`, `acquire`, or `down` on the semaphore. However, if the counter is already down to zero, the thread goes to sleep and is put into an OS waitqueue until the wakeup notification arrives. The notification is initiated by some thread calling `release`/`up` on the same semaphore. This operation atomically increments the counter value and also allows some of the waiting threads to continue execution. The most used type of semaphores is called the **mutex**, and it allows only a single thread to enter and also mandates the implementation to check that the thread that releases the mutex is the one that has previously acquired it. There are also other types of semaphores or more complex locks built on top of them, such as the read-write lock or a monitor.

Semaphores are an alternative to a lower-level **spin-lock** primitive that uses **busy waiting**, that is, constant checking of the counter variable until it increases above zero.

Another, more general name for this method is **polling** that refers to constantly querying the state of some resource (a lock, a network socket, a file descriptor) to know when its state changes. Polling has both drawbacks and advantages: it occupies the thread instead of yielding CPU to other workers, which is a serious downside, but it also avoids expensive utilization of the OS context-switching required by semaphores.

So both semaphores and spin-locks find their place. In the low-level OS code, spin-locks prevail, while semaphores are a default synchronization primitive in the user space.

Mutual Exclusion Algorithms

Relying on hardware features for synchronization is a common approach taken by most software systems. However, since the beginning of work on this problem, computer scientists, including such famous algorithmists as Dijkstra and Lamport, proposed mutual exclusion algorithms that allowed guarding the critical sections without any special support from the platform. One of the simplest of them is Peterson's algorithm.

It guarantees mutual exclusion of two threads with the use of two variables: a two-element array interest and a Boolean turn. A true value of the interest item corresponding to a thread indicates that it wants to enter the critical section. Entrance is granted if a second thread does not want the same or it has yielded priority to the first thread:

```
(defparameter *interest* (rtl:vec nil nil))
(defparameter *turn* nil)

(defun peterson-call (i fn)
  (let ((other (abs (1- i))))
    (setf (aref *interest* i) t
          *turn* other)
    ;; busy waiting
    (loop :while (and (aref *interest* other)
                      (= *turn* other)))
    ;; critical section start
    (funcall fn)
    ;; critical section end
    (setf (aref *interest* i) nil)))
```

The algorithm satisfies the three essential criteria to solve the critical section problem: mutual exclusion, progress, and bounded waiting. Mutual exclusion means that several competing threads can never be in the critical section at the same time. For Peterson's algorithm, if thread 0 is in its critical section, then (aref *interest* 0) is true. In addition, either (aref *interest* 1) is nil (meaning thread 1 has left its critical section and isn't interested in coming back into it) or *turn* is 0 (meaning that thread 1 is just now trying to enter the critical section but waiting) or thread 1 is trying to enter its critical section, after setting (aref *interest* 1) to true but before setting *turn* to 0. So if both processes are in the critical section, then we conclude that the state must satisfy (and (aref *interest* 0) (aref *interest* 1) (= *turn* 0) (= *turn* 1)), which is, obviously, impossible. That is, only one of the threads could have entered the section. The condition of progress, basically, says that only those threads that wish to enter the critical section can participate in making the decision as to which one will do it next and that this selection cannot be postponed indefinitely. In our case, a thread cannot immediately reenter the critical section if the other thread has set its interest flag. Thus, the thread that has just left the critical section will not impact the progress of the waiting thread. Bounded waiting means that the number of times a thread is bypassed by another thread after it has indicated its desire to enter the critical section is bounded by a function of the number of threads in the system. In Peterson's algorithm, a thread will never wait longer than one turn for entrance to the critical section.

The drawback of Peterson's algorithm is busy waiting.[4] So it may be compared to a spin-lock. There are a number of other similar algorithms, including Dekker's and Lamport's ones, which also share this property. A newer Szymański's algorithm is designed to avoid busy waiting, but it requires access to the OS scheduling facilities to make the thread sleep, waiting for the wakeup call, making the algorithm similar to semaphores.

High-Level Synchronization

All the mentioned synchronization primitives don't solve the challenges of synchronization completely. Rather, they provide tools that enable reasonable solutions but still require advanced understanding and careful application. The complexity of multithreaded programs is a level-up compared to their single-threaded counterparts, and thus much effort continues being spent on trying to come up with high-level ways to contain it. That is, remove it from the sight of a regular programmer by providing the primitives that handle synchronization behind the scenes. A simple example of that is Java synchronized classes that employ an internal monitor to ensure atomic access to the slots of a synchronized object. The major problem with regular locks (like semaphores) is that working with them brings us into the realm of global state manipulation. Such locking can't be isolated within the boundaries of a single function—it leaks through the whole caller chain, and this makes the program much harder to reason about. In this regard, it is somewhat similar to the use of goto, albeit on a larger scale, and so a push for higher-level synchronization facilities resembles Dijkstra's famous appeal to introduce structured programming ("goto considered harmful"). Ironically, Dijkstra is one of the creators of the classic synchronization mechanisms that are now frowned upon. However, synchronization has intrinsic complexity that can't be fully contained, so no silver bullet exists (and hardly will ever be created) and every high-level solution will be effective only in a subset of cases.

---

[4]The other apparent limitation of supporting only two threads can be lifted by a modification to the algorithm, which requires some hardware support.

I have seen that very well on my own when teaching a course on system programming and witnessing how students solve the so-called classic synchronization problems. The task was to apply both classic synchronization techniques (semaphores and others) and the new high-level ones (using Erlang, Haskell, Clojure, or Go, which all provide some of those). The outcome, in terms of complexity, was not always in favor of the new approaches.

There are a number of these classic synchronization problems, and I was even collecting them to be able to provide more variants of the tasks to diminish cheating. :) But, in essence, they all boil down to just a few archetypal cases: producer-consumer, readers-writers, sleeping barber, and the dining philosophers. Each problem demonstrates a certain basic synchronization scenario and allows the researchers to see how their approach will handle it. I won't include them in the book but strongly encourage anyone interested in this topic to study them in more detail and also try to solve using different synchronization mechanisms.

Now, let's talk about some of the prominent high-level approaches. Remember that they try to change the paradigm and avoid the need for explicit locking of critical sections altogether.

Lock-Free Data Structures

My favorite among them is lock-free data structures. This is a simple and effective idea that can help deal with many common use cases and, indeed, avoid the necessity for explicit synchronization. Still, their use is limited and, obviously, can't cover all the possible scenarios.

The most important among them is arguably a lock-free queue. It can be implemented in different ways, and there's a simple and efficient implementation using cas provided by SBCL in the sb-concurrency contrib package. Here is the implementation of the main operations (taken from the SBCL source code and slightly simplified):

```
(defstruct lf-queue
  (head (error "No HEAD.") :type cons)
  (tail (error "No TAIL.") :type cons))

(defconstant +dummy+ '.dummy.)
```

```
(defun lf-enqueue (value queue)
  (let ((new (cons value nil)))
    (loop (when (eq nil (sb-ext:compare-and-swap
                          (cdr (lf-queue-tail queue))
                          nil new))
            (setf (lf-queue-tail queue) new)
            (return value)))))

(defun lf-dequeue (queue)
  (loop (rtl:with ((head (lf-queue-head queue))
                   (next (cdr head)))
          (typecase next
            ;; the queue always has at least one element:
            ;; a +dummy+ node, thus a non-empty queue
            ;; will have at least two elements,
            ;; so a null NEXT means that the queue was empty
            (null (return (values nil
                                  nil)))
            (cons (when (eq head (sb-ext:compare-and-swap
                                   (lf-queue-head queue)
                                   head next))
                    (let ((value (car next)))
                      (setf (car next) +dummy+)
                      (return (values value
                                      t)))))))))
```

An important precondition to understand this code is knowing that (car (queue-head queue)) is +dummy+ and its cdr points to the first data node in the queue. By using compare-and-swap, we know definitely whether we are accessing the most recent version of the head (with a correct pointer to the next element) or if it has already become stale. In the latter case, we'll just retry, and in the former, we'll also need to cut off the current head by setting (car next) to +dummy+.

The value of this structure lies in that it enables the implementation of the master-worker pattern that is a backbone of many back-end applications, as well as, in general, different forms of lock-free and wait-free coordination between the running threads. Basically, it's a lock-free solution to the producer-consumer problem. The items are put in the queue by some producer threads (masters) and consumed by the worker threads. Such an architecture allows the programmer to separate concerns between different layers of the application: for instance, one type of threads may be responsible for handling incoming connections and, in order to ensure system high availability, these threads shouldn't spend much time processing them. So, after some basic processing, the connection sockets are put into the queue, from which the heavy-lifting worker threads can consume them and process in a more elaborate fashion. That is, it's a job queue for a thread pool. Surely, a lock-based queue may also be utilized as an alternative, in these scenarios, but the necessity to lock from the caller's side makes the code for all the involved threads more complicated: what if a thread that has just acquired the lock is abruptly terminated for some reason?

Data Parallelism and Message Passing

Beyond thread pools, there's a whole concept of data parallelism, which, in essence, lies in submitting different computations to the pool and implementing synchronization as an orchestration of those tasks. In addition, Node.js and Go use lock-free IO in conjunction with such thread pools (and a special syntax for its seamless integration) for an efficient implementation of user space green threads to support this paradigm.

Even further along this direction is Erlang that is a whole language built around lock-free IO, efficient user space threading, and a shared-nothing memory model. It is the language of message-passing concurrency that aims to solve all synchronization problems within this single approach. As discussed in the beginning, such stance has its advantages and drawbacks, and so Erlang fits some problems (like coordination between a large number of simple agents) exceptionally well, while for others it imposes unaffordable costs in terms of both performance and complexity.

I won't go deeper into this topic as it is not directly related to the matter of this book.

STM

Another take on concurrency is the technology that is used, for quite a long time, in the database systems and was reimplemented in several languages, being popularized by the author of Clojure—Software Transactional Memory (STM). The idea is to treat all data accesses in memory as part of transactions, computations that possess the ACID properties: atomicity, consistency, and isolation (minus durability, which is only relevant to the database systems persisting data on disk). These transactions should still be initiated by the programmer, so the control over synchronization remains, to a large extent, in their hands with some portion of the associated complexity. The transactions may be implemented in different ways, but they will still use locking behind the scenes, and there are two main approaches to applying locking:

- Pessimistic: When the locks are acquired for the whole duration of the transaction, basically making it analogous to a very conservative programming style that avoids the deadlocks but seriously hinders program performance—acquiring all locks at once and then entering the critical section. In the context of STM, each separate variable will have its own lock.

- Optimistic: When the initial state of the transaction variables is remembered in the thread-local storage and locking occurs only at the last (commit) phase, when all the changes are applied—but only when there were no external changes to the transaction variables. If at least one of them were changed, the whole transaction would need to be rolled back and retried.

In both cases, the main issue is the same: contention. If the number of threads competing for the locks is small, an optimistic approach should perform better, while, in the opposite case, there will be too many rollbacks and even a possibility of a livelock.

The optimistic transactions are, usually, implemented using the Multiversion Concurrency Control (MVCC) mechanism. MVCC ensures a transaction never has to wait to read an object by maintaining several versions of this object. Each version has both a Read Timestamp and a Write Timestamp which lets a particular transaction read the most recent version of the object which precedes the own Read Timestamp of the transaction.

STM is an interesting technology, which hasn't proven its case yet beyond the distinct area of data management systems, such as RDBMs and their analogs.

Distributed Computations

So far, we have discussed synchronization mainly in the context of software running in a single address space on a single machine. Yet, the same issues, although magnified, are also relevant to distributed systems. Actually, the same models of computation are relevant: shared-memory and shared-nothing message passing.

However, for distributed computing, message passing becomes much more natural, while the significance of shared memory is seriously diminished and the "memory" itself becomes some kind of a network storage system like a database or a network filesystem.

However, more challenges are imposed by the introduction of the unreliable network as a communication environment between the parts of a system. These challenges are reflected in the so-called "fallacies of distributed computing":

- The network is reliable.

- Latency is zero.

- Bandwidth is infinite.

- The network is secure.

- Topology doesn't change.

- There is a single administrator.

- Transport cost is zero.

- The network is homogeneous.

- Clocks on all nodes are synchronized.

Another way to summarize those challenges, which is the currently prevailing look at it, is the famous Brewer's CAP Theorem, which states that any distributed system may have only two of the three desired properties at once: consistency, availability, and partition tolerance. And since partitional tolerance is a required property of any network system as it's the ability to function in the unreliable network environment (that is the norm), the only possible distributed systems are CP and AP, that is, they either guarantee consistency but might be unavailable at times or are constantly available but might be sometimes inconsistent.

Distributed Algorithms

Distributed computation requires distributed data structures and distributed algorithms. The domains that are in active development are distributed consensus, efficient distribution of computation, and efficient change propagation. Google pioneered the area of efficient network computation with the MapReduce framework that originated from the ideas of functional programming and Lisp, in particular. The next-generation systems such as Apache Spark develop these ideas even further.

MapReduce is primarily targeted at large-scale distributed computing, but it can be run and demonstrated on a single machine also. If you remember the parallel merge sort example, it can be alternatively expressed as a MapReduce computation in the following way (using the primitive from the lparallel multiprocessing library). This function is intended to be run in parallel using N threads on a single machine. However, if we had access to a distributed underlying implementation, it could be transparently swapped in without the need for any changes to this code:

```
(defun mapreduce-merge-sort (list n &key (pred '<))
  (lparallel:pmap-reduce
    (lambda (x) (merge-sort x pred))           ; map step: solve a
                                               ; subproblem
    (lambda (x y) (merge (type-of x) x y pred)) ; reduce step: combine
                                               ; solutions
    (group (ceiling (length list) n) list)))   ; divide data into
                                               ; sub-problems
```

Yet, the primary challenge for distributed systems is efficient consensus. The addition of the unreliable network makes the problem nontrivial compared to a single-machine variant where the consensus may be achieved easily in a shared-memory setting. The world has seen an evolution of distributed consensus algorithms implemented in different data management systems, from the 2-Phase Commit (2PC) to the currently popular RAFT protocol.

2PC is an algorithm for coordination of all the processes that participate in a distributed atomic transaction on whether to commit or roll back the transaction. The protocol achieves its goal even in many cases of temporary system failure. However, it is not resilient to all possible failure configurations, and in rare cases, manual intervention is needed. To accommodate recovery from failure, the participants of the transaction use logging of states, which may be implemented in different ways. Though usually intended to be used infrequently, recovery procedures compose a substantial portion of the protocol, due to many possible failure scenarios to be considered.

In a "normal execution" of any single distributed transaction, the 2PC consists of two phases:

1. The "commit-request" or voting phase, in which a coordinator process attempts to prepare all the participating processes to take the necessary steps for either committing or aborting the transaction and to vote, either "Yes" (commit) or "No" (abort).

2. The "commit" phase, in which, based on the voting of the participants, the coordinator decides whether to commit (only if all have voted "Yes") or roll back the transaction and notifies the result to all the participants. The participants then follow with the needed actions (commit or roll back) with their local transactional resources.

It is clear, from the description, that 2PC is a centralized algorithm that depends on the authority and high availability of the coordinator process. Centralized and peer-to-peer are the two opposite modes of the network algorithms, and each algorithm is distinguished by its level of centralization.

The **3PC** is a refinement of the 2PC which is supposed to be more resilient to failures by introducing an intermediate stage called "prepared to commit." However, it doesn't solve the fundamental challenges of the approach that are due to its centralized nature, only making the procedure more complex to implement and thus having more failure modes.

The modern peer-to-peer coordination algorithm alternatives are Paxos and RAFT. RAFT is considered to be a simpler (and, thus, more reliable) approach. It is also, not surprisingly, based on voting. It adds a preliminary phase to each transaction, which is leader election. The election, as well as other activities within a transaction, doesn't require unanimous agreement, but a simple majority. Besides, execution of all the stages on each machine is timeout-based, so if a network failure or a node failure occurs, the operations are aborted and retried with an updated view of the other peers. The details of the algorithm can be best understood from the RAFT website, which provides a link to the main paper, good visualizations, and other references.

Distributed Data Structures

We have already mentioned various distributed hash-tables and content-addressable storage as one of the examples of these types of structures. Another exciting and rapidly developing direction is eventually consistent data structures or **CRDTs** (conflict-free replicated data types). They are the small-scale representatives of the AP (or eventually consistent) systems that favor high availability over constant consistency, as they become more and more the preferred mode of operation of distributed systems.

The issue that CRDTs address is conflict resolution when different versions of the structure appear due to network partitions and their eventual repair. For a general data structure, if there are two conflicting versions, the solution is either to choose one (according to some general rules, like take the random one or the latest one, or application-specific logic) or to keep both versions and defer conflict resolution to the client code. CRDTs are conflict-free, that is, the structures are devised so that any conflict is resolved automatically in a way that doesn't bring any data loss or corruption.

There are two ways to implement CRDTs: convergent structures rely on the replication of the whole state, while commutative use operation-based replication. Yet, both strategies result in the CRDTs with equivalent properties.

The simplest CRDT is a **G-Counter** (where "G" stands for grow only). Its operation is based on the trivial fact that addition is commutative, that is, the order of applying the addition operation doesn't matter: we'll get the same result as long as the number of operations is the same. Every convergent CRDT has a merge operation that combines the states of each node. On each node, the G-Counter stores an array that holds the per-node numbers of the local increments. And its merge operation takes the maximums of the elements of this array across all nodes, while obtaining the value of the counter requires summing all of the cells:

```
(defstruct (g-counter (:conc-name nil))
  ccs)

(defun make-gcc (n)
  (make-g-counter :ccs (make-array n)))

(defun gcc-val (gcc)
  (reduce '+ (ccs gcc)))

(defun gcc-merge (gcc1 gcc2)
  (rtl:map* 'max gcc1 gcc2))
```

The structure is eventually consistent as, at any point in time, asking any live node, we can get the current value of the counter from it (so there's constant availability). However, if not all changes have already been replicated to this node, the value may be smaller than the actual one (so consistency is only eventual once all the replications are over).

The next step is a **PN-Counter** (positive-negative). It uses a common strategy in CRDT creation: combining several simpler CRDTs. In this case, it is a combination of two G-Counters: one for the number of increments and another decrements.

A set is, in some sense, a more sophisticated analog of a counter (a counter may be considered a set of 1s). So a **G-Set** functions similar to a G-Counter: it allows each node to add items to the set that are stored in the relevant cell of the main array. The merging and value retrieval operations use union. Similarly, there's **2P-Set** (2-phase) that is similar in construction to the PN-Counter. The difference of a 2P-Set from a normal set is that once an element is put into the removal G-Set (called the "tombstone" set), it cannot be readded to the set. That is, addition may be undone, but deletion is permanent. This misfeature is amended by **LWW-Set** (last-write-wins) that adds timestamps to all the records. Thus, an item with a more recent timestamp prevails, that is, if an object is present in both underlying G-Sets, it is considered present in the set if its timestamp in the addition set is greater than the one in the removal set, and removed in the opposite case.

There are also more complex CRDTs used to model sequences, including Treedoc, RGA, Woot, Logoot, and LSEQ. Their implementations differ, but the general idea is that each character (or chunk of characters) is assigned a key that can be ordered. When new text is added, it's given a key that is derived from the key of some adjacent text. As a result, the merge is the best-possible approximation of the intent of the edits.

The use cases for CRDTs are, as mentioned in the preceding text, collaborative editing, maintaining such structures as shopping carts (e.g., with an LWW-Set), counters of page visits to a site or reactions in a social network, and so on and so forth.

Distributed Algorithms in Action: Collaborative Editing

In fact, CRDTs are a data structure–centric answer to another technology that is used, for quite some time, to support collaborative editing: operational transformation (OT). OT was employed in such products as Google Docs and its predecessors to implement lock-free simultaneous rich-text editing of the same document by many actors.

OT is an umbrella term that covers a whole family of algorithms sharing the same basic principles. Such systems use replicated document storage, that is, each node in the system operates on its own copy in a non-blocking manner as if it was a single-user scenario. The changes from every node are constantly propagated to the rest of the nodes. When a node receives a batch of changes, it transforms the changes before executing them to account for the local changes that were already made since the previous changeset—thus the name "operational transformation."

The basic idea of OT can be illustrated with the following example. Let's say we have a text document with a string `"bar"` replicated by two nodes and two concurrent operations:

```
(insert 0 "f") # o1 on node1
(delete 2 "r") # o2 on node2
```

Suppose, on node 1, the operations are executed in the order o1, o2. After executing o1, the document changes to `"fbar"`. Now, before executing o2 we must transform it against o1 according to the transformation rules. As a result, it will change to (delete 3 `"r"`). So the basic idea of OT is to adjust (transform) the parameters of incoming editing operations to account for the effects of the previously executed concurrent operations locally (whether they were invoked locally or received from some other node) so that the transformed operation can achieve the correct effect and maintain document consistency. The word "concurrent" here means operations that happened since some state that was recorded on the node that has sent the new batch of changes. The transformation rules are operation-specific.

In theory, OT seems quite simple, but it has its share of implementation nuances and issues:

- While the classic OT approach of defining operations through their offsets in the text seems to be simple and natural, real-world distributed systems raise serious issues: namely, that operations propagate with finite speed (remember one of the network fallacies); states of participants are often different, thus the resulting combinations of states; and operations are extremely hard to foresee and understand.

- For OT to work, every single change to the data needs to be captured: obtaining a snapshot of the state is usually trivial, but capturing edits is a different matter altogether. The richness of modern user interfaces can make this problematic, especially within a browser-based environment.

- The notion of a "point in time" relevant to which the operations should be transformed is nontrivial to implement correctly (another network fallacy in play). Relying on global time synchronization is one of the approaches, but it requires tight control over the whole environment (which Google has demonstrated to be possible for its datacenter). So, in most cases, a distributed solution instead of simple timestamps is needed.

The most popular of these solutions is a **vector clock** (VC). The VC of a distributed system of n nodes is a vector of n logical clocks, one clock per process; a local "smallest possible values" copy of the global clock array is kept in each process, with the following rules for clock updates:

- Initially all clocks are zero.

- Each time a process experiences an internal event, it increments its own logical clock in the vector by one.

- Each time a process sends a message, it increments its own logical clock in the vector by one (as in the preceding bullet, but not twice for the same event) and then sends a copy of its own vector.

- Each time a process receives a message, it increments its own logical clock in the vector by one and updates each element in its vector by taking the maximum of the value in its own vector clock and the value in the vector in the received message (for every element).

You might notice that the operation of vector clocks is similar to the CRDT G-Counter.

VCs allow the partial causal ordering of events. A vector clock value for the event x is less than the value for y if and only if for all indices the items of the x 's clock are less or equal and, at least for one element, they are strictly smaller.

Besides vector clocks, the other mechanisms to implement distributed partial ordering include Lamport Timestamps, Plausible Clocks, Interval Tree Clocks, Bloom Clocks, and others.

Persistent Data Structures

To conclude this chapter, I wanted to say a few words about the role of the functional paradigm in synchronization and distributed computing. That's no coincidence that it was mentioned several times in the description of different synchronization strategies: essentially, functional programming is about achieving good separation of concerns by splitting computations into independent referentially transparent units that are easier to reason about. Such an approach supports concurrency more natively than the standard imperative paradigm, although it might not be optimal computationally (at least, in the small). Yet, the gains obtained from parallelism and utilizing the scale of distributed computing may greatly outweigh this low-level inefficiency. So, with the advent of concurrent and distributed paradigms, functional programming gains more traction and adoption. Such ideas as MapReduce, STM, and message passing–based coordination originated in the functional programming world.

Another technology coming from the functional paradigm that is relevant to synchronization is purely functional data structures. Their principal property is that any modification doesn't cause a destructive effect on the previous version of the structure, that is, with each change, a new version is created, while the old one may be preserved or discarded depending on the particular program requirements. This feature makes them very well suited for concurrent usage as the possibility of corruption due to incorrect operation order is removed, and such structures are also compatible with any kind of transactional behavior. The perceived inefficiency of constant copying, in many cases, may be mostly avoided by using structure sharing. So the actual cost of maintaining these data structures is not proportional to their size, but rather constant or, at worst, logarithmic in size. Another name for these structures is persistent data structures—contrast to "ephemeral" ones which operate by destructive modification.

The basic persistent functional structure is, as we already mentioned in one of the preceding chapters, a Lisp list[5] used as a stack. We have also seen the queue implemented with two stacks called a **real-time queue**. It is a purely functional data structure, as well. The other examples are mostly either list- or tree-based, that is, they also use the linked backbone structured in a certain way.

To illustrate once again how most persistent data structures operate, we can look at a **zipper** that may be considered a generalization of a real-time queue. It is a technique of representing a data structure so that it is convenient for writing programs that traverse the structure arbitrarily and update its contents in a purely functional manner, that is, without destructive operations. A list-zipper represents the entire list from the perspective of a specific location within it. It is a pair consisting of a recording of the reverse path from the list start to the current location and the tail of the list starting at the current location. In particular, the list-zipper of a list (1 2 3 4 5) when created will look like this: (() . (1 2 3 4 5)). As we traverse the list, it will change in the following manner:

- ((1) . (2 3 4 5))
- ((2 1) . (3 4 5))
- And so on

If we want to replace 3 with 0, the list-zipper will become ((2 1) . (0 4 5)), while the previous version will still persist. The new zipper will reuse the list (2 1) and create a new list by consing 0 to the front of the sublist (4 5). Consequently, the memory state after performing two movements and one update will look like this:

5If we forbid the destructive rplaca/rplacd operations and their derivatives.

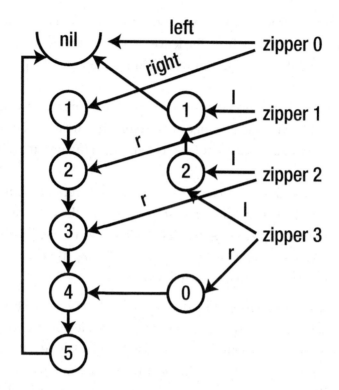

It is apparent that each operation on the zipper (movement or modification) adds at most a single additional element. So its complexity is the same as for normal lists (although with larger constants).

Zippers can operate on any linked structures. A very similar structure for trees is called a **finger tree**. To create it from a normal tree, we need to put "fingers" to the right and left ends of the tree and transform it like a zipper. A finger is simply a point at which you can access part of a data structure.

Let's consider the case of a 2-3 tree for which the finger approach was first developed. First, we restructure the entire tree and make the parents of the first and last children the two roots of our tree. This finger is composed of several layers that sit along the spine of the tree. Each layer of the finger tree has a prefix (on the left) and a suffix (on the right), as well as a link further down the spine. The prefix and suffix contain values in the finger tree: on the first level, they contain values (2-3 trees of depth 0); on the second level, they contain 2-3 trees of depth 1; on the third level, they contain 2-3 trees of depth 2, and so on. This somewhat unusual property comes from the fact that the original 2-3 tree was of uniform depth. The edges of the original 2-3 tree are now at the top of the spine. The root of the 2-3 tree is now the very bottom element of the spine. As we go down the spine, we are traversing from the leaves to the root of the original 2-3 tree; as we go closer to the root, the prefix and suffix contain deeper and deeper subtrees of the original 2-3 tree.

Now, the principle of operation (traversal or modification) on the finger tree is the same as with the zipper: with each change, some elements are tossed from one side of the spine to the other, and the number of such elements remains within the $O(\log n)$ limits.

Finally, another data structure that is crucial for the efficient implementation of systems that rely solely on persistent data structures (like the Clojure language environment) is a **hash-array mapped trie** (HAMT). It may be used both in ephemeral and persistent modes to represent maps and sets with $O(\log n)$ access complexity.[6] HAMT is a special trie that uses the following two tricks:

- As an array-mapped trie, instead of storing pointers to the children nodes in a key-value indexed with their subkeys, it stores a list, an array of pointers, and a bitmap that is used to determine if the pointer is present and at what position in the array it resides. This feature requires limiting the number of possible subkeys (e.g., individual characters, which are the dominant use case for tries) to the length of a bitmap. The default length is 32, which is enough to represent the English alphabet. :)

- However, the hash feature gives us a number of benefits including limiting the limitations on the subkeys. Actually, in a HAMT, all values are stored at the leaves that have the same depth, while the subkeys are obtained by, first, hashing the key and then splitting the obtained hash into n -bit ranges (where n is usually also 5).[7] Each subkey is used as an index into the bitmap: if the element at it is 1, the key is present. To calculate the index of a pointer in the pointer array, we need to perform popcount on the preceding bits.

---

[6] …and a quite high algorithm base—usually 32—that means very shallow trees resulting in just a handful of hops even for quite large structures.

[7] Except for the length of the leftmost range that depends on the number of bits in a hash. For instance, for a 32-bit hash, it may be 7, and the depth of the whole HAMT would be 5.

With such a structure, all major operations will have $O(\log 5)$, that is, $O(1)$ complexity. However, hash collisions are possible, so the hash-table–related collision considerations also apply to a HAMT. In other words, HAMTs are pretty similar to hash-tables, with the keys being split into parts and put into a trie. However, due to their tree-based nature, the memory footprints and the runtime performance of iteration and equality checking of the HAMTs lag behind array-based counterparts:

- Increased memory overhead as each internal node adds an overhead over a direct array-based encoding, so finding a small representation for internal nodes is crucial.

- On the other hand, HAMTs do not need expensive table resizing and do not waste (much) space on null references.

- Iteration is slower due to non-locality, while a hash-table uses a simple linear scan through a continuous array.

- Delete can cause the HAMT to deviate from the most compact representation (leave nodes with no children, in the tree).

- Equality checking can be expensive due to non-locality and the possibility of a degenerate structure due to deletes.

So what's the value of this structure if it's just a slightly less efficient hash-table? The difference is that a HAMT can not only be implemented both with destructive operations, but also, being a tree, it can be easily adapted to persistent mode with a usual path-copying trick that we have already seen.

Complexity estimations for persistent data structures use amortized analysis to prove acceptable performance ($O(\log n)$). Another trick at play here is called **scheduling**, and it lies in properly planning heavy structure-rebuilding operations and splitting them into chunks to avoid having to execute some at a time when optimal complexity can't be achieved. To learn more about these topics, read the seminal book by Chris Okasaki, *Purely Functional Data Structures*,[8] that describes these methods in more detail and provides complexity analysis for various structures.

---

[8]His thesis with the same title is freely available, but the book covers more and is more accessible.

Besides, the immutability of persistent data structures enables additional optimizations that may be important in some scenarios:

- Native copy-on-write (COW) semantics that is required in some domains and algorithms.

- Objects can be easily memoized.

- Properties, such as hashes, sizes, and so on, can be precomputed.

The utility of persistent data structures is only gradually being realized and apprehended. Recently, some languages, including Clojure, were built around them as core structures. Moreover, some people even go as far as to claim that git is a purely functional data structure due to its principal reliance on structure-sharing persistent trees to store the data.

Takeaways

We have covered a lot of ground in this chapter at a pretty high level. Obviously, you can go much deeper: whole books are written on the topics of concurrency and distributed computing.

Overall, concurrency can be approached from, at least, three different directions:

1. There's a low-level view: the means that should be provided by the underlying platforms to support concurrent operation. It includes the threading/process APIs, the atomic operation, synchronization, and networking primitives.

2. Then, there's an architecture viewpoint: what constraints our systems should satisfy and how to ensure that. At this level, the main distinctions are drawn: shared-memory vs. shared-nothing, centralized vs. peer-to-peer.

3. And, last but not least, comes the algorithmic perspective. What data structures (as usual, they are, in fact, more important than the algorithms) can be used to satisfy the constraints in the most efficient way possible or to simplify the architecture? We have seen several examples of special-purpose ones that cater to the needs of a particular problem: lock-free data structures,

eventually consistent ones, and purely functional persistent ones. And then, there are some areas where special-purpose algorithms also play a major role. Their main purpose, there, is not so much computational efficiency (like we're used to), but, mostly, correctness coupled with good enough efficiency.[9] Mutual exclusion and distributed consensus algorithms are examples of such targeted algorithm families.

There's a lot of room for further research in the realms of synchronization and, especially, distributed computation. It is unclear whether the new breakthroughs will come from our current computing paradigms or we'll have to wait for the new tide and new approaches. Anyway, there's still a chance to make a serious and lasting contribution to the field by developing new algorithm-related stuff. And not only that. Unlike other chapters, we haven't talked much here about the tools that can help a developer of concurrent programs. The reason for that is, actually, an apparent lack of such tools, at least of widely adopted ones. Surely, the toolbox we have already studied in the previous chapters is applicable here, but an environment with multiple concurrent threads and, possibly, multiple address spaces adds new classes of issues and seriously complicates debugging. There are network service tools to collect metrics and execution traces, but none of them is tightly integrated into the development toolboxes, not to speak of their limited utility. So substantial pieces are still missing from the picture and are waiting to be filled.

---

[9]The reason for that might be relative immaturity of this space, as well as its complexity, so that our knowledge of it hasn't been developed enough to reach the stage when optimization becomes the main focus.

Afterword

This book is, surely, not perfect. Hopefully, most of the mistakes in it were fixed with the help of many nice people who commented on the chapters as they were published on my blog.

Also, the book is terribly incomplete. Almost every chapter could be expanded by a factor of 2 or 3 with relevant details and concrete implementations of some of the general ideas that are presented, currently. But neither did I have the time to write those down nor, what's much more important, anyone would have had the time to read them, in entirety. I believe I have put enough concrete examples with executable code to illustrate all the important concepts in each part. This is a great advantage of using Lisp for the book: the code is clear and compact enough to serve both to explain the algorithms and to permit testing them for real, in the REPL. The main compromise each author has to make is between brevity and completeness. I hope that I made the right choices in this regard, but, for sure, there's much more to learn about every piece of technology mentioned. My hope is that the book lays a solid groundwork to facilitate further deeper exploration.

There are also a couple of topics that I would have liked to cover but couldn't find a good place for them. Probabilistic data structures is the most important of them. Yet, they are not big enough to justify a separate chapter and, also, don't fit into any of the existing chapters.

But enough with the whining. :) In fact, I'm quite satisfied with the end result as my main goal was to sufficiently develop the following key themes:

- The main one, obviously, was the description of all the important data structures and the associated algorithms.

- The next, also very important, was the demonstration of the essential tools that help in the development, testing, and verification of the produced algorithmic code: tracing, profiling, pretty-printing, and so on.

V. Domkin, *Programming Algorithms in Lisp*, https://doi.org/10.1007/978-1-4842-6428-7

- We have also discussed, when it was relevant, the real-world engineering considerations and constraints that influence the programs using our algorithms. And sometimes these constraints have more impact than the purely theoretical complexity calculations.

- Finally, in each chapter, I tried to present the practical use case of the algorithms we have studied, showing the broad variety of such applications. In fact, it spans all the different corners of the software landscape we're used to. We have talked, albeit briefly, about such different domains as neural networks, plagiarism detection, web search, mapping, chess-playing, image compression, and many others.

There are a lot of books on algorithms, but I haven't seen any that primarily aims to bridge the gap between theory and practice. This is one of the key distinctions of *Programming Algorithms in Lisp*. It is definitely not the best exposition of the theoretical ideas, but I hope that, instead, it builds sufficient understanding and skill for the common developer to start writing efficient algorithmic programs.

I wanted to finish the book with the following statement: programming craft is primarily about making choices. What approach to prefer, which algorithm to choose, what trade-offs to make. And, at the other level, what properties to give more priority: speed or safety, brevity or consistency, space or debuggability, clarity or conciseness, and so on and so forth. Lisp is one of the few languages that are "pro-choice." Its authors understood very well the importance of freedom to make the critical choices, and it is felt in the design of the language. For instance, with the help of `declaim,` we can even signal our preferences to the compiler, to some extent, at the level of a single file or even an individual form. `(declaim (optimize (speed 3) (safety 1) (debug 0) (compilation-speed 0)))` will ask the compiler to produce the fastest possible code. Yes, this language will not guard you against poor choices as some others claim to do. Sometimes, you're not wise enough to make a correct choice, but, much more often, every choice just has its pros and cons, so someone will approve of it and someone won't. And that's what freedom is about: ownership and responsibility. So use Lisp if you liked it. And if you prefer other languages, I'd urge you to still take advantage of the concept of freedom of choice in programming. Don't be constrained by the prevailing paradigms, and try to use the best parts of all the different approaches you know...

Index

A

Abstract Syntax Tree (AST), 153
Aging, 116
Aho-Corasick (AC), 223, 229, 233
Algorithms
    complexity, 3, 7
    importance of, 1
    value of, 2
Allocation profiling, 317
Amortized analysis, 172, 173, 363
Approximations
    branch/bound, 290–292
    combinational optimization, 277–281
    evolutionary algorithms, 288, 289
    GDf
        definition, 293
        framework patters, 293
        improve, 295, 296
        procedures, 294
        sampling, 296, 298
    locator search, 282–285, 287
Arrays, 41
    aref, 42
    0-based indexing, 50
    constant, 42, 43
    creation, 41
    element type restriction, 42
    initialization, 41
    intervals, 49
    length function, 44
    multidimensional, 49–51
    mutable, 42
    RUTILS, 43
    segment, 49
    sequence, 43
    slice, 44
    subseq function, 44
    taste/convenience, 49
    vector, 41
Associative arrays, 102, 153
Avalanche effect, 122
AVL trees, 163, 175–177

B

backptrs array, 263
Balance factors, 175
Big-O complexity, 8, 9
Binary search trees (BSTs)
    advantage, 163
    arbitrary element, 53
    AVL, 164
    bignums, 55
    comparisons, 54, 55
    complexity, 53
    divide/conquer, 53
    elements, 163, 164
    example, 53
    find function, 52
    geometric progression, 164

© Vsevolod Domkin 2021
V. Domkin, *Programming Algorithms in Lisp*, https://doi.org/10.1007/978-1-4842-6428-7

T, U

V, W, X, Y, Z